SONGS OF NASHVILLE

ALSO BY JAKE BROWN

Rick Rubin: In the Studio

*Nashville Songwriter: The Inside Stories Behind
Country Music's Greatest Hits*

Heart: In the Studio (cowritten with Ann and Nancy Wilson)

Strange Beautiful Music: A Musical Memoir by Joe Satriani
(coauthor)

Motörhead: In the Studio (cowritten with Lemmy Kilmister)

SONGS OF NASHVILLE

....

THE REAL STORIES BEHIND COUNTRY MUSIC'S GREATEST HITS

JAKE BROWN

DIVERSION
BOOKS

Diversion Books
A division of Diversion Publishing Corp.
www.diversionbooks.com

Copyright © 2025 by Jake Brown

All rights reserved, including the right to reproduce this book or portions thereof in any form whatsoever. No part of this publication may be reproduced or transmitted in any form or by any means, electronic or mechanical, including photocopying, recording, or any other information storage and retrieval, without the written permission of the publisher.

Diversion Books and colophon are registered trademarks of Diversion Publishing Corp.
For more information, email info@diversionbooks.com

First Diversion Books Edition: June 2025
Hardcover ISBN: 9798895150436
e-ISBN: 9798895150245

Cover design by Jonathan Sainsbury // 6x9 design
Design by Neuwirth & Associates, Inc

Printed in the United States of America
1   3   5   7   9   10   8   6   4   2

Diversion books are available at special discounts for bulk purchases in the US by corporations, institutions, and other organizations. For more information, please contact admin@diversionbooks.com.

The publisher does not have any control over and does not assume any responsibility for author or third-party websites or their content.

This book is dedicated to my parents, James and Tina Brown, for their tireless support of my creative pursuits over the past quarter century; my brother, Ret. Sgt. Joshua T. Brown, for helping foster a love of country music during our teens; and my late grandmother Jacqueline and grandfather Armand Thieme (especially for introducing me to Outlaw Country, Merle Haggard, Willie Nelson, and more during trips to Carlyle Lake as a kid).

CONTENTS

INTRODUCTION 1

The ABCs of Writing Country Music's Greatest Hits
Merle Haggard, Ashley Gorley, Cole Swindell,
Dallas Davidson, Shane McAnally, Craig Wiseman,
Dean Dillon, Matraca Berg, Sonny Curtis, and More

CHAPTER 1 11

Backroad Baptism
Jelly Roll

CHAPTER 2 23

Girl Power
Hillary Lindsey, Liz Rose, Lori McKenna,
and Natalie Hemby

CHAPTER 3 35

The Natural
Vince Gill

CHAPTER 4 53

I've Come to Expect It from You
Buddy Cannon

CHAPTER 5 60

Country Music Lover
Bobby Braddock

CHAPTER 6 76

The Way I Am
Sonny Throckmorton

CHAPTER 7 85
Average Joe
Colt Ford

CHAPTER 8 98
Everybody Oughta Sing a Song
Dallas Frazier

CHAPTER 9 111
I Did It My Way
Clint Black

CHAPTER 10 123
Resurrection
Kinky Friedman

CHAPTER 11 131
Friends in Low Places
Earl Bud Lee

CHAPTER 12 136
Peaceful, Easy Feeling
Jack Tempchin

CHAPTER 13 143
King of the Juke Joint
Wayne "The Train" Hancock

CHAPTER 14 147
Lost in a Song
Willy "Tea" Taylor

CHAPTER 15 154
Midnight Plane to Houston
Jim Weatherly

Contents ix

CHAPTER 16 161
Oklahoma Swing
Tim DuBois

CHAPTER 17 167
Cotton Belt Music
Rock Killough

CHAPTER 18 175
Here in the Real World
Mark Irwin

CHAPTER 19 182
Murder on Music Row
Larry Cordle

CHAPTER 20 187
Americana's Ambassador
Jim Lauderdale

CHAPTER 21 200
Lookin' for Love in All the Wrong Places
Wanda Mallette

CHAPTER 22 205
A Bridge That Just Won't Burn
Jim McBride

CHAPTER 23 211
Gentle on My Mind
Carl Jackson

CHAPTER 24 224
Grandma Got Run Over by a Reindeer
Randy Brooks

x   SONGS OF NASHVILLE

CHAPTER 25 232
Talkin' to the Moon
Larry Gatlin

CHAPTER 26 238
Brand New Man
Don Cook

CHAPTER 27 247
Play It Again
Jeff Stevens and Jody Stevens

CHAPTER 28 268
The New School
Will Weatherly, Drew Parker, Josh Thompson,
Matt Rogers, and Steve Moakler

Acknowledgments   *289*
About the Author   *293*

INTRODUCTION

THE ABCs OF WRITING COUNTRY MUSIC'S GREATEST HITS

Merle Haggard, Ashley Gorley, Cole Swindell, Dallas Davidson, Shane McAnally, Craig Wiseman, Dean Dillon, Matraca Berg, Sonny Curtis, and More

Country music at its core has long been common sense put to melody, whether writing about love or heartache, life or death, dreams or disappointments. Reflecting the real lives of its listeners in a way that's unique compared to arguably any other musical genre of songwriting, the translators of those emotions and experiences as they move from reality into recorded form are Nashville Songwriters. Dazzling us for decades with their Music Row magic, here the curtain is pulled back on decades of country music's greatest hits written directly from the memories of those who penned them.

Merle Haggard begins our conversation about songwriting by revealing that his songs come to him from the mysterious musical beyond many songwriters refer to as the muse: "I don't have no recollection at all of writing 'Mama Tried.' I don't have any idea what caused me to write 'Mama Tried.' I don't know why I wrote 'The Bottle Let Me Down.' We wrote songs all the time. My best friend Freddy Powers and I lived during the 1980s on houseboats out on Lake Shasta. I've got a song called 'Favorite Memories' that was a number one song, that came out of the lake life. It was very fertile songwriting ground." Merle Haggard, then owner of the Silverthorn Resort with a private dock, and Freddy Powers wrote signature hits including "I Always Get Lucky with You," "Silver

2 SONGS OF NASHVILLE

Eagle," and "Let's Chase Each Other Around the Room Tonight," while living the lake life.

Merle Haggard: The lake itself was just a different life than anything I'd ever experienced, and I think for Freddy too. It's one of the most beautiful places in the world. After we wrote "I Always Get Lucky with You," we played nonstop for about five years. Sometimes we'd eat, sometimes we'd have a drink, but mostly we played all the time. Living out on the lake there, we had the boats hooked up to the shoreline where we had phones down there so we could call up and get whatever supplies we needed while we worked. We wrote songs all the time. We didn't have no reason beforehand; we just wrote songs, and a lot of the sons of bitches we never heard again. "Natural High" was a good song. It was peaceful, and it kind of captured the mood that we had going out there at the lake. Everything we wrote didn't go to number one. A lot of them we threw in the God damn lake, because all of it was not good.

Freddy Powers: From the beginning, Merle and I were almost inseparable. Where one went, we both went. We would do an occasional tour where I would play guitar and sing a few songs in the show. Somehow, I knew that it was more than just a friendship with Merle, it was a mutual respect for each other's talents. He is such a great and profound writer, and with that in your mind at all times, it was overpowering. And just think how I felt when Merle Haggard looked at me and said, "I like your writing." After that my confidence grew and I felt very comfortable telling him any song idea I had, and I'm proud to say we used a lot of them. By 1983, Merle and I were living on the boats full-time, writing and partying. We called it "The

Spree of '83." For all the good times, many of the songs we wrote during that time were about lost loves or love experiences. Some we wrote during that time were like an audio-biography of our lives. Together, we collaborated on some thirty songs he had recorded on albums as well as some that I wrote by myself. We had five number one hits, Song of the Year, and received the Triple Play Award for writing three number one songs in a twelve-month period. And [we] have since become what is called "Members of the Million Air Play Club" for over one million plays on the radio with "Let's Chase Each Other Around the Room Tonight."

While Lake Shasta proved a beautiful backdrop for Merle Haggard to write number one hits against, it's common knowledge within country music that the first rule to making it as a Nashville Songwriter is to "Always Be Writing!" It's an edict echoed by Big Loud Shirt (now known as Big Loud Publishing) owner / legendary hit writer Craig Wiseman, who offers his philosophy that "when you're stylizing a song, you can take an idea, and write a real retro-type country song with it, or do things a little more pop, you can kind of mess with that some too, but that's kind of what you're supposed to do: You're a Carpenter. When Tim Nichols and I wrote 'Live Like You Were Dying,' we had a friend of ours who'd just had a huge misdiagnosis, if you can imagine. This guy was a young father and all this stuff, went to the doctor, who told him 'Oh, you have this weird thing on your X-ray,' and this guy was sort of a hypochondriac anyway, so, he freaked out! They sent him to an oncologist and this guy took some other X-rays a week or ten days later, and [they] told him 'No, dude, this is a little birth mass that everybody's born with. Most people it goes away; it didn't with you. This is not going to kill you, you're fine.' So, we were talking about him—'What would that be like?'—and then that led us to talk about other people, like my uncle, who got leukemia and had to go to Mayo Clinic, and luckily it was treatable, but he retired and went shark diving. So, we just started talking about people who responded in that type of way, 'Wow, it's time to get busy,' as opposed to 'I'm going to go lay down in my bed and freak out,' and our talks just turned in that direction of people that just sort of respond to that news in a really cool way. And at some point, we knew there was a song there, like 'Dying to live.' I think I mumbled 'Live like you were dying,' and Tim said 'Yeah, that!' And as soon as he stopped me, I grabbed the guitar and just kind of started scatting some stuff out, and next thing you know, we finished the second verse at midnight on the phone. I was laying in my living room in the pitch dark on the phone, and the song within a few days of that, and the rest is really history."

The 2005 Grammy winner for Song of the Year, Chris Stapleton, would repeat that honor in 2015 when he was nominated in the same category for his career-making rendition of "Tennessee Whiskey." Selling fourteen million copies and pushing his *Traveller* LP to victory in the Album of the Year category, a reflection cowriter Dean Dillon muses of the timelessness a great song can carry through the ages in country music, especially given he'd first written it twenty-five years earlier in 1981 after "I had gone to a listening room, and the reason I'd gone there that night was, I had heard this song called 'Is There Anybody Out There Who Can Shine?' by Olivia Newton John. It was a big hit at the time, and the girl who wrote that song was going to be there that night playing. Her name was Linda Hargrove. So, I went, saw the show, went up to her after the show, we got to talking, went out and got coffee, and she invited me over to her house and at 3:00 or 4:00 in the morning, wrote 'Tennessee Whiskey.' I'd had that idea for a while, 'You're as smooth as Tennessee whiskey,' I think that's about all I had of it, and we sat down and wrote that song. I had the melody for 'Smooth as Tennessee whiskey, Sweet as strawberry wine,' and basically, I can tell you this, of all the songs I've written, I can't name you very many where I did not write the melody too. I've written so long it

The ABCs of Writing Country Music's Greatest Hits   5

can work anyway, but normally I've got that melody with that hook, so when I sit down to write, 99.9 percent of the time, the melody's present, at least the verse melodies are anyway. I've always been a melody man from the word go."

A golden rule in country that has long carried the day, Luke Bryan's 2013 seven-million-selling single "Play It Again" proved just how infectious melodies can become in a winning chorus. Songwriting icons Dallas Davidson and Ashley Gorley, as Gorley recalls, "[were] just kind of playing the keyboards on this one, messing around, and we were writing with the idea that the song we were writing was going to be somebody's favorite song, some way to kind of put that. It was a really, really loose idea, about when a girl says, 'This is my song, this is my song!' And we both kind of landed on that, 'Oh, my God, this is my song' thing with the melody both at the same time, and it took off from there chorus-wise. We both kind of said it at the same time, and once we had the chorus going, we spit out 'Play It Again' at the end of it. It was kind of a little extra bonus at the end that wound up being what everybody called it."

Both recognizing they were crafting something instantly memorable in the song's addictive chorus, Dallas Davidson describes a writing routine where "we started that song just like Ashley and I always do, where we just start jamming, he played the piano and I played the guitar, and we just start mumbling stuff and then words start coming out, 'She was sitting all alone on a tailgate, tan legs swinging by a Georgia plate . . .' That song was written kind of backward, and I don't think we said the title first and then wrote to it. We wrote it and then the title popped out, so, we started with the verse and then worked our way to writing a chorus, and then when we got to 'Oh my God, this is my song,' that kind of became a hook, 'This is my song.' I think we were going to call it 'This Is My Song,' but then Ashley started singing 'Play it again, play it again, play it again,' and that became the title. That's what really drove that song, because that's how people talk, 'She was like, Oh my God,' that's how this generation speaks. I guess it's my generation too, but once we hit 'Oh my God, this is my song,' we knew we were on to something for sure on that."

While some country hits come together inside one inspired session, others like Sam Hunt's "Body Like a Back Road" spent thirty-four weeks at number one courtesy of careful compositional consideration and care over multiple writing sessions, with cowriter and *Songland* TV show judge Shane McAnally confirming that "the writing of that song went on for a really long time. My memory of it the first time is being over at Zack's place, he lived in East Nashville at the time, and Sam came in and we just talked and threw around things. He told us about this title, 'Body Like a Back Road,' and this is what Sam always does, he doesn't walk into the room and say, 'I've got an idea!'—which is different from most writers. For most writers, that's how we start, but he will take two hours going down a road about different things, and then say 'Oh, I also had this idea, "Body Like a Back Road . . ."' The reason he does it that way with us is because when our antennas go up, he goes 'Okay, now I have something.' We don't just write the first thing that comes to mind, or he doesn't just come in and say, 'This is what we're writing!' That's usually what Josh Osborne and I do, completely ring out the idea and then give Sam so many options and he would go away with it, and then come back and say, 'Okay, when we say this it's too funny, when we say this it's too far, but this is right on it, we need more stuff like this.' So, we just have a whole bunch of conversation, and he'll throw things out until we light up, and on 'Body Like a Back Road' we all lit up! Just the title, so we started googling first to make sure it hadn't been recorded already because it sounded like it would have been."

Proving the timeless importance that a title can play in not only selling a song but shaping its writing in the first place, legendary songwriter Sonny Curtis knew he was onto something with the title of his signature hit, "I Fought the Law (and the Law Won)," sharing that he wrote the song not long after "Buddy Holly had moved to New York, the Crickets asked me back into the group. Before Buddy and the Crickets had taken off, I had been in the group with Buddy called The Three Tunes, and we'd gone to Nashville to record for Decca. So, they called me to join the group just a couple of months before Buddy died in that plane crash, and we were due to cut an album for Coral Records. We recorded the album in mid-July of 1959, and I wrote the song just before we left for New York. I wrote 'I Fought the Law' as a country song originally. I was just sitting in my house in the living room one afternoon, and I remember it was hot, and the sand was blowing, which is often the case in West Texas. I just sort of started picking, and I kind of wrote it as a country song first, and it came to me awfully quick—it only took about fifteen or twenty minutes, and I had it. I think my attention span at that time, when I was twenty-one years old, was not very long, and if I didn't write it pretty fast, I would have probably given up on it. When I'm writing, I don't think about harmonies, I just try to think of a good melody, and I hummed that one out with a melody as I was sitting there picking, and when I write—and I probably write maybe a little differently than a lot of people. With 'I Fought the Law,' I don't even think I wrote it down, which is kind of dangerous. Then when we were on our way to New York, and we were trying to think of songs to record, I said 'Hey, I got this country song we might change,' and sang them 'I Fought the Law,' and they thought it was great. So we changed it to a straight-eighth feel and Jerry Allison put those triplet gunshots at the front, but we were really flying by the seat of our pants, as they say."

A 24-7 songwriting machine that never stops, while many of country music's greatest hits have been written in the famed writing rooms on Music Row along 15th and 16th Avenues, just as many have been written on the road as songwriters travel with artists and bands to write during downtime between shows. One of the most successful examples in recent times comes with Florida Georgia Line's "This Is How We Roll." Celebrated as a "a modern, genre-busting pop song" by the *New Yorker*, cowriter and future country star in his own right Cole Swindell remembers being "out writing with Luke Bryan and Florida Georgia Line on the road on their Dirt Road Diaries Tour. It was the second night of that weekend run of shows, and I was sitting in the back of the bus with Brian Kelly. It was just him and I at the time, and we were getting ready to write, waiting on Tyler. So, it was just going to be us three, and BK said, 'Man, I heard something Luke was talking about last night at the show, about being out in the country, out where nobody can bother you, and you could shoot bullets at the moon if you wanted. I just thought that was such a cool thought,' and that's how the whole song started, was from something Luke said onstage the night before. I remember Luke saying that it was part of the show, but that's the funny thing about how songwriting works. So, we started writing around that, and had a melody kind of, and BK threw out the title 'This Is How We Roll' and wanted to see what we could come up with. He was singing 'This is how we roll,' the first line of the chorus, but that's about all we had melody-wise. Then Tyler came in and he loved it, so we started writing the song, and we got into the first verse, and out of nowhere, Tyler said, 'Man, I wonder if Luke would like this?' So, I happened to send a text from the bus and said, 'Hey, the guys are asking, you want to come check out what we're working on?' So, sure enough, he came over, and we had just started it, so, he listened to what we had and was like 'I'm in!'"

Country fans were, too, sending the song to number one for four weeks, selling six million copies and establishing Florida Georgia Line as a major radio act, a magic spot that every new country act or artist covets and requires to get their career rolling, as Matraca Berg helped Martina McBride do with her first number one hit, "Wild

The ABCs of Writing Country Music's Greatest Hits 9

Angels," which she credits once again to the all-important routine of cowriting after "that song came from my head, and I started it with Harry Stinson, and we wrote this kind of more alternative song where the lyrics were kind of . . . not my best effort, but the melody was killer. People kept putting it on hold, and then they'd call and say, 'What's this song about?' So, I'm terrible at rewrites, once I get something in my head, and so I call Gary Harrison. Gary is the song doctor, and he came in and the chorus was off, and 'Wild angels on blue horses,' I don't know where that came from or what I was smoking, but he said 'Well, you just repeat "wild angels,"' and it was like 'Oh! You're right.' He had a really neat first couple of lines, and after that, everything was super easy. He has a remarkable sense that way; he just gets down to the brass. I feel that chemistry is really hard to figure out, and it could be somebody who's very similar to you that you have your sensibilities click. I've found myself in rooms where I removed myself from the situation, because I just don't think I have anything to offer, and the cowriter's pretty dug in to where they are. Sometimes they're open to help and I've helped, but you have to find there's an open mind there. I'm getting to where I'm more of in a mentor situation, so I'm writing with a lot of young writers, and becoming a song doctor."

We'll talk to many here who share the real stories behind the songs and songwriters that over the past fifty years have helped make country the biggest-selling genre in the United States today.

CHAPTER 1

BACKROAD BAPTISM

· ·

Jelly Roll

Country Rap — that's one of those catchphrases that Jeff Foxworthy would have thrown into his famous "You Might Be a Redneck" jokes twenty years ago, but today, its success is nothing to laugh at. Among the mainstream, just hearing about the biggest underground phenomenon since hip-hop in the early '80s, when rappers were selling tens of thousands of tapes out of their car trunks, country rap has broken through thanks to much of the same kind of grassroots fan base. From more than a billion YouTube views, this new sound rose up from the underground and into the mainstream as what is today an established commercial subgenre. Led by genre pioneers like Colt Ford, Big Smo, and producers Jon Conner, Ray "DJ Orig " Riddle, and David Ray, Bubba Sparxxx, Haystak, The LACs, Lenny Cooper, Upchurch the Redneck, Jawga Boyz, and Demun Jones, Jelly Roll has become without a doubt the biggest star to burst onto mainstream stardom out of this underground movement he helped pioneer for more than twenty years!

Star of his own Super Bowl commercial in 2024, the *New York Times* the same year spotlighted the rapper-country singer-songwriter as "one of the year's biggest breakout stars," with three number one hits in 2023, multiple Grammy nominations for New Artist of the Year and Best Country Duo/Group Performance for "Save Me." It's a viral smash with more than 200 million views on YouTube and 137-million-plus streams on Spotify, while "Son of a Sinner" has racked up more than 177 million streams and counting, with *Entertainment Tonight* even reporting on Jelly's "Epic night at

12   SONGS OF NASHVILLE

the 2023 CMA Awards," taking home the New Artist of the Year from the Country Music Association.

Shaking his head in amazement on the evolution of his own career in real time with country rap's fusion into the mainstream listening of country music fans, Jelly muses: "Man, it's been crazy to watch this thing grow from fucking nothing into something, and also to watch the evolution of how the music genre's changing with the people and the crowds, and everything's kind of coming together. It's been a unique experience, man; I've been really blessed."

Jelly Roll, born Jason Bradley DeFord in the 1980s, grew up in Antioch, Tennessee, outside of Nashville, as blue collar as the audience he represents and for whom he has written throughout his career and catalog. Raised on a blend of country and hip-hop that informs his sound, he counts his mother's influence as pivotal, too, in rounding out the hybrid breakthrough music he makes today, recalling that "When I grew up, I used to tell people my mom listened to old rock and roll, old Southern rock, or straight oldies. My mother's an older woman, so we would literally come up with 'Splish, splash, I was taking a bath!' So, I've just been brought up into that for so long, I've seen so much of that, and I've heard so much of that growing up, but I didn't realize how influenced by it I was till I got older. Because then, when you get older, you're in the store and you hear 'Backfield in Motion,' singing along, asking 'How do I know this?' Or you're singing 'Mama said there'd be days like this, there'd be days like this . . .' And I'll ask, 'How do I know that record?' Because I grew up listening to that music."

Making music in bedroom studios like many artists at the dawn of the digital recording generation, Jelly first began laying his voice on tape via the tried-and-true, hip-hop tradition of mixtapes, beginning in 2003 with *The Plain Shmear Tape*, 2004's *Gamblin on a White Boy*, Vol. 1, *The Halfway House* in 2005, *Street Flavor* with Charlie P and Haystak, whom Jelly counts as an early influence among others who taught him the game of independently releasing his sound to the streets:

I was in my early teens when I really started to realize I had a gift for making music, when I realized I had a way of putting words together, I was probably thirteen, fourteen. I had a different philosophy.... For me, the difference from mixtapes to albums was next to nothing, it didn't matter what it was, you just put it out, man. I came up under a lot of peers where I got to watch a lot of different people do a lot of different ways of making music, and I thought the only mistake they'd make is they wouldn't take the content to the people.

Haystak: It was inevitable, I just got lucky in the fact that I met him first. He was going to entertain and do his thing regardless, but Jelly, I've been down with him twenty-five-plus years. Jelly showed up the first time I met him on a pass from a maximum-security juvenile facility, and he just had this look in his face.... People think shit has been sweet for Jelly, but no, and this is the time we really need to push him to the next level. Back then, that was the ambition and that was the vision, that he would do something that I was not able to do. So, I'm proud of him.

I know he can be on D-Block, or he can be on the stage, the kid is a fucking miracle. He's a character, he's bold. All of us are brave, all of us have a little courage, but Jelly's bold. Jelly has achieved his position like I have achieved mine, through poise and audacity. And that means we know how to sit still until it's time to move. There's an art to sitting still, and the audacity just stems from being willing to do what the next man's not. Jelly has that.

14 SONGS OF NASHVILLE

So, no matter what I'm able to accomplish, and what doors that would open for, say, Ritz, who opens the door for Lil Dicky, or Lil Wyte who opens this other artist, and my being from Nashville and Wyte being from Memphis, and both of us feeling the best thing we can do is support Jelly Roll, because he is the best parts of us. He is the best parts of our message. Of course he's his own man, but in that, there's similarities. If I were to pass, if Lil Wyte were to pass, God forbid, Jelly would be here and through that, we'd still have some sort of life.

Collaborating with both Haystak and Lil Wyte on full-length albums like *Year Round* with Wyte in 2011 and *Strictly Business* with Haystak in 2011, for years before then, he met the street demand for more with a steady outflow of other mixtapes like *House Arrest* in 2007, *Gamblin on a White Boy*, Vol. 2, and Vol. 3 in 2008 and 2009 respectively, *The Hate Goes On* in 2009, *Therapeutic Music: The Bipolar Edition* in 2010, *Therapeutic Music 2: The Inner Struggle* and *Deal or No Deal* in 2010, and *Mr. Controversy* in 2010. *Eleven on the Come Out* released in 2011, which produced three more that year with *Gamblin on a White Boy*, Vol. 4, *The Collection*, and *Therapeutic Music 3: Road to Vol. 4.* The fearlessness Jelly Roll points to as one of his greatest strengths is one he addresses head-on and made him stand out from the crowd of peers trying at the same time to break through: "It's like they were so afraid of failure, they were scared to drop a mixtape and have only thirty people listen to it. Even now, I hear people say, 'We can't let that record go, what if nobody hears it, we wasted the record.' Well, letting the motherfucker sit in your hard drive's wasting the record. So, I just took it to the people, fourteen mixtapes deep, just taking it to the people."

Equally impressive as Jelly Roll's output is that he recorded so much music while dealing with repeat incarcerations throughout this musically productive period. *American Songwriter* magazine reported that "before Jelly Roll became a household name in country music . . . he struggled to stay on the right side of the law as he found himself in and out of correctional facilities for numerous offenses like drug dealing, shoplifting, drug possession, and aggravated robbery." *People* magazine spotlighted the head-turning fact that "the singer has been to jail some 40 times for various drug charges," and *CBS News* coverage amid his mainstream breakout added that "if you're wondering where Jelly Roll came from, one answer is the Metro-Davidson County Detention Facility in Nashville. Jelly Roll was in and out of facilities for ten years, starting at age 14. . . . He says he wrote hundreds of songs in his cell. He was twenty-four when he left prison for the last time. In 2010, Jelly Roll had his first minor hit, a hip-hop track called 'Pop Another Pill.'"

Courtesy of the same mixtape culture and plentiful crop of new music he kept pushing with a dream, as *GQ* magazine recently painted it, of making the "unlikely transformation . . . [of] a former Nashville ne'er-do-well [to] a 21st-century country superstar" courtesy of "the years spent honing his creative and commercial instincts on the Southern-rap, mixtape circuit. . . . Where he once trafficked certain drugs and rapped about his proclivity for others, he earlier this year testified before a Senate committee about the fentanyl crisis; a juvenile facility in which he was locked up is now outfitted with a recording studio he funded. And to produce the hits that have precipitated this fame and fortune, Jelly had to for the first time welcome others into what had previously been a hermetic creative process." *Southern Living* magazine recently, in rounding out headlines on his full-circle journey to redemption, added that "the crooner uses his experience to bring hope to others that are struggling to find the right path in life, and to show them that it's never too late to turn things around, often visiting those currently incarcerated."

Revisiting those years and how they helped shape the songs he writes today, Jelly Roll begins by revealing that clinging to his dream of one day becoming a breakout star with his music was the hope he held on to while serving time, addressing his past in the streets head-on with the admission that "it's not hidden, I don't hide the fact that I sold drugs before I was a rapper. There was actually a point in my career where I could have been taken as glorifying that. There's *no* glory in that. A lot of people asked me why my music changed, and I was like, 'Why the fuck would you want to go relive the worst moments of your life in a studio every day?' I got out of that, why would I want to keep rapping about that? I didn't want to be there in the first place. I think rappers are humble when they say they've never seen it, and I appreciate that humility because I'm a humble guy myself, but I did, I prayed about it. I laid in a steel bunk in jail doing a year day for day the last time I went to the county jail. I just sat there, and I seen it, and you know what, the crazy thing is: Everything I've seen is coming to life!"

Once he was released and returned to the studio to continue his prolific output of mixtapes that had first made him a known quantity on the Southern rap circuit, he began to spread his wings creatively. He showcased the soulful country voice he's known for today on albums as well as where he began experimenting with writing and recording in different musical styles and fusions courtesy of early albums like *The Big Sal Story* in 2012, *No Filter* with Lil Wyte in 2013, *Business as Usual* with Haystak in 2013, *Sobriety Sucks* in 2016, *No Filter 2* with Lil Wyte in 2016, *Addiction Kills* in 2017, collaborations with Struggle Jennings over *Waylon & Willie* in 2017, *Waylon & Willie II* in 2018, *Waylon & Willie III* in 2018, *Goodnight Nashville* in 2018, *Whiskey Sessions II* in 2018, *Waylon & Willie IV* with Struggle Jennings in 2020, *Self Medicated* in 2020, and more mixtapes like *Therapeutic Music Vol. 4: Just My Thoughts* in 2012, *White Trash Take* in 2012, *Mid-Grade Miracle: The Boston George Story* in 2012, *Whiskey, Weed & Women* in 2013, *Biggest Loser* in 2014, and *Therapeutic Music Vol. 5* in 2015.

As his profile grew based on the strength of early singles like "Smoking Section" in 2015, certified gold without charting along with three street hits off the *Addiction Kills* album in 2017 with "Hate Goes On," "Only," and "Wheels Fall Off," "Fall with the Fall" with Struggle Jennings in 2017 off the *Waylon & Willie II* LP, "Same Asshole" off *Crosses and Crossroads* in 2019, "I Need You," "Creature," and "Bottle and Mary Jane" off *A Beautiful Disaster* in 2020, "Son of the Dirty South" with Brantley Gilbert in 2022, along with charting hits like "The Lost," "Behind Bars" with Brantley Gilbert and Struggle Jennings in 2022, "Hold On" and "Kill a Man" from the *Whitsitt Chapel* LP, and "I'm On It" featuring cowriter David Ray. Friends for the better part of twenty-five years, David "D-Ray" Ray and Jelly cowrote his breakout underground hit "Save Me" in 2020 with more than 200 million YouTube views before it was re-released in 2023 to smash chart success, hitting number one on *Billboard*'s Country Airplay Chart and Canada's Country Chart and even cracking the Top 20 of the *Billboard* Hot 100 Chart. Using the hit to give fans a look at how his songwriting process works in action, Jelly begins by explaining the important point that whenever he goes into a new writing/recording session:

> You just go into the studio, and you hear it, and you feel it, and you flow with it. It's like a puzzle for me when I write. I just take rhyme words and fill in the blanks, because I came up freestyling. So, I just believe music's organic, man. I believe it's something you don't put a lot of time and energy into, I hate to say it that way, but I think it's something you just do. I love D-Ray a lot—that's my brother—and musically, I think he's one of the most talented singer-songwriters in Nashville. I like working with people who are really hands-on, that I can really sit down and gel with, and he's definitely one of those guys.

David Ray: My dad was a big George Jones / Merle Haggard fan, so a lot of the outlaw Waylon Jennings and traditional country stuff I definitely came up on. I've got a taste for Al Green and a lot of the Motown sounds, which is where a little more of the soul and bluesier side of what I do probably comes in. On the hip-hop side, my influences are just so vast. The first records I ever bought were Erik B & Rakim and The Fat Boys, and obviously earlier in my career, everything was so East Coast driven with the Biggie/Puffy era, Nas, and Twista, a fast rapper who was always one of my favorites. Then as a consumer, there was the N.W.A. craze that I really adapted to. It depends on what we're working on, I draw from different sources, but if there's something soulful, if it's a bluesy guitar lick, I'm probably just naturally gonna go there. That's what I channel, that's what I hear.

Jelly Roll: I was eating dinner with my father and brother this afternoon, and I told my father, "The greatest gift that God has given me is I have the ability to change how people feel for three minutes and forty-five seconds at a time." The fact that I have the ability to, whatever they're going through, however sad they are, their old lady's yelling at them, whatever the bad moment is in life, I have the ability for three minutes and thirty seconds at a time to change the way that person feels.

Inviting fans inside the studio for a look at his approach to writing and producing hits with Jelly Roll like "Save Me" and "Son of a Sinner," which hit number one on the *Billboard* US Country Airplay Chart and broke through on the US Hot Rock & Alternative Songs Chart, staying there for twenty weeks before peaking in the Top 5 and cracking the Top 40 of the US Hot 100 Singles Chart, David

Ray first takes us on a walk down memory lane into his own musical roots where, "First off, I learned time and again that to have a hit hook, someone's gotta be able to sing along with it, and every hook's gonna be different. Every hook is what the music just tells you to do, but some of it needs to be catchy and repetitive so that person can learn it even the next time it comes around. On a producer's side, being in the Atlanta scene, a lot of people would say a lot of that music is dumbed-down and loses some respect away from the lyricism side, because we've seen the South come in and kind of take over with these trap beats and really melodic but easy-to-learn hooks, and that's definitely one thing that I've taken from it that's helped me be 'the hook guy.' As a producer, just watching other people vibe in and not trying to be the lyrical miracle on every song, if you know what I'm saying. . . . There's so much more to a producer than just making a hot beat, so cool drums over guitars or whatever. A producer—in the insane environment—will help create and write that song, coach the delivery of vocals, the whole nine. I can draw obviously from my years of singing hooks too for that, because I've picked up so many tricks in the studio. For instance, one thing I tell a lot of new artists a lot is that you can recite the most emotional quote ever written over the most emotional track, but if you just say it, it has no meaning. You've got to have that melody, and sometimes we'll have a subject matter, and a beat will kind of speak to us and let us know."

As Jelly Roll continues his ascension toward becoming one of the biggest music stars in the United States, he does so proudly with his daughter as one of his biggest fans, beaming that "I get a kick out it now when my daughter recognizes one of my songs, I didn't always because they were so vulgar and bad, but now that I've got more lighthearted music, I really get a kick out of seeing her resonate with certain kinds of songs." Along with seeing the reaction of his daughter to his music, Jelly gets a natural high from seeing the very real way his songs connect with listeners, explaining his popularity with fans as one based on a successful combination of accessibility and relatability, whereby "I was blessed that I think it was more to do with how I approached people, that made people connect with me. And there's something about imperfections that people fuck with. I wear my inequities and inadequacies on my sleeve, and I think people are like 'Fuck, yeah! We're just like that too. . . . What excites me about making new music is changing people and knowing that I can help people. At first, it was just a music thing, I was helping myself and helping the people that listened. Now I'm changing people's lives."

Bonds he's built for the better part of two decades are now based on a core philosophy where Jelly reasons, "We're building it one fan at a time. Taylor Swift once said, 'If you want a million fans, sign a million autographs.'" As he's graduated from playing before three hundred people to playing before tens of thousands, Jelly relishes his relationship with his loyal and ever-growing live audiences around the country, confirming that "shows are probably my favorite part of this besides actually making the music. I appreciate going and taking the music to people. I appreciate taking that music to people and getting to feel them. I walk the line every night when I do a Jelly Roll show and there's a line of kids. I walk that line and shake those kids' hands, and go meet those fans, that's just what I do. I remember taking DJ Highlight to California for the first time in his life. I remember his eyes being lit up the whole trip. The different places we travel across this country, the places that we got to see that music made happen for us, the lives that are changing, if this thing keeps going, we're going to make multiple millionaires, that's crazy, dude! Doing something we love; I'd do it for free. I'd stand on a car rapping for the same kids who pay to see me, no bullshit."

The *Arizona Republic* recently captured a sense of why Jelly Roll's popularity has spread with such even flow across the genres and generations, reporting on his 2024 headlining set that "Jelly Roll drew a huge crowd for the weekend's most anticipated set at Country Thunder Arizona, taking the stage with arms outstretched to thunderous applause as he launched his performance with 'Halfway to Hell,' the gospel-tinged country rap anthem that opens his first full-blown country album, last year's *Whitsitt Chapel*.... He's like a gospel tent revivalist with way more face tattoos than your typical preacher. And before the night was through, he'd delivered an uplifting sermon or two for a crowd he said numbered as many as 26,000, framing his darkest hours as a pathway to enlightenment."

Reflecting on how far he's come over the course of his twenty-year-plus journey to the top of the charts, Jelly triumphantly points to "a song me and David Ray did years ago where I said, 'Rappers are writing their way into a life we're trying to write our way out of, . . .' and I wrote my way the fuck out of it! I have the ability to make men that don't want to dance, dance. I have the ability to make people that cry themselves to sleep at night happy . . . and that's not just me, that's music! Music has given us that ability. I sang 'Sunday Morning' once at a funeral in Murfreesboro, Tennessee, the song was 'Sunday Morning'—we all know it, it's a happy, hung-over song—and when I sang that song, for three minutes and thirty seconds at that funeral, people clapped. For three minutes and thirty seconds at that funeral, people shed tears of joy, I did it right next to an open casket. God rest his soul, his name was Eli. He was a tattoo artist and a great dude, and when his homies called me to do it, I didn't have a hesitation. He and his little girl sang that song every Sunday, and I came and sang it for her. So, to watch these 225 people at this funeral, just in there clapping, 'It's Sunday morning,' it was just crazy! I walked out of there and, man, I probably cried for two hours. If everything I've seen so far is coming to light, that means my dreams are limitless, with what I've seen sitting in that prison cell, man, we're on our way. Everything I visualized is happening, so, dude, we're on our way to a fucking arena!"

Variety's headline that "the roll that country star Jelly Roll is on will make itself felt in arenas in the late summer and fall of 2024. . . . Although this will be Jelly Roll's first all-arenas tour, he had a good chance to become accustomed to them on his 2023 'Backroad Baptism' tour, which found him playing a mixture of amphitheaters and arenas, with almost entirely different routing than he has scheduled for 2024," would seem to confirm that Jelly Roll has arrived!

Circling back to his daughter as a driving force for what inspires the music he makes today, country music's newest sensation keeps his head out of the clouds and feet on the ground, firmly rooted in the outlook that "my daughter, she changed everything, she changed my perspective of people, and what life's really about. Life's about love, dude, everything else is just fucking cosmetics. They're eyeliner, they're lip gloss, they're whipped cream on a good Boston Crème pie, baby. It's all about love."

CHAPTER 2

GIRL POWER

· ·

Hillary Lindsey, Liz Rose,
Lori McKenna, and Natalie Hemby

C ountry music has long been dominated on the charts by just as many women stars as men, but within the world of Nashville songwriting, in the last twenty-five years, a generation of female songwriters has reshaped that landscape forever, anchored by a handful of Music Row legends like Hillary Lindsey, Liz Rose, Lori McKenna, Natalie Hemby, and more who gather to talk about writing some of their signature hits and dish on direction for the modern-day Nashville Songwriter.

Songwriter Liz Rose's life would change forever after she had a chance meeting with a then-unknown teenager in the mid-2000s looking to cowrite, sharing a now-iconic musical moment in country music when "I'd played a couple of songs at a Writer's Round and this teenager approached me and said, 'You know, I really like your songs. I'm Taylor Swift, would you write with me sometime?' The funny thing was, after we had our first writing session, I walked out of there saying, 'Well, what was I doing there?' because she was so fast and knew what she wanted to say, but it was a great hang. She was talented and it was fun, so I just kept doing it! She's a storyteller. She had such a great imagination, and still does, and she could take an idea or an emotion and turn it into a song and tell a story. It just blew me away. We wrote every week, and some days we would write a couple songs."

A few short years later, *Rolling Stone* magazine would recognize Rose for "co-writing some of the biggest country songs of the 21st century," with "Tim McGraw" and "Teardrops on My Guitar" standing out as two early favorites of the cowriter where with the former, "Taylor came in that day and said 'I was in math class today and I started this idea,' so, she had that verse started and said 'It's called, "Tim McGraw,"' and I was like 'Okay . . .' I wasn't crazy about the idea, but I knew enough that I was not trying to write my song, that we were writing Taylor's song. So, I went with it, but what you're thinking is, 'Okay, we're writing this song about Tim McGraw, and if you don't cut it, then nobody else is gonna cut it [*laughs*]!' But I didn't care, I always went with it with Taylor, and knew we were writing the song for Taylor and that's all I really cared about. Whereas a lot of people at that time were thinking, 'Well, if the artist doesn't cut it, you can demo it, and pitch it somewhere else,' but I never felt that way with her. I always felt like these songs were special, and to sit back and see what she does with it, which is always cool. With 'Teardrops on My Guitar,' that song was about a guy named Drew that she dated, and she wanted to put his name in it, and I was like 'Really?' It was so cute. Taylor always had her experiences, but she also embellished."

Synching with the songwriter more and more synergistically as time went on, she proudly points to another early Swift smash, "Pictures to Burn," as a number one hit that was born after "she came in with the melody and we wrote it fast. Taylor always showed up with an idea, with an emotion, with something going on in her mind. I always say these songs were Taylor stories, not mine. I think Taylor writes little movies, she sees the whole story and it comes out of her mouth, so you just follow her emotion and I pay close attention, because she starts playing and starts saying words, and you just write down everything she says as fast as you can, and then I helped her put the story together, and then you put a song together. It's an amazing process with her, there's nothing like it."

Seeing songwriting in similarly cinematic terms, Music Row legend Hillary Lindsey has been shaping country music's landscape for more than a quarter century. *Rolling Stone* magazine concluded that she "helped chart the genre's current course," describing her natural writing style as one where "singing and songwriting both came hand in hand with me, like the melodies would always just kind of fly out and the words would a lot of times come with it. So it was weird, I don't know, but I just did it. The funny thing was, I assumed at a young age that everybody who sang just wrote their own songs." Once she arrived in Nashville and landed at Belmont University, Lindsey found a similar sense of community within the other then-unknown songwriters looking to land their first cut: "I met this amazing community of being around people who were like you, and they were so supportive. They couldn't wait to hear whatever new song you wrote, some of the kids I went to school with, and I wanted to hear theirs, and then somebody would say, 'Ooh, I want to play this part on this,' so, it was just a community of musical people. I got drug to my first writers' round, but I think because you would just get the feedback, you could tell obviously from just the reaction from the crowd whether or not they liked it or different, from 'Only one person clapped, oh, that song must have sucked . . .' or afterward where, yet again, the community of people you would meet—which were all the other songwriters in the room—where you would end up talking about maybe the song you had written and they would say something about it, or next thing you know, somebody would say, 'Well, hey, you want to come over and write something together sometime?' It was just the community of being out there, I think, and it just improves your skills the more you're around other songwriters."

Counting among her circle some of the biggest writers of the millennium to come, Lindsey fondly counts among "the crew I came up with: Troy Verges, Aimee Mayo, Chris Lindsey, Brett James, Gordie Sampson, and Angelo Petraglia, we were all really tight. It's like a safe place to be. A couple of them had a few hits, but nobody had really, like, all the way blown up, and so you were kind of just creating from this space of everybody was a little green but so excited. I think that's the beauty of having your tribe of cowriters, because it's just people that are in the same boat with you. It's just like this huge, beautiful experiment of trying to make some music together." As she racked up major early hits in her catalog like the number one smash "Jesus, Take the Wheel," Lindsey points to the 2005 Best Country Song Grammy winner as one of those songs from the beyond that she counts as among "a handful of them where you don't really know how they were written when it's over. It's like 'Wait a minute, did we do that?' because it seems so powerful, and I really think it's God, I think we're just vessels—all of us are, whether we write music or we don't. I think that that, to me, is what's so crazy about that song is that it truly helped people. There was something on CNN with two girls who got kidnapped and sang the lyrics to that song back and forth to each other during the ordeal. It was just unbelievable."

Fellow superstar songwriter Brett James took fans inside a daily writing routine where "we were just showing up for work on a very typical writing day. That day we were working at Hillary's house, and so we showed up that morning like we always do, made the coffee, and sat around and shot the bull for a half hour about what's going on, talking about life, and finally sat down and someone said, 'Well, what do you want to do today, what do you want to write about?' And we usually keep some titles lying around, or some concepts or places to start, and started going through ideas to write that day, and Gordie had this idea. So, Hillary was sitting over by the fireplace, and Gordie was sitting in his chair, and I'm sitting on her couch, and this was a tiny little living room, and Gordie says, 'Man, I got this little idea called "When Jesus Takes the Wheel.""

Reminding aspiring songwriters of the importance of taking chances in the writing room, Hillary felt the trio pooling their

Girl Power   27

cosmic songwriting talents: "There was so much freedom in writing that song because, back then, we were all so willing to just try anything, and everybody supported everybody in such a beautiful way that I still say, 'Dare to suck, when you have an idea, just go for it.' Whether it's a line you think is stupid, say it out loud, or if it's a melody that you think might be absolutely ridiculous, sing it. Probably a year after it had become a hit, I was driving home to Georgia in my beat-up Ford Explorer for Christmas, and I remember I was in a dark place in my life. Some of us songwriters, sometimes we get a little twisted in our head, and it came on the radio, and it spoke to me in that moment like no other song had ever spoken to me. It was so strange because I helped to create it, but it was as if it were going, 'Hey, Hillary, you need to pay attention.' It was just the strangest thing, and I don't know if that has ever happened to Gordie or Brett but it's weird when you create something and then it turns around and tries to teach you a lesson."

Aiming to relate to the listener in a real way every hit out, Lindsey would team up with a super-group of cowriters to create the Grammy-and-Oscar-nominated "Always Remember Us This Way" alongside Natalie Hemby, Lori McKenna, and Lady Gaga. Lindsey offers that, with any ballad she's sitting down to write, "I love when the heart is really in a song. Whether that's a love song or advice song, or a song about drinking and trucks—which I wish I was good at, I'm not great at—but even those songs have a lot of heart in them. It's true; it's real life, so that's what I love, when the heart makes the connection in the song. That's when I think people can really identify with it, and it makes them feel something. Sometimes I hear somebody in my head, where I can actually hear their voice singing what I'm singing. I'm not trying to do that, but sometimes it just kind of pops into my head, not all the time, but there are times where I'll say, 'Oh, my God, so-and-so would sound so good singing this.'"

As Lindsey was working together on the song with Lady Gaga, Natalie Hemby, and fellow cowriter McKenna, Lori succeeded

28   SONGS OF NASHVILLE

with her troupe of collaborators in capturing what she felt was "this amazing and crazy story that I think every single one of us has. Those are my favorite stories to hear, just like a glimmer of regular life, and you have three and a half minutes to magnify it, set it on fire, and make a little moment of it so we can understand the emotions of that character in that three and a half minutes."

When navigating a high-profile assignment like the one Hemby and her cowriters had been handed, Natalie for her part reveals of her songwriting process that "sometimes writing a song feels like a dare to see what you can get away with. You just go for it, almost like you don't really care what people think, because you are just having a good time writing it. The same goes for a song that is so personal. You just say what you want, like therapy. And it doesn't really matter what people think, because you know it was something you had to write or had to tell. I love both extremes." She comes at music from a purehearted place where she always felt it calling out to her as a natural gift, where "as a kid, I grew up, going to Puxico, Missouri, where my grandparents lived, and I would play the piano, make up songs, get up and sing or play the piano in church. It was a safe place to learn and make mistakes. The best thing my parents ever did for me was put a piano in my room. You could always tell if I was grounded because I'd play the piano for hours and hours. It became my favorite thing to do!"

Within the same mystical musical universe in which she helped create *A Star Is Born*'s signature song, Hemby—who from the same muse produced number one hits like "Pontoon" by Little Big Town, "Bluebird," "Baggage Claim," "White Liar," and "Automatic" by Miranda Lambert—offers helpful guidance to aspiring songwriters who might be worried about coming up with a new idea with which to walk into a cowrite with. Pointing to the very same spot she found herself in with Gaga, McKenna, and Hillary Lindsey, Natalie begins with the importance of "cowriting, for me, it's all about the cowriters. Depending on who it is, I can't wait to either share my ideas with them, or to hear their ideas. No matter who you are, you want to be inspired, and that's what I love about cowriting. I get inspired by my buddies. They make my songs better, and I want to make their songs better. There are so many ways to write a song. I have pages and pages of titles I write down. Sometimes when I'm working with someone who has a track, I see which title feels like the song and go from there. I've heard melodies in the middle of the night, I've had lyrics come to me when I'm in the shower or hiking or sitting up late at night thinking. They all have a common theme: In order to be a good writer, in any capacity, you need time alone with no distractions. And that's hard to do these days. Also, you need to be a good listener, an observer of life and people. I get so many ideas from conversations and stories I hear people tell. The world is one giant song waiting to be written, but you have to look in the most remote places."

Lori McKenna agrees, pointing to the inspiration behind one of her biggest hits, Tim McGraw's Grammy-winning number one hit for Song of the Year, "Humble and Kind," as coming to her far away from Nashville "back home in Massachusetts. I don't live in Nashville, so I write a lot by myself up here at home. That day, I had a rare moment of calm; I'd just gotten all my kids off to school, and I was sitting in my house thinking about the things that we want to tell our kids. At the time, my youngest was ten and my oldest was twenty-five, and we have all these different ages going on and the things my husband and I try to tell them and want to tell them, and decided to make a list. It took me the day to write it, and I went and picked them up from school, cooked dinner, and all that stuff, and when my husband came home, I was still tweaking it and finishing it up and played it for him, and he said, 'Man, that's good!' So, I sang it in my phone and emailed it to McGraw, and I still see that song as such a simple, little prayer I always call it: 'This is what I want you to know, this is what I want you to believe in yourself, and I want you to be a good person,' and Tim thought in such a bigger way. That was another blessing, because 'Humble and Kind' is another example of someone in the universe being really nice to me [*laughs*] and letting me write that song and be in a position where I could forward it to someone like Tim and for him to see it in such a huge way and make such a beautiful moment of it, it's all been so magic."

Dazzling everyone so that she took home the 2016 American Music Award for Favorite Country Song and the CMA's prized Song of the Year, she would repeat the honor alongside her fellow Love Junkies after the songwriting troupe comprising McKenna, Hillary Lindsey, and Liz Rose wrote "Girl Crush" for Little Big Town, taking home the Grammy Award for Best Country Song. Written within the sort of inspirational incantation that came to life when the three got together "at Liz's house, where the Love Junkies camp," Lori affectionately recalls, painting a picture for fans where "we'll sleep over and we write all day and night. The first song we wrote together as a threesome was 'Silver,' and that of course was cut by Little Big Town, and we knew sort of right away that we clicked musically, we all had different strengths, and we all can flip our strengths to one another depending on the song."

Liz Rose, reflecting the true synergy a group of gifted songwriters can conjure together when channeling all their talents into a song, feels "when we get in a room together, I feel like we're one songwriter, I really feel that. We talk about everything, and we probably talk 90 percent of the time, and write 10 percent [*laughs*], but we get so many ideas out of it, it's so fun! That's my wish list, is to have that feeling every time I write a song. When we're writing, the places they go are very different because of the kind of singers that they are—they're very different. So, for instance, there's never an 'artist' in the room, if you know what I mean, it's really the Love Junkies, it's really what the three of us do together. In that case, when Lori came in and said, 'Hey, I want to write a song called "Girl Crush,"' I went, 'No, that's not a good idea, how would we write that?' and she protested, 'No, no, no, I really do,' and I said, 'That sounds really hard.' We didn't have a lot of time that morning."

Lori McKenna welcomed the challenge of taking on such a simple-seeming subject from its title and creating the far-more-layered song that followed after "we woke up at Liz's house, and I always get up a little bit earlier than Hillary because I'm on Boston time. So, Liz and I were awake and making breakfast and we knew we had a couple hours and so it was like, 'Are we going to write, are we going to hang out? Were we gonna girl talk, what were we going to do?' And I said, 'I want to write a song called "Girl Crush,"' but I hadn't thought about it at all. I just thought it could be fun, really cool, it's a great title. I knew it would be a girl singing it, but other than that, I didn't really think anything else about it, and the title came just from like people saying that term. It was a popular term at the time, and I'm a woman that's inspired by other women. I'm like a girl's girl in that way. There's this blogger I follow, and everyone asks me what the big deal is, and I'd say, 'No, she dresses so nice, everything she does is great, that's my girl crush.' So, it's like, I don't know her, but I always thought of it in a positive way. Liz didn't like the idea at first and was like 'I don't know, man, I don't even know what that means, I don't know lyrically where you would go with that.'"

The answer would arrive with Hillary and a spontaneous burst of inspiration that gave the song idea its wings after Lindsey recalled "that day, when I woke up, after Lori told her she wanted to write a song called 'Girl Crush' and apparently Liz had said 'That sounds like a hashtag. I don't want to write anything that sounds like a hashtag.' Well, Lori always says, 'You know how you ask your mom or your dad something, and when one says no, you go to the other parent?' So, she went to the other parent, which was me, and said, 'Hey, I want to write a song called "Girl Crush."' As soon as I heard that title, I picked up the guitar, and I don't know how or why but I just played the chords and the first four lines of the melody just kind of came out. When I sang that line, Lori said *'Yes!'* and Liz said 'Oh, my God, I love that, we are writing that, we've got to write that now.' So, we wrote it really quickly, and didn't even talk about it. So this was probably around nine o'clock, and within forty-five minutes to an hour, we recorded the demo on one of our iPhones and that was that, and [we] didn't think anything else about it at all. Then when Karen [Fairchild] and Kimberly [Schlapman] from Little Big Town showed up to write, they asked us if we'd written anything cool that week and Liz said, 'Actually, we wrote something this morning if you want to hear it.' I wanted to kill her because I had a cold, and initially protested, 'Please don't play this in front of Karen and Kimberly,' because they're amazing singers and I sounded terrible, but she played it anyway, and they instantly freaked out and were like 'We have to have this, we have to have this,' and Liz, Lori, and I were all like 'Wait a minute, what just happened? This never happens, ever, ever, ever.' So, that one was another song that just wrote itself. We had to write it fast and had no time to second-guess ourselves, no time to filter ourselves, it just came out so quickly because they were showing up to write."

Pointing to the number one smash that was so popular with country fans, they made it the second most played single of 2015—one of those shooting stars songwriters catch and capture together during a write. McKenna acknowledges it to date as "just a gift. It wasn't like one person came in with that song and the other two helped it, because if it wasn't for the three of us sitting there, and Hillary being a genius and the songwriting gods being nice to us that day, none of it would have happened." Whether sitting behind the scenes writing a new hit single or onstage performing one on *The Late Show with Stephen Colbert*, Lori offers as advice for other songwriters looking to follow in her storied footsteps that her key has come with balancing "the two things I have in my life that are the most important, my family and my music. They work together so well, and I'm lucky because I've rarely felt like one has taken away from the other. I feel like one has helped the other. On the family side of it, music has brought us so much, from taking us to places we never would have been able to go and has brought both my husband and I friendships we wouldn't have been able to have otherwise. So, they really do enrich one another, especially when you've done it as long as I have. I think you have to be in it for the long haul to see the payoff in that way."

As important as her considerable creative counsel is, Hillary Lindsey offers the following from the business side of making sure the songs you write wind up being heard by those who might want to cut them, beginning with the importance of "this thing in town that publishers do called a pitch sheet. You can look on there and see who's cutting, who's about to cut, who's in the studio at that time, so sometimes you do go, 'Oh, man, Keith Urban's cutting in a couple weeks, we should try to write something for him.' Every songwriter is like this. Especially being a songwriter, sometimes it's like 'Dammit, I wish I wrote that.' I think that's why people connect to music in general. I know I do when I hear other people's songs and say, 'Oh, my God, that's exactly how I feel, I wish I could have found a way to say that!' You never let yourself sit in it long enough because you've just got to write the next song."

Liz Rose continues to marvel at the magical nature of songwriting rooted in the fact that "you never know when or where a song's going to come from. I think you'd be silly to think, no matter where you are in your career, you're never too big or too small for any artist to write with or for, and you should never think you're too big of a songwriter to write with a new artist. I think you've got to write with all of them, and you've got to get in a room with everybody you can because you never know who you're going to click with, and who you're going to be that conduit for. You could be the person that helps them tell their story, so you've got to get in those rooms and figure out what works."

Once a song is written, Natalie Hemby brings the conversation full circle by placing an emphasis every time out on getting and staying in the practice of "playing your songs live, it's so important! It is the ultimate sounding board. No one will sell your song more than you. You are the translator. And it opens doors that you didn't realize existed. Other writers are sometimes in the audience, and they might hear a song they love and come up to you and ask you to write. It's how you find your niche, your tribe. Songs are meant to be sung, not kept hidden away, and the world is always in need of a good song."

CHAPTER 3

THE NATURAL

. . . .

Vince Gill

"Oklahoman Vince Gill is among the most talented and successful country artists of the last few decades. Hugely popular in contemporary country—with more than 40 singles on the US Billboard charts—he has won 18 CMA awards, including the highly coveted Entertainer of the Year award two years in a row (1993 and 1994), and 21 Grammys, virtually monopolizing the award for Male Country Vocal Performance between 1989 and 1997."
—PBS.com

Vince Gill has a voice that just sounds like it belongs on country music radio. He's as revered a six-string slinger, giving the world for decades what *Guitar World* magazine has hailed as "his virtuosic and sweetly expressive solos—whether flat-picked or played fingerstyle," so sweet to the ear that he made *Rolling Stone*'s 250 Greatest Guitarists of All Time, and traces his roots there, so young in fact that

I have a picture of me when I was a baby, probably a year and a half old, and I'm asleep face-down on the couch and have my arms wrapped around a guitar. I don't remember an age where I can say I started playing the guitar, five or whatever, but my dad played with me a little bit, and his mom played a little bit, my dad's brother played a little bit, so it was always a part of our lives.

I think my first conscious memory of music was hearing my grandmother play "How Great Thou Art" on the piano. If you go back into the '50s, there wasn't much else to do but listen to records, and that was the case with our family, it was often playing records. I had a big brother and sister and long before I could buy my own records, I was at the mercy of whatever records my older siblings and mom and dad were playing.

I don't ever remember not trying to play the guitar. I've got a picture my mom saved of me playing a tiny little parlor guitar and it had a lampshade for a strap, and I used to drag it around by that lampshade [*laughs*]! So, I've been about it my own life.

As *Billboard* has astutely observed in comparison, "Just like Marty Robbins before him, there is no style of music that Vince Gill hasn't mastered. Whether it be his home base of country music, his first love of bluegrass, rock or blues, Vince Gill is an artist who can do it all—and do it very well." Reflective of his grounding in a keep-your-boots-on-the-stage-and-cowboy-hat-out-of-the-clouds mentality that has served him royally throughout his career-long loyalty to it, Gill affirms decades after his live performing career began as an early teenager that

I don't care about being front and center when it comes to music, I just like being a part of it. Honestly, I just stumbled into being an artist, I guess. It wasn't my plan when I left home [*laughs*], I never sat in front of the mirror pretending I was Elvis. I just kept my nose down, trying to play the guitar and just be part of the process. I'm still part of a band in my 60s.

Born and raised in Norman, Oklahoma, Gill found his way into his first group as a teenager playing guitar with the bluegrass band Mountain Smoke, finding a home away from his own onstage and the road he's followed ever since. Paying his proverbial dues as a road player from the mid- through late-1970s, playing first as a member of the Louisville-based Bluegrass Alliance and then with Ricky Skaggs's Boone Creek band, he next found himself out West in Los Angeles playing with Sundance and famed fiddler Byron Berline.

Still, though he felt he was born with a natural ability to play guitar, when he began trying to extend that gift into writing songs on the six-string, Vince confesses that "it's like anything else, you're not automatically a songwriter or a good one. I think that came last for me, the process of thinking about writing a song. I do have a silly thing I did as a grade-schooler where I changed the words to 'Old Shep' for some school project I had to do. I don't think I really started to try and write songs until I was late into my teens. It takes years and years and songs and songs to really learn how to put them together."

Gill made his way to Nashville, Tennessee, in 1983 after scoring his first charting hit, "Let Me Love You Tonight," with his band Pure Prairie League in 1980 off the album *Can't Hold Back*, gaining his first national radio and TV exposure with appearances on *American Bandstand* and *Solid Gold*. Singing lead on the hit, he was already showcasing the winning teaming of his extraordinary guitar-playing and gifts as a lead vocalist with a hit already under his belt. Sharing his earliest memories of discovering he had his own unique way of singing a song, the superstar remembered it was "pretty early on. I was a guitar player first and then began singing. I didn't have the courage to sing at first, it takes a lot of guts to sing in front of people. I don't think people understand how hard that is, the courage to do that. So that was excruciating,

38 SONGS OF NASHVILLE

finding the courage to sing in front of people, but in the bands I was in, I was usually the guy who could kind of sing the best. So I wound up singing the songs, and got over my fears and everything was fine."

Spotlighting an important distinction, he learned to draw early on between a well-sung and well-written song that served him well throughout his career. Vince offers that "for me, both of those things, my playing ability and my singing ability, always overshadowed my songwriting, and probably that's because sometimes a great voice can fool you. You're not quite so in tuned to a lyric, but the guy singing can really sing, so people say, 'The guy could sing the phone book and he'd probably be okay . . .' So, again, it took a long time for the songs to show up and get good, and I think that's the case for everybody. Through that, I think that it made me work harder, because people didn't respond to my songs as quickly as they did the other things I could do, and I don't mind that because there's a lot of truth in it."

He found more successful employment in the music business as lead guitar player in Rodney Crowell's Cherry Bombs (later known as the Notorious Cherry Bombs), where he played with Emory Gordy Jr. and Tony Brown. Ironically, both Gordy and Brown would go on to produce albums with Gill, who scored his first publishing deal and record deal with RCA in 1983. Navigating his way through the politics of the publishing business early on, he won Top New Male Vocalist from the Academy of Country Music in 1984, and first broke through on radio as a solo star once he was given the green light to record his own songs. Scoring his first Top 40 solo hit in 1985 with "True Love," he then made the Top 10 on the *Billboard* Hot Country Songs Chart debut courtesy of a ballad he cowrote with Rosanne Cash, titled "If It Weren't for Him" off *The Things That Matter* LP.

He would give his fast-growing fan base an encore when his second Top 10 hit arrived in the form of one of those classics that's still playing on radio today, "Oklahoma Borderline," one of Gill's most requested live staples. Proudly pointing to the cowriting team of himself, Rodney Crowell, and Guy Clark as jointly responsible for penning the smash, Gill quips that his primary role in the song's writing session was "to shut up and keep up [*laughs*]! Both Rodney and Guy were great mentors of mine. I met them both when I was nineteen years old, played guitar on their records, and was around all these great songs. And they were kind enough to help me along and get one written. That one is a really cool lick because of Rodney and Guy and has always been a staple in my repertoire. I always play it every night I play live music, and I think it might have been the first song I ever got a BMI [Broadcast Music, Inc.] award for one of the most played songs in a year. It's meant everything to me and has sentimental value to me too, and once again is kind of a guitar showpiece song for me over the years. It has a lot of history with me."

Following the release of 1987's *The Way Back Home*, which produced more early chart hits with Top 20 placements "Everybody's Sweetheart" and "Let's Do Something"—the first written solo and the second cowritten with Reed Neilsen—Gill would hit the Top 5 with "Cinderella." Gill's next monster radio hit would be a precise reminder of why he held the respect of both the veteran and new eras of country music fans with "When I Call Your Name," recalling of its creation that "it's just your typical country music sad song. Country music is legendary because of those kinds of songs, and those are the ones I've always been most drawn to, the saddest songs of all. 'He Stopped Loving Her Today' by George Jones or 'Gospel Girl' or whatever sad, morbid songs you want [*laughs*], the sadder the better. And that's what 'When I Call Your Name' was meant to be. I'm not saying the song wasn't there without it, but it became my first big breakthrough, monster record, and that it was something traditional was something I really, really loved. That song, as we recorded it, nobody thought a whole lot of it, nobody was going 'Here's our breakthrough song!' not one time. Then three things happened to it that changed the face of that song. The first was, we didn't have an intro for that song, so I called my friend Barry Beckett late one night, it was 1:00 or 2:00 in the morning, and he'd been in a session all day, and I said: 'Man, we're slaving away. We need a really cool intro for this song,' and he came over sleepy-eyed and played that intro, and we said: 'There we go, it finally has its definition. It has that thing that is going to identify that song that a musician played.' Then, as a finishing touch, Paul Franklin came in and did the pedal steel solo, but I actually called him afterward and said, 'Hey, man, would you mind coming back down here and playing the solo on this Waltz?' And at first he said, 'I liked what I played,' and was kind of mad about it, so I said, 'Well, I like it too, but I really want the instrument to do what it used to do, I want it to be that emotional, swelling, sweeping high, beautiful thing that a steel guitar does that nobody does much anymore.' He begrudgingly came back in and redid it. Then when it was done and he heard it, he said, 'Thank you for asking me to come back in and replay that solo [*laughs*]!' It's one of the twenty iconic steel guitar solos ever to musicians and steel players, and then the gem on top was Patty Loveless's voice. The interesting thing about that being the breakthrough song for me is how traditional it was, and that wasn't really the norm in 1989, 1990. Anything that 'traditional' was really not that common, and whether you sing it by yourself or with a band or great harmony singers, it's still in the song. It doesn't need all those things, but it's all of those things that kind of made it the classic that it is."

Taking country music's collective breath away when it hit radio waves, high school prom, and wedding dance floors. PBS soon thereafter reported that Gill broke through into mainstream country music stardom with "When I Call Your Name": "The title cut firmly established him as a new force on the scene, peaking at number two and earning Gill his first CMA Award (Single of the Year) and first Grammy (Best Male Country Vocal Performance). The

The Natural   41

album, certified platinum, revealed what would become Gill's trademark mix of country-pop, rock, bluegrass, and hard country songs."

Gill found himself in the same position every newly minted country star with high expectations does: follow up the last hit with a new chart topper that MCA Records was certainly hoping sold even bigger than the last LP. And he succeeded with the two-million-selling album *Pocket Full of Gold* and the four Top 20 hits that followed. "Liza Jane," which was cowritten with Reed Neilsen, became a Top 10 hit along with the title track "Pocket Full of Gold," cowritten with Brian Allsmiller, plus the solo-written "Take the Memory with You," and "Look At Us," cowritten with Max Barnes, which peaked at number four, and which Gill singles out as "a gift! I wrote that with Max D. Barnes, and I'd been working on this idea and knew from 'Chiseled' that he liked sad songs, so it went, 'Look at us, after all these years together,' and the way I'd originally started it, the intent of it was, 'We're not gonna make it, after all these years are gone . . .' And I took it to him and sang him the verse I had going. After I got through singing him the first verse of the song, I stopped and asked, 'What do you think?' and he replied, 'That's a great idea but that's too sad . . .' [*laughs*]. I said, 'What are you talking about, sad songs? You *love* sad songs!' and he said, 'Yeah, but you got a great idea going here, you're just going about it the wrong way.' I asked, 'What do you mean?' and he said, 'This couple needs to stay together.' So, we flipped it around and it became a positive love song, and I bet I've had a thousand people send me their fiftieth wedding anniversary picture and all this kind of stuff, saying, 'The song we danced to, . . .' so Max was spot on as usual."

Gill topped the year off with another round of awards for his trophy shelf, including arguably the grandest distinctions for any rising country star: induction into the Grand Ole Opry, along with CMA's Male Vocalist of the Year nod and his second Grammy win for Best Country Vocal Collaboration for "Restless," a duet with

Ricky Skaggs and Steve Wariner. Still, it was with his sixth studio album that Vince Gill would become one of country music's biggest stars and reach the top of the proverbial mountain that every songwriter and recording artist on the rise in Nashville aims to reach, that of number one on the *Billboard* Hot Country Songs Chart! He would do so handily with the release of the *I Still Believe in You* album, which delivered future *Greatest Hits* album highlights that drove Gill's fifth LP to five million copies sold based on the chart strength of four back-to-back number one smash hits—"I Still Believe in You," "Don't Let Our Love Start Slippin' Away," "One More Last Chance," and "Tryin' to Get Over You," along with the Top 5 hit "No Future in the Past."

Giving his fans around the world an in-depth look at the writing of the album's title track, "I Still Believe in You," his first number one hit, Gill—who admits he was feeling the pressures that come with stardom and the expectations of those around him and poured them therapeutically into the song—recalled that the lyrics led the way, where "the first line of the song sort of points where it goes, and it just has to be an idea. The truth doesn't need to necessarily be there at every turn, and the day I wrote that with John Barlow Jarvis, I'd just had a huge blowout with my first wife, and just felt like 'Everything's wrong. . . .' I was in the midst of really turning my life around professionally, and when I walked in, he asked, 'How's it going?' and I said, 'Man, everybody wants a little piece of my time,' and he said, 'Okay, that's the first line!' He already had some music going for that, and that song was actually not a ballad when we wrote it, it was a more up-tempo song. It's funny sometimes how the music of something will take it where it needs to go. A friend of mine, Mark Foster, used to say: 'You can take a song anywhere you want. You can play it fast, play it in a different time signature,' and it's interesting how that's so true."

Gill would pick that tempo up for the weekend dance floor and main street cruising crowds with "Don't Let Our Love Start Slippin'

Away," with Vince teaming up with "my old friend Pete Wasner," with whom he identified an especially kindred musical connection with the two channeled together into what became his second number one hit: "There's something about we play music together that was probably unlike anything else. We wrote songs together, but we also played music together, and he's a great piano player, and whether it's groove-wise, feel-wise, we both love the same thing. So, we complement each other really, really well musically, and that was a song that really was more about the groove that we had built. I actually took two old verses from another song and used them in that song, and then the chorus just laid over the top of that groove. It was as easy as anything you ever hope to find. That's one of those things that's not going to make you think of Bob Dylan's lyric [*laughs*], but there's something about all of it put together—the groove and the feel, and that makes it work."

Following the release of his first Christmas-themed album, a long-standing standard for any country music star who wants to truly hang around through the ages, Gill delivered with the two-time, platinum-selling *Let There Be Peace on Earth* before returning to the studio to record his seventh studio album, the aforementioned *When Love Finds You*, which sold a staggering four million copies and added another five hits to Gill's catalog, beginning with "Whenever You Come Around," which remains close to the legendary star's heart as a favorite: "That one's really special. That's arguably one of my very favorite songs, and the one I prefer singing over all of them, maybe, because it was written simply from being taken with Amy's smile, my wife, Amy Grant, the first time I saw her. Innocently, I thought it was the most beautiful song I'd ever sung, went home and wrote this song about it. So, once again, the very start of this song was about something very real, then the rest of it was just songwriters making a story that was hopefully compelling. So, it was a simple inspiration, the beauty of a smile, that turned into a really aching, yearning love song."

44   SONGS OF NASHVILLE

Vince's hit streak would continue to blaze up the charts with follow-up smashes "You Better Think Twice" and "What the Cowgirls Do," both of which peaked at number two on the *Billboard* Hot Country Songs Chart, the title track "When Love Finds You," which reached number three, "Which Bridge to Cross (Which Bridge to Burn)," which was close behind at number four, and among Gill's most celebrated songwriting and vocal accomplishments to date, "Go Rest High on That Mountain." A tribute by Gill to his stepbrother's tragic passing just before he wrote the ode, it would eventually rank at number seventeen on *Rolling Stone* magazine's Saddest Country Songs of All Time, and would appropriately win the Country Music Association Song of the Year Award in 1996, two Grammys for Best Male Country Vocal Performance and Best Country Song, and the BMI Trophy for Most Performed Song in 1997.

Already receiving an early version of the "Greatest Hits" treatment with the three-million-selling *Souvenirs* album, released in 1996 in reflection of Gill's popularity as a swooner with listeners, as Vince Gill entered the second half of the 1990s, fans heard *High Lonesome Sound* on the horizon. His eighth studio album pulled into town and took over the charts as it reached number two with the self-penned "A Little More Love," number five with "Worlds Apart"—which earned him another Grammy for Best Male Country Vocal Performance—and the Top 10 with "You and You Alone," and again peaking at number two with "Pretty Little Adriana." The title track, "High Lonesome Sound," would earn Gill his second Grammy for Best Country Collaboration with Vocals thanks to his duet with Alison Krauss on the song's soaring lead vocals. Celebrating Gill's love of Krauss's native genre, he recalls "that song came from my history of bluegrass. I played a lot of bluegrass in my teenage years, and the first three bands I played in after I left home were bluegrass bands, and so if I hadn't done anything in bluegrass music, I wouldn't know how to write a song like that. There's nothing better than singing with Alison, it doesn't get any better. And it was all her band too, the Union Station guys all played on that record, and I still love bluegrass and being a small part of it from time to time. For me, the way I've always approached what I do, I think it's harder to sing with someone than people realize, to blend, to make your voice work and do what theirs does, and at the same time, not sing too hard. I've worked on I think a thousand different artists' records in my career. So, I've got years and years and years and years of experience of being a supporting cast member, and that's something I've always loved doing. I think I was always trying to be Phil Everly for people, or what Don Rich was to Buck Owens, and I just wanted to be a great, seamless harmony singer, and always had an ear for it, a knack for it, and always had a love for it. That saying, 'High Lonesome Sound,' comes from Bill Monroe, and the song is very much a nod to him."

Pointing to the inspiration behind another of the album's standout hits, "Pretty Little Adriana," Gill gives fans an insight into his personal life and how fatherhood influenced him as a songwriter: "I don't think a lot of people know the history of that song, but the inspiration behind it was: I was home watching the news, and this was back in the early 1990s, and a young African American girl had been killed in a drive-by shooting, which you never really saw happen much here. I saw the pictures of this kid on TV with a beautiful smile, and it was actually 'Adrienne,' but I needed an extra syllable for the song to make sense, so, I changed her name to 'Adriana.' My daughter Jenny was the same age as this kid, so the real intent of that song is so different from what most people assume it is when they hear it. It's really written from the perspective of a parent losing a child, so, it's not quite a simple little love song. It's deeper and different than that, and after the song had come out and was successful, I found Adrienne Dickerson's family and let them know that their daughter inspired this song. So, there was beauty to it."

In making creative decisions before beginning any new album, Vince credited his confidence within his vocal and guitar-playing abilities as a key to opening any new writing session, reasoning that "the important thing to the way that I write songs is that, because of the singer that I am and the musician that I am, I can take melodies that go and do things that suit what I can do and what I'm good at. A lot of times, I don't think songwriters have the range melodically to sing certain things, so they might stay in their own little place and not go very far. But think of somebody like Roy Orbison, listen to the songs he wrote and the way he could sing—he could take the melodies and the crying and all the tender songs, go up there and blow the roof off. I'm not saying I can, but I am saying because I play and because I have the range that I have, I can melodically take songs to some good places that suit me. Not because they're better, it just suits what I do musically and what I hear, and what I like. That's all we have."

Triumphantly hitting number one on the US Top Country Albums Chart with *The Key* in 1998, Gill would once again give his fans another era of hits to round the dance floors with fast or slow, courtesy of "If You Had Forever in Mind," which hit number five. Vince remembered "writing with Troy Seals, and I had nothing to do with that lyric. I was the music for that song, melody, and feel. Troy and I messed around and wrote some songs together a long time ago, and that's the song that probably just found the lyric and added the music to maybe ten years later when we'd gotten together. It reminded me of when Ray Charles did that great country record, with that kind of feel, real bluesy and slow."

The superstar would rack up another smash ballad with Patty Loveless on "My Kind of Man, My Kind of Woman," which he revealed was not originally intended to be a duet, going so far as to offer that when he's first sitting down to begin work on a ballad, "I don't think songs are written very often with the thought of being duet songs. Some of them make great duet songs, people make them

The Natural   47

whatever they want them to be, change the key. I've always sung as high as a woman anyway [*laughs*], so I could be singing with a girl, and you wouldn't have to change keys. So, it worked out pretty good. I always knew I was going to sing that one with Patty, it was a no-brainer, and that was written as a duet, which was fun to incorporate both points of view and tailor make it for our two voices."

The Oklahoman would crown *The Key* as "one of the best albums in country music history," followed by another platinum holiday release, *Breath of Heaven: A Christmas Collection,* and then Gill's first album release of the 2000s, *Let's Make Sure We Kiss Goodbye.* Years removed from the thunderstorm that followed his being lit by a lightning bolt of love that sparked a lifelong love song between Gill and longtime wife and partner Amy Grant, in reflecting on how songwriting provided a badly needed refuge from the first negative headlines he'd received in his superstar career, specifically in the form of one song of the many songs he'd go on to write for her: "At that time in my life, Amy and I hadn't been married that long, and so I wrote, 'I'll take these days, over any other days I've ever known,' and that was true. That was my truth, it was real. So, 'These Days' is one of my favorite songs, lyrically."

Following the release of *Let's Make Sure We Kiss Goodbye,* which gave the hit songwriter another one when "Feels Like Love" became a Top 10 hit, Gill gave fans *Next Big Thing.* Then he spread his creative wings even further in a demonstration of both his vast influences stylistically and prolific ability to celebrate them musically. Vince Gill would do just that—and ambitiously—on *These Days,* released over four albums as a boxed set, ranging across forty-three songs all penned solo by Gill. It made number ten on *People* magazine's "Top 10 Best Albums of the Century (So Far)," sharing space on a list that featured everyone from Jay-Z to Amy Winehouse. Speaking to the strength of mainstream popularity and staying power, the four albums are *Workin' on a Big Chill,* known as "The

48   SONGS OF NASHVILLE

Rockin' Record," *The Reason Why*, alternately known as "The Groovy Record," *Some Things Never Get Old*, known as "The Country and Western Record," and *Little Brother*, alternately known as *Little Brother*.

In selecting those he felt best reflected each of the four records within the collection, Gill spotlights a teachable moment for aspiring songwriters as he was writing the forty-three tunes that span this one-of-a-kind collection, offering his learned opinion that "the most important advice is your ears won't lie to you. They'll generally tell you the truth. Now, your eyes will lie to you all the time. What you think you see and precondition you to judge before anything even happens. But your ears won't, and I think what I've learned most is being patient, waiting for a lyric to come, don't settle, and be willing to work even a little harder, finding a little bit of a different way to say something. Or, in a lot of cases, being willing to edit yourself. It's not how much information I give, it's the correct information that I give, and all you need to do is tell the story, that's all you need to do. It's the same way with a guitar solo; you don't feed thirty-eight notes in there if ten will do great. There are things that show up in life at times when you need them, and you don't always know that you need them. Back in the 2000s, when radio kind of stopped playing my records, I wasn't a big hit country guy like I had been, and that was starting to weigh a little bit, and I get a call from Eric Clapton [who]asked me to play with him, and I thought, 'Wow, one of the best guitar players in the world likes what I do,' and my answer was 'Yeah, I'll come, of course!' Then something like the Eagles opportunity shows up, and all it is to me is an affirmation of a lifetime of work."

As he reached the point heading into the mid-2000s, following his taking home the Grammy Award for Country Album of the Year, Vince Gill had earned the freedom to head wherever he wanted to, and he chose to join The Time Jumpers, an all-star Western swing group that recorded albums including the live

The Natural   49

Jumpin' Time album in 2007. He then released *The Time Jumpers* in 2012 and *Kid Sister* in 2016, eventually earning Gill another Grammy for Best American Roots Song with "Kid Sister," which the superstar penned. The *Guitar Slinger* LP marked Vince Gill's most direct celebration of his six-string roots as a lifelong axe-slinger, while National Public Radio would spotlight a superstar teaming where "country-music star Vince Gill and steel guitarist Paul Franklin have teamed up to record a new concept album called *Bakersfield*. Their idea is to cover hits from the 1960s and '70s by two artists who helped define the Bakersfield, California, country sound: Merle Haggard and the Strangers, and Buck Owens and the Buckaroos." Gill calls the collection part of "the journey, all records are the journey, and the one I make next will be different than the one I made previously. To me, it's like when I made *Bakersfield* with Paul Franklin, and scratched that real traditional place, 'Now I want to go make this record,' and it was very different. I've seen that pattern my whole life, trying to do something a little bit different. I like all kinds of things."

As Vince Gill reached his fourteenth studio album, *Down to My Last Bad Habit,* and then *Okie* in 2016, it was a vision he detailed as one where "the whole premise of this record *Okie* was to only have it be about the songs, there was not any blazing solos, there weren't big backgrounds, there weren't hit driven/proven recording tricks of the trade to try and do anything. It was simply a guy singing these songs and standing out of the way of the lyric. The lyrics were to me fairly substantial in reflection and in honesty, and things like that. More than anything it wasn't trying to wow you, because I think great records move you, rather than impress you."

To little surprise, Gill would keep racking up more Grammy wins heading into the 2020s, including in 2020 the Grammy for Best American Roots Song "I Don't Wanna Ride the Rails No More" and again in 2021 for Best Male Solo Performance on "When

My Arms Pray." In 2023, his next collaboration with Paul Franklin on the *Sweet Memories* LP earned the pair the trophy for Best Country Duo / Group Performance for "Kissing Your Picture (Is So Cold)." When Gill is asked about his status as the most awarded Grammy country music artist in history, he begins by quipping, "I don't gloat about it [*laughs*]! What I'm proudest of is the diversity of them. They're for writing songs, they're for being a musician, they're for instrumental tracks, they're for producing records, for being an artist, so the fact that they encapsulate everything that it is I do, that's what means the most to me. It's an unreal feeling to have people respond, and the neat thing about all that kind of stuff—awards—is that people get to vote for what they like."

Gill would find himself entering a whole new level of spotlight when he was suddenly faced with a call he never expected or hoped to receive following the *Los Angeles Times* cover story asking the classic question: "Can an iconic rock band that's lost a key member continue? Or should it? Founding members of the Who—Pete Townshend and Roger Daltrey—have kept that band alive despite the deaths of drummer Keith Moon in 1978 and of bassist John Entwistle in 2002. The Grateful Dead essentially retired that band's name after lead guitarist Jerry Garcia died in 1995. Queen has found new life and new fans touring with *American Idol* alum Adam Lambert singing the parts originally voiced by Freddie Mercury, who died in 1991. And now the Eagles are about to fly again without a musician widely viewed as its leader and chief musical architect. . . . Surviving members have turned to one family member and one longtime friend to help it through this transition: Deacon Frey, the twenty-four-year-old son of Eagles cofounder Glenn Frey, who died [in 2016], and country music star Vince Gill." He was instantly catapulted from arenas to stadiums, playing with arguably the biggest country rock band of all time. Vince confesses to feeling a little surreal when they pulled

The Natural 51

his name out of the cosmos of stars the band could have had, but from day one he followed his tried-and-true formula of keeping his feet on the ground and head out of the clouds after he'd quickly accepted the position in the band:

> The only reason I got to do it was out of something tragic with the passing of Glenn, and I think those songs are the most important of all of it. We're all going to fail to live forever, that's just not going to happen, but the songs will. There's a lot of naysayers out there, and I don't blame them. That's my favorite band, and if a key member of the band was gone like Glenn Fry, I wouldn't be too keen either on some knucklehead showing up and singing their songs, but I was grateful.

> I don't think it really ever felt at any point like trying to fill someone's shoes, as much as it was "Hey, we need somebody to show up and play these songs." Those songs are so great, and they'll never be the same, the original is never going to be surpassed, and I knew that going in. It was just a great lesson to learn, again, even at sixty years old, how important songs are, and that's a catalog of songs that can't be touched by any American band in history. So, just to be the guy they called to come help out was pretty amazing. I feel like it's a good fit, what I do is well within their wheelhouse, so, it's been a great thing!

While he's given plenty of those sorts of timeless moments and memories to generations of his own fans around the world in song on record and stage over the past forty-plus years, when asked in closing about advice he's given and continues to give to the kid dreaming of playing out a path in Nashville and country music more broadly, Gill sticks to the basics that have always served him solidly: "What I would tell a young person is, it doesn't have to be a certain way. I was nothing like Merle Haggard and Merle was nothing like Roy Acuff. The way life evolves, the kids today are nothing like I've been, and they shouldn't be. They should be themselves and be what it is they're inspired to be!"

CHAPTER 4

I'VE COME TO EXPECT IT FROM YOU

· ·

Buddy Cannon

B uddy Cannon's career in Nashville, in the estimation of the Country Music Hall of Fame, has been "marked by longevity, affability, and excellence." Judging his caliber as a producer by the nearly twenty-five years Kenny Chesney has been working with him, or the last two decades he's been Willie Nelson's exclusive man behind the boards, Cannon has earned the right to become what CMT recently spotlighted as "one of Nashville's most sought-after producers." Before he began producing hits, Cannon spent the 1980s and 1990s writing a catalog full of them, ranging from "Give It Away" and "I've Come to Expect It from You" by George Strait, "Anywhere But Here" by Sammy Kershaw, "Naked in the Rain" by Loretta Lynn, "Dream of Me" by the Oak Ridge Boys, "She's Not Crying Anymore" by Billy Ray Cyrus, "I'm Still Crazy" and "Set 'Em Up" by Vern Gosdin, "She Meant Forever When She Said Goodbye" by Mel Tillis, for whom Cannon additionally wrote the number one smash "I Believe in You," to more recent Willie Nelson cuts, including "The Wall," "It's All Going to Pot," and "Roll Me Up and Smoke Me When I Die."

Finding a fit with the guitar at the same natural age many kids are finding it within a baseball glove, Cannon remembers: "I bought my first guitar when I was eleven. It was a Silvertone that I ordered from the Sears, Roebuck and Company catalog for $13, and when I got it in the mail, I started learning how to make chords, and one of my mother's brothers was a really good musician. He could have been a pro if he'd chosen to, but he wanted to stay at home. But he

54 SONGS OF NASHVILLE

could play well any instrument with strings on it, and when he saw I was kind of getting the hang of the guitar, he came over one day and had a different guitar, an old Gibson that one of his musician friends had gotten drunk one day and stomped. It had a big hole in it, and it looked kind of like Willie Nelson's guitar, Trigger, in reverse, but it was a Gibson, and he told me, 'Here, you give me that guitar and you take this one.' So, my uncle Dalton Tate was my musician mentor."

Within his record collection, Buddy counts as equally important and influential the music he heard, "listening to everything growing up! Even before rockabilly had broken out, I was listening to Hank Williams and whatever the popular country record was. That's where I started was Hank, and I remember finding out he'd died by listening to a song myself on the radio called 'The Death of Hank Williams.' I was about four, and I remember being brokenhearted and crying, because he'd influenced [me] from three years old on. We had an old battery-operated radio at home, but my uncle Dalton Tate had a nice, big-cabinet stereo with a bunch of 78 RPMs, and he had everything from bluegrass to Bob Wills and the Texas Playboys. I'd go to his house, lay down in front of that thing, and just play those 78s, and it went into my heart. That early on, I was just listening to the emotion of the song, I hadn't gotten yet into dissecting the record. But to me, throughout my career, capturing the emotion of the song has been everything."

Landing in his first band doing that firsthand while still in his teens, Buddy recalled that "I was in my junior year of high school when a bunch of local guys and I formed this little rock band called the Lyndels I played guitar in. We were playing teen dances and gigs like that, and by that time the Rolling Stones and the Beatles were starting to pop, [and] the Animals, the popular rock of the day on the radio is what we were playing." Cannon wound up thereafter in his migration to Music Row as journeyman musician in bands like the Fabulous Bobby Pierce and the Nashville Sounds playing bass.

Cannon reveals that, once he'd arrived in Nashville with a group of Grand Ole Opry regulars The Four Guys, "I actually replaced Don Cook!," giving him his first experiences playing live at the legendary Opry:

> They were a quartet like the Oak Ridge Boys, and they played at a club out on Murfreesboro Road five, six nights a week, and not only were we playing at the club at night, but every time an Opry spot [came up], we played there. I had actually started writing songs while I was on the road with Bob Luman, riding a thousand miles and nothing to do, and didn't really think of myself as a songwriter, but I was writing a few things. Through a connection with a guy named Jimmy Darrell, who worked for Mel Tillis at his publishing company, I'd given Jimmy a demo of four or five songs I'd written. Well, he played those for Mel, and he loved them, and they actually called me up at a gig and told me Mel had just recorded one of my songs called "Golden Nugget Gambling Casino"!

> I'd written the song with a buddy of mine named Gene Dunlap, and back in those days in Las Vegas, the show-room curtain was on a timer. So, if you were supposed to start playing at nine o'clock, no matter what you were doing, that curtain went up. For the forty-five-minute shows, at the end of the forty-five minutes, even if you were still playing, that curtain would come down [laughs]! So, people were always getting caught in the middle of a song, and that's what it was about. It had happened to Mel Tillis a couple times, because he had a stutter and couldn't really regulate time very well, so he identified with that song and recorded it. Then the next day he had another session and recorded three more songs off my demo, one

56 SONGS OF NASHVILLE

called "Everyone Needs Someone" and "It's Just Not That
Easy to Say."

It was a big break Buddy now still shakes his head in amazement
at, given the fact that "here Mel's one of the greatest songwriters ever
to come to Nashville, and all of a sudden, out of nowhere, he records
my song. When he called me up that first night he cut my song, I
thought somebody was pulling my leg when he said, 'We're down
here at my office listening to what we cut tonight, come on down!' I
went down there about 10:30, 11:00 at night." Cannon immediately
felt a kindred spirit in Mel Tillis, and the feeling was mutual. Cannon
shares that, "I didn't leave till the sun came up, and when I did, I had
a job. Mel Tillis signed me as a songwriter back in 1976, and coinci-
dentally, that was the same time he hired Jimmy Bowen to produce
his records. So, every time Mel was in the studio working, I was in
the studio hanging out and Jimmy was the guy driving the ship. That
was kind of my introduction to the whole Music Row scene, and I
just started soaking up everything like a sponge. That's where I started
learning how the studio ran. Soon enough I started helping produce
the demos for Mel, and it just kind of morphed into that because I
had musical instinct, and me and Jimmy Darrell, the two of us started
ramrodding the demo sessions, and that's really where I got bit by
the bug of being in the studio. The biggest things I learned from Mel
over those years ranged from me showing Mel a song I'd written
and him pointing out a little two-word thing that I might have had
backward or something. I remember one time I had a song Don Lee
had recorded called 'Woman, You Should Be in Movies,' and I had
the verses written in the second and the chorus was in third person,
and as soon as I heard it, he pointed it out to me and a big light went
off. I worked for Mel Tillis for twelve or thirteen years. During that
time, I also played in Mel's band."

The equivalent of earning a master's degree in how the business
worked from the songwriting to performing to producing sides of

creating a hit record, Buddy continued to find country music that radio loved as his earliest charting singles and hit records began to turn into gold and platinum smashes like "I Believe in You," which Buddy remembers first writing "in 1977 with Gene Dunlap, and Mel loved the song when we turned it in, but he wanted Glen Campbell to cut it because he and Glen were buddies. So, he sent it to Glen, and he listened to it, then called Mel and said, 'Yeah, I like it but there's a couple of lines in there I don't think I want to say.' So, Mel said, 'I'll get them to rewrite it and see what happens. . . .' So, he came back to us and that happened two or three times, where we'd rewrite it, Mel would send it back and Glen would say, 'No, that's not it.' Finally, Mel said, 'I'm cutting it myself,' and he did, and it was a number one hit for a few weeks. That was a giant thrill, and it happened to be at the same time while I was out playing on the road with Mel, so I was getting to play my own song every night! We were doing a lot of symphony gigs and getting to play it with a huge orchestra. Mel cut a lot of my songs on albums, quite a few songs, and I loved every one of them."

Hitting number one with his first charting single, Cannon was on a roll, following it up with a Top 40 hit by Loretta Lynn with "Naked in the Rain," then a duet between Nancy Sinatra and Mel Tillis, "Texas Cowboy Night," and another Top 10 for Vern Gosdin with "Dream of Me." He is proud of the way the song has stood the tests of time as he recalls that "I got acquainted with Vern Gosdin in 1980, 1981, and I had just written a song, 'Dream of Me,' and I played it for Vern and he flipped out over it, and had a hit record on it. The Oak Ridge Boys cut it, there were a lot of cuts on that song."

Buddy would rack up another early '80s Top 20 hit, "Whiskey Chasin'" by Joe Stampley, before scoring two more back-to-back number one hits with Vern Gosdin over "Set 'Em Up" and "I'm Still Crazy" before cracking his first number one hit with George Strait over "I've Come to Expect It from You," quipping that "back in George's heyday, everybody wanted a George Strait cut!"

58 SONGS OF NASHVILLE

Tracing the roots of his relationship with the superstar back a decade earlier, Buddy recounts that "I was lucky enough to get to know George in the very beginning, when he was doing his first demo session before he had a record deal. I was writing with Dean Dillon back then a lot, and I had a song on his first album, and through the years, he's cut several of my songs." Giving fans a look at the creation of one of those, the subsequent number one smash "Give It Away," cowritten among the superstar writing team of Cannon, Jamey Johnson, and the great "Whisperin'" Bill Anderson, Cannon remembers an immediate meeting of musical minds once the talented trio sat down to begin to write:

Jamey and Bill and I got together one morning over at my office at 19th and Grand, and we neither one of us has an idea to write, and Jamey was in the middle of getting divorced, and he started talking, telling us about a conversation with his ex-wife the night before. She didn't want any of their possessions, just told him to give it all away, and that thing kind of started writing itself. I thought it would be cool to do that recitation kind of thing, setting the verses up, I don't know why. .... Most people think Bill did that, because he does a lot of that. He always tells everybody I thought of doing that, and it worked out. We wrote it that morning, made a little guitar/vocal demo on it that afternoon, and George's manager, Erv Woolsey's office was across the street from my office, and I would always see Erv come and go. So, the next morning, I got to my office early, had a CD and sat there and waited till Erv drove in, walked out on the porch and hollered at him, and we met out in the middle of the street, and I said, "Hey, man, I just wrote this with Jamey and Bill," and he said, "I'll send it to George ..." and when he heard it, he called and put a hold on it and cut it shortly after that.

To this day, as serendipitous as any song sale ever goes, Buddy has lasted six decades in the business by sticking to the same rules of the songwriting road he always has, beginning amid his wildly successful career transition in the 1990s through the past thirty years producing tens of millions of albums sold with Kenny Chesney and Willie Nelson. First, he says, "I don't pitch my own songs to artists I record, not unless I think it's right. So, with Kenny Chesney, for instance, his music—the path it took—is different from the songs that I write. I've been fortunate to have some really good records cut on songs of mine, but they are all on artists I'm not working with."

Touching on his long-term record-making relationship with Willie Nelson, Cannon felt from the beginning of their acquaintance that "We could have been brothers. The first time I ever heard him sing, I was instantly a fan. I love the improvisation of everything he done playing or singing, and his songwriting is total genius." Whether he's been a songwriter in the session as a band member cutting one of his own hits or sitting behind the boards cutting his next number one hit with any of the stars he works with today in the studio, Buddy sticks to the bottom line of "just knowing I have a good song in my back pocket. With Kenny, I never have to worry about him wanting to cut anything else. With Willie, he and I just talk about it and then do it, and he's fun. How much better can it get working with your hero fifty years after he became your hero!"

CHAPTER 5

COUNTRY MUSIC LOVER

Bobby Braddock

The Country Music Hall of Fame has crowned Bobby Braddock "one of country music's most prolific, imaginative, and successful songwriters" in Music Row history. *Rolling Stone*, clearly in agreement, muses that "Braddock's tunes have not only inspired generations of other songwriters, they have served as solid building blocks for some of Nashville's finest singers of the past six decades." His greatest hits catalog features "He Stopped Loving Her Today" by George Jones, "The Bird" by Jerry Reed, "The Night Hank Williams Came to Town" by Johnny Cash, "Faking Love" by T. G. Sheppard and Karen Brooks, "Time Marches On" and "Texas Tornado" by Tracy Lawrence, "I Wanna Talk About Me" by Toby Keith, "D-I-V-O-R-C-E" by Tammy Wynette, "Golden Ring" by George Jones and Tammy Wynette, "I Feel Like Loving You Again" by T. G. Sheppard, "People Are Crazy" by Billy Currington, "Thinkin' of a Rendezvous" by Johnny Duncan, and "Come On In" by Jerry Lee Lewis.

Pointing to the Top 10 hit "The Killer" made out of his song, Braddock still beams to this day, regarding it as a full-circle moment of sorts given that Jerry Lee Lewis "was one of my rock and roll heroes. When I was in high school, my buddies used to come over to the house and say, 'Play that Jerry Lee thing on the piano!' My second wife, who was the inspiration for 'I Feel Like Loving You Again,' this was about her, following that song. That was a poem I put on my door when I went down to Alabama to get her and bring her back to Nashville, so when she went in the door, the first thing she saw was those words, and I turned that poem into a song!"

Having long perfected by then the art of pulling his muse out of real life, a key conduit that has made country music so long a mirror of its listeners' real lives, in love and in heartbreak, Bobby points to T. G. Sheppard's "I Feel Like Loving You Again" as the perfect example wherein "Sonny Throckmorton and I were sitting down to write together, and just trying to figure out what to come up with, we were just in the initial stages where we hadn't settled on anything. I had a girlfriend at the time, who became my second wife, we'd had this torrid affair and then she went back to her husband, and it wasn't working out. I had not heard from her in two or three months and got a phone call. And I told the girl at the front desk, 'I'm working. What did she call me?' and she said 'Sparky . . .' and I said, 'Oh, let me talk to her.' So, we talked for a while and she said she wanted to see me, and when I hung the phone up, I said 'Sounds like she's coming back again,' and then I thought 'I feel you coming back again,' so, we wrote the song that way: 'I feel you coming, I feel you coming, I feel you coming back again. . . .' Then Sonny's wife told him, 'You can't do that, y'all need to change that . . .' and she suggested to him, 'I feel like loving you again.'" Sonny Throckmorton shares his own fond memory of that particularly inspired writing session because "while we were writing that, we wrote 'Fadin' In, Fadin' Out' in the middle and it was perfect to have the analogy of a radio station that goes in and out and sometimes you're here, sometimes you're not. It didn't take us fifteen, twenty minutes to write that. So at the end of the three hours, we had two songs, and one went number one, and the other was a Top 5! That's kind of amazing."

Long a songwriter with sharp sensibilities to know when it was time to broaden the borders and barriers around what country music had been used to hearing based on writing something that took the genre somewhere new, Braddock spotlights Toby Keith's number one smash "I Wanna Talk About Me" as one where

> up to that point, there had only been two number one country rap songs, and that was the first one before "Dirt Road Anthem" by Jason Aldean. At the time, I was trying to get a deal for a young man named Blake Shelton, and eventually did and produced a lot of hits on him for the first four or five years. Blake would go around singing this real dirty rap song, and honestly, I don't know if it was something he wrote or something he heard, but it was amazing hearing this country white boy with an Oklahoma drawl doing a rap song. It was hilarious, but he did it good. So, I thought, "I'm going to write a rap song for him," and then I got a call from a very close friend of mine in Richmond, Virginia. The place [where] she worked, there was a girl who had been fired and that doubled her workload. It's all she could talk about, and she went on and on and on talking about that and nothing else. After I hung up, I started thinking, "I want to talk about me sometime," and that thing came to me, and turned into the rap song I wanted to write for Blake.

> After I wrote it, I called her and played it for her, but she didn't say much. Then she called me the next day and said, "That song you played for me yesterday, did you write that about me?" and I said, "That's right [*laughs*]." So, I went in to do the demo, and Giant [Giant Music, an independent music label] had already signed him, but were taking forever. It took two and a half years for them to get a record out on him, and Blake and I did a demo on the song. We

liked it so much that I said, "Do you want us to go ahead and upgrade this and present it to Giant to put out on you?" and he said, "Hell, yeah!" So, we did. They did research on it, and Doug Johnston, the label head, said, "Man, the research is coming back saying that shouldn't be a single, and probably shouldn't even go on the album. . . . The reaction to it is not good." By then, the song plugger at Tree [Tree Publishing] had gone and played it for Toby Keith's A&R [artists and repertoire division in a music publishing company] person and, initially, they passed on the song. So, I heard Toby Keith did this thing called "Get Ya Some" and it was kind of a talking thing, and since A&R has passed, and I knew his producer James Stroud, but James was not listening to songs, he had so many artists, he didn't have time to listen to songs. But he's a nice guy, and I ran into him at a convenience store and said "James, I have a song I really think you would like, it's one song, and you gotta hear this!" I kind of had him in a corner so he flipped open his phone, called his assistant and said, "Find me five minutes somewhere, anywhere, so Bobby Braddock can come in and play me this song." Well, when I did, he jumped over his desk and grabbed my hand and said, "Man, this is a damn hit!" Next, he called up Toby and played it for him over the phone right then, and Toby said, "I want to cut that!"

Long a master at the art of Music Row hit-making by then, turning the dial back in time six decades to 1965, he scored his first charting hit as a songwriter for Marty Robbins with "While You Were Dancing" and 1966 with "The Last Laugh" by Jim Ed Brown, marking the beginnings of Braddock's long-term cowriting relationship with Nashville songwriting legend Curly Putman. The dynamic duo would write a second smash for the

Statler Brothers with "You Can't Have Kate, and Edith Too," and what would become one of their signature collaborations and Braddock's first number one hit with "D-I-V-O-R-C-E" by Tammy Wynette:

> Curly was maybe ten years older than me and had a two-year head start on me with songwriting in Nashville. I think Curly was probably better at cowriting than I was. He could write with just a number of people, and I always liked writing alone better. I had no cowriter on "I Don't Wanna Talk About Me" or "Time Marches On" or "Texas Tornado." There's something to be said for cowriting, if you get two people who home in on an idea, it can be an exhilarating experience. I cowrote with Curly a lot of times out of a matter of convenience, because he was there when I first went to Sony, which then was Tree Publishing. Curly was the sole country song plugger employed there, and was very objective about it, and as prone to pitch somebody else's song as he was one of his own—if he really liked it and felt it was a good pitch.

> With "D-I-V-O-R-C-E," I had written the song and thought there was something to it, but no takers, so I finally asked Curly, "Why is nobody recording that song? It's kind of a clever song . . ." and Curly said, "It's just a small place on there, but that title line, and then it comes around in verse two, it's a sad song, but the melody gets kind of happy there." So, what you hear on the song now is exactly what I wrote, except for the title line, "Oh, I wish that we could stop this D-I-V-O-R-C-E," which was a very important piece of real estate in the song. I asked, "Curly, well, what would you do?" and he took a guitar, and there was something eternally sad about Curly that came

Country Music Lover   65

through in his singing, and he made a slight change to that melody, and so I said "Well, let's put it on tape."

So, he sat with his guitar, and I sat at the piano, and that's when I came up with what became the signature hook on the record. Then we took it down to Billy Sherrill and he loved it and cut it on Tammy Wynette. Curly told me, "What I did was so small, I don't think I should take any of it. I have more of a track record than you. . . ." I was still new then, I had three or four Top 10 things, and "D-I-V-O-R-C-E" became my first number one. So, then he said, "If my name's on there, I'm going to probably end up getting the credit, you know?" So, we compromised. He took 25 percent and had his name on the song, and what he said would happen didn't happen, because before long, I had a bunch of hits myself. But also, at the same publishing company, alphabetically my name came before Curly's [*laughs*]! I think because we became friends, it was sort of a natural thing to do. We wrote enough songs that you could say we were a songwriting team. Out of maybe a couple thousand songs Curly wrote—I'm sure he had at least that many—we may have written seventy together. A whole lot!

Indeed, the dynamic duo's other hits written together throughout the late 1960s and 1970s include "Ballad of Two Brothers" by Autry Inman, "A Funny Thing Happened (on the Way to Miami)" by Tex Ritter, and the monster number one smash "He Stopped Loving Her Today" by George Jones, which went to the top of the *Billboard* Hot Country Songs chart in 1980. He quipped that, inspired by how big the song became for him, "George Jones used to say, 'When are you going to write me another 'I Stopped Loving Her Today'? I told him, 'Well, you said when you heard that, you didn't like it.' Billy Sherrill kind of forced him into it." Highlighting the song's composition as an illustration of what first gets a song roaring to live in his imagination, in the case of "He Stopped Loving Her Today," Braddock offers that "what gets me started is if I get a concept that's really exciting, and more often than not that will entail the title itself, not always. Curly always said I brought this idea to him, and the concept was of [a] guy who never stopped loving her and wouldn't stop loving her until he died. Then when he died, he didn't love her anymore, he stopped loving her. So, the title and the concept came about the same time. I had a writing session with Curly Putman, and I told him about the idea, and we wrote it. With that one, Curly wanted to take a lesser amount of the publishing and ended up taking a quarter on that. But then, when Billy Sherrill wanted a recitation thing there, we worked further on it, and I said 'Curly, you need more of the song now,' and he went from 25 percent to 33 percent. People I don't think do that that much today, but back then, we did."

One especially memorable number one party Braddock recalls he and Curly attended together came with the chart-topping success of Jerry Reed's "The Bird," which had a unique compositional makeup as the original song was co-penned by Hal Coleman and Barry Etris before Reed added impressions of Willie Nelson's "Whiskey River" and "On the Road Again" and Jones's aforementioned "He Stopped Loving Her Today," resulting in Johnny Bush, Paul Stroud, Braddock, Nelson, and Putman being added as songwriters, and producing "one of my favorite memories of winning a BMI award because I was standing there with Willie, and asked him 'Have you ever gotten an award this easily?' and he said 'No, I don't think I have [laughs].'"

Picking "I Believe the South Is Gonna Rise Again" by a young Tanya Tucker as another of his personal favorites from this early era of his songwriting career and catalog, Bobby mused that "that's one I'm proud of. You don't see multiple cuts of the same song much anymore, Tanya was like twelve years old when she sang that, but she just sang it great, she was a great singer when she was a kid too. But the version I love, it never made the charts, but a singer named Molly Ridgeway cut it, Johnny Slade went in and cut it with her, and she had the most unusual voice in the world, but, oh, my God, I loved it."

At the same time he was churning out hits for other stars, Bobby charted for the first time as a solo artist with two of his own songs in 1967 with "I Know How to Do It" and "The Girls in Country Music" but kept his irons in the songwriting fire for other artists, continuing with another Top 10 hit for the Statler Brothers with "Ruthless" the same year along with "Jump for Joy" alongside "You Pushed Me Too Far" by Ferlin Husky and His Hush Puppies, and "Country Music Lover" by Little Jimmy Dickens. He'd finish out the 1960s establishing himself as one of the hottest new writers on the country charts via writing other early hits between 1968 and the 1970s for everyone from "How Sweet It Is (To Be in Love with You)" and "I Want One" by Jack Reno, "Joe and Mabel's 12th Street Bar and Grill" by Nat Stuckey, "Something to Brag About" by Charlie Louvin and Melba Montgomery, "Did You Ever" by Lee Greenwood and Nancy Sinatra, "Nothing Ever Hurt Me (As Bad as Losing You)" by George Jones, "We're Not the Jet Set" by George Jones and Tammy Wynette, sending the duo to number one once again with another smash hit in "Golden Ring." Pointing to that hit as an example of a songwriter targeting a specific star when writing the hit, Braddock begins by revealing:

> It's unusual for me to write a song for a specific artist. With the original concept of "Golden Ring," my idea was to write kind of a country gospel-sounding song for George and Tammy. I was thinking of a group you've probably never heard of that was popular way, way back—The Chuck Wagon Gang. They were a country gospel group, kind of like the Southern Gospel Quartet, but they were family.

So, I made it that kind of a song, and the idea came from a TV show about the biography of a gun. It was about this handgun that ended up in a pawn shop, and it belonged to a cop, it belonged to a criminal, it passed hands to a lot of different people, and at the end of the show, it showed this little three-year-old kid climb up in a chair and finding the gun in this cabinet, and pulling it out. That was how the show ended, so I thought "How about making this song about the fate of a wedding band. That's where it came from, so I had it started but never could finish it. I was at Tree Publishing, and I called Curly up and said, "I got this idea, you want to come in and write with it?" and he said, "No, Bobby, I think I'll just hang around the farm today." Right about that time Rafe Van Hoy came in the door, and I said, "Hey, I got a song started. You want to finish it with me?" and he said "Yeah." So, that's how it happened.

Bobby would continue decorating the charts with more musical artwork in the form of "Tonight Someone's Falling in Love" by Johnny Carver, "Moontan" by Jeris Ross, "Peanuts and Diamonds" and "Head to Toe" by Whisperin' Bill Anderson. And there was "Her Name Is" by George Jones, another number one smash with "Thinkin' of a Rendezvous" by Johnny Duncan, "My Better Half" by Del Reeves, "Something to Brag About" by Mary Kay Pace, "Georgia in a Jug" by Johnny Paycheck, "Womanhood" by Tammy Wynette, "Fadin' In Fadin' Out" by Johnny Paycheck, more of his own charting singles with "Between the Lines" and "Nag Nag Nag," and "Hard Times" by Lacy J. Dalton.

The 1980s would be equally good to Braddock as he logged another decade of singles on the charts, helping raise a new generation of stars to the top like John Anderson with "Would You Catch a Falling Star," "I Don't Remember Loving You" by John Conlee, "Faking Love" by T. G. Sheppard and Karen Brooks, "Honky

Tonk Women Made Honky Tonk Men" by Craig Dillingham, "I'd Rather Be Crazy" by Dana McVicker, "Hillbilly Hell" by the Bellamy Brothers, and he even scored a Johnny Cash single with "The Night Hank Williams Came to Town"! Reflecting on his staggering catalog, Braddock points to some features of his songwriting that have stayed the same throughout, beginning with his visual nature as a composer: "When I write a song, there's usually an arrangement that comes with it, I hear the whole thing. To me, producing a demo and producing a master is exactly the same thing, except with the master you have the luxury of time. You have the budget, and more time to do it, that's simply the only difference with me. Over all of my hits, it's pretty much the same kind of pride and ego trip. Of course, when I first heard songs I wrote on the radio, I was very young and very green, and it was just pure magic and has remained so to this day!"

Braddock's multi-decade hit streak would continue as he kept writing number one smashes throughout the 1990s, like "Old Flames Have New Names" by Mark Chesnutt, "Hurt Me" by LeAnn Rimes, "People Are Crazy" by Billy Currington, and back-to-back chart-toppers for Tracy Lawrence with "Texas Tornado" and "Time Marches On," selecting the latter chart victory as one "when people ask me what's the favorite song I've written, I tell them the favorite *hit* I've written is 'Time Marches On.' I have songs I've written I don't particularly like, that one I like. Where it started was, I was born and raised in a small town in Central Florida, and while I was growing up—this was pre–Disney World—it was a very Southern-cultured town. The area was agricultural, and my father was a citrus grower, and I was middle-aged when I wrote the song. And people who are middle-aged, they're our teachers, and of course all the older people were long gone. Physics is kind of an inspiration to me, time is fascinating. So, that's where that started, and then 'The South moves North, the North moves South, a star is born, a star burns out' was also true. Where I

70   SONGS OF NASHVILLE

came from, a lot of people when they came of age would go north looking for work, making cars in Michigan. I had a couple uncles who went up there. But there again, there were a lot of people from the North who moved South to Florida, older people from everywhere, so that's where that came from. 'The only thing that stays the same is everything changes,' that's my favorite bridge I ever wrote. I had an in-law from my first marriage, this woman who had a bumper sticker on her car that said, 'Sexy Grandma,' and we got a big kick out of it. So, that's where the line 'Sister calls herself "Sexy Grandma"' came from [*laughs*]!"

At the same time, Braddock began showing up as a producer as he helped launch the career of what would become one of country music's biggest stars, Blake Shelton, producing his first three studio albums, including his self-titled debut LP, featuring the three hit singles "Austin," "All Over Me," and "Ol' Red," *Blake Shelton's Barn & Grill*, which took "Some Beach" to number one and "Nobody But Me" to number four and *The Dreamer* LP, which boasted the number one smash "The Baby," which Bobby remembers playing a serendipitous songwriting role in, literally, following "the first time Blake and I heard it, we both liked it, and that's the only time that's ever happened. That was written by Michael White and Harley Allen, and Harley sang it, and his demo was great, he was a great singer. But it was hard to get a song that Blake liked. Throughout the whole process, we knew that was one we were going to cut. Once we got in and cut that record, I was walking around in the studio and, for some reason, just started singing and it was kind of an addendum to the song that went 'Mama's died and gone to heaven,' and went over to the piano and started playing that. Every syllable was a different chord, which made it sound really regal and churchy, almost like a hymn from the nineteenth century. Blake was in the room when I played it, and when he heard it, said, 'Man, I like that, do you think that's the intro?' And I said, 'Yeah, and we'll do it again at the end and get strings to come in there to do it exactly note for note,' and that came out right before the session was set to start."

Whether he was writing or producing hits, Braddock marvels at his one-of-a-kind success among Nashville Songwriters, closing with what amounts to the kind of balanced outlook that should serve as an example for anyone following in his storied footsteps: "It's pretty much the same kind of pride and ego trip, of course. Then as I got older and got producer creds, there was still a feeling of immense pride, especially knowing that it was a hit I'd produced, hearing it a lot, that was a good feeling. After a few years, I realized producing pulled me away from songwriting, so after we'd done the third album. I feel like the creative part of me is just as good now as it ever was, in some ways it may be better. What I'm doing now is spending longer with a song, because I've got songs in my past I wish I could go back and change. If you want to do it more than anything in the world, come on!"

Ashley Gorley
(Photo credit: Kenley Flynn)

Craig Wiseman
(Photo credit: Big Loud Shirt)

Sonny Curtis
(Photo credit: Sonny Curtis.com)

Dallas Davidson
(Photo credit: Dallas Davidson)

Dean Dillon
(Photo credit: J. C. Leacock)

Cole Swindell
(Photo credit: KP Entertainment)

Hillary Lindsey
(Photo credit: Concord Music Publishing)

Lori McKenna
(Photo credit: Becky Fluke)

Matraca Berg
(Photo credit: Glen Berg)

Merle Haggard (left) and the author
(Photo credit: Catherine Powers)

Jelly Roll (center right) (Photo credit: Jake Brown)

Liz Rose
(Photo credit: Liz Rose Music)

Shane McAnally
(Photo credit: Jake Brown)

Natalie Hemby
(Photo credit: Natalie Hemby FB)

CHAPTER 6

THE WAY I AM

. . . .

Sonny Throckmorton

"I may be old-fashioned, but I don't write anything, I'm just a reporter."

In the history of Texas country music, which anyone from the state will tell you is a self-contained music scene unto itself, you don't even have to break out big nationally to be a star locally, and songwriters are as revered as cowboys or football players. Legendary Texas Longhorns coach Darrell Royal was one of the songwriters' biggest fans, known for decades for his charity golf tournaments where a who's who of country music hit-makers, actors, and even astronauts would descend on Willie Nelson's golf course in Spicewood, Texas, to golf by day and hold now-mythic pickin' parties all night.

One regular attendee for decades was lone star state songwriting legend Sonny Throckmorton, who in the world of country hit-writing has done it all. He saw a record ninety songs cut in a two-year period in the late 1970s alone, has penned multiple number ones and Top 10 hits, and collected every award under the sun, from being named Songwriter of the Year by the Nashville Songwriters Association three years in a row between 1978 and 1980, and then, in 1977, winning the same designation in *Cashbox* magazine and by BMI in 1980. He won the Academy of Country Music's Song of the Year in 1980 and 1985, and was nominated for a Grammy as recently as 2019 for cowriting Willie Nelson's "Ride Me Back Home." Taking fans behind the scenes inside Coach Darrell Royal's storied pickin' parties, Throckmorton begins by confirming that

Coach Darrell Royal was a great influence for music in Texas. He was a big part of Texas music over the thirty years, he had a big hand. He knew all the entertainers and was always friendly because Coach just loved singers/songwriters—he just loved them and treated them good and gave them breaks and invited them to do things they probably wouldn't have gotten to do otherwise. I met characters like Freddy Powers at Darrell Royal's golf tournaments down in Houston, he and so many fellow songwriters would come down and entertain and play golf, as we all did, and first they were Coach Darrell Royal Golf Tournaments, then became Darrell and Willie Nelson, and then it was a Ben Crenshaw, Darrell, and Willie, but those twenty-five-plus years of tournaments were all one and the same because they all had Darrell. So, I got to be friends with him and his wife, Edith.

Edith Royal: After the children were out of school, we had eventually moved out by Willie and had a house on the lake out there, so we all hung out together all the time, and Darrell played golf with Willie nearly every day. He always went to the studio with Willie after their golf game was over, and Darrell loved being around music. Then, after the Longhorn games, we'd always have pickin' parties at our house with Willie and the boys playing songs all night.

Austin City Limits, 1988: Freddy Powers hosted two songwriter shows: On the first, a bearded Merle Haggard and Willie Nelson joined him, and the three traded solos, duets, and trios. The concert turned into an impromptu tribute to Floyd Tillman, present in the audience, whose melodic complexities and popular lyrics had influenced both Nelson and Haggard. "Pure magic," judged Darrell Royal, "pure magic." The following year, Powers brought

78 SONGS OF NASHVILLE

back Haggard and Nelson and expanded the circle to include Whitey Shafer and Spud Goodall in a program that crossed the borders between country and jazz.... In the eleventh season, Merle Haggard repaid Freddy Powers's hospitality by inviting him to be a special guest on his own *Austin City Limits* show—his third.

Sonny Throckmorton, exploring his own history within playing *Austin City Limits*, proudly points to the fact that "we did the first one they ever did for songwriters. We wound up doing that, and Whitey was on that show and wore Lefty Frizzell's boots. Darrell Royal's the one who put that show together, and it had Willie Nelson, Floyd Tillman, Red Lane, Whitey Shafer, Hank Cochran, and myself, and that's the very first one they'd ever done. We shot for about an hour, and then they liked it so much, they asked us if we'd do another hour, so, we did, and then they put that out, and it won the Chicago Film Festival. So, that kind of put them on a different course to start thinking about songwriters. On that show, everybody had major hits, so there was nobody on that stage that night who was going to sing anything other than a major hit. Willie could go all night if nobody stopped him, and by that time, I'd had a bunch of hits, and Whitey had hits, so that was the first one. Now it's grown to where it's shown in a lot of countries around the world who get to see a lot of American talent in that one show. So, ACL [*Austin City Limits*] has endured the test of time, and they've been so lucky to have so many people come in and do that show."

For decades, Throckmorton has been known for his famous nickname for himself, and everybody in time, "Puddin'." Sonny credits fellow Texas songwriter Whitey Shafer for giving him that name, affectionately recalling that "I met Whitey when he started going down to the Darrell Royal / Willie Nelson golf tournaments, and that's where I really got to know Whitey. He was a great guy. It was actually Whitey who nicknamed me 'Puddin',' I nicknamed him 'The White Man.' We'd gone to one of the golf tournaments down in Houston, and we got to acting silly, and started singing a song that was out that year called 'I Beg Your Pardon (I Didn't Promise You a Rose Garden),' so we started singing 'I Beg Your Puddin', I didn't promise ya a good'in,' and we sang it so much and did it so much that somehow or another, I wound up being puddin'. So, he nicknamed me 'Puddin',' and to this day, a lot of people still call me 'Puddin'.' So, both those nicknames stuck, which I think speaks to our friendship and our enduring love for each other. I loved Whitey, as I do so many writers and good people in Nashville, and Whitey was certainly one of them. We wrote a thing Merle Haggard did one time, which is a pretty good song, 'When I'm Out of You (I'm Out of Love),' so, we wrote a couple of songs, but our thing wasn't about writing, our deal was hanging out and acting silly."

Traveling back in time to the dawn of his discovery of his gifts as a songwriter, Sonny confesses that "It took a while for me to really start doing it. I played bass first and then guitar. The first song I ever wrote, I wrote while my dad was preaching. It was a gospel song. I was about seventeen years old when I started writing songs, so didn't really pick it up until I was almost out of high school. I first moved to Los Angeles, signed a record deal but only stayed about a month and left. Later on, a friend of mine, Will Henry, brought some of my tapes to Nashville. Pete Drake heard them and invited me to move there, and that's how I got to town."

Throckmorton would go on to have more than a thousand of his songs recorded throughout a songwriting career that first made its debut in 1967 with his first Top 10 hit for Bobby Lewis on "How Long Has It Been" before following with the Top 40 hit "Ordinary Miracle" by the same star in 1968, and continued writing charting singles into the early 1970s. Other hits from this early era included "That's Your Hang Up" by Johnny Carver, "Come and Get It Mama" and "It Almost Felt Like Love" by Charlie Louvin,

"We're Back in Love Again" by Johnny Bush, the Top 20 hit "Here We Go Again" by Brian Shaw, "Easy Look" by Kenny Price, "Fine Time to Get the Blues" by Jim Ed Brown, "I'm Knee Deep in Loving You" by Jim Mundy, and "Rosie (Do You Wanna Talk It Over)" by Red Steagall.

Still, by the mid-1970s, Throckmorton decided despite his first era of success to "move back to Texas. See, I first moved to town when I was writing for Tree [Publishing]. The first time I left because I wasn't really making it, I think I was getting 60 or 70 percent of my songs cut. I just wasn't having any big hits, there wasn't any big artists doing them, and I hadn't quite reached the ear of the Merle Haggard and people like that. I had a deal with myself that if I turned thirty-five and hadn't been successful, I was going to get out of the business. Curly Putman was an early supporter of mine too, and he was the kind of songwriter that believed in other writers. He was my champion. He always championed the cause of Sonny Throckmorton. When I left Tree the first time, he went over there to tell them every day, 'You need to get Sonny back here!' He and Dave Kirby and a few people, the great Don Gant, and writing with Curly was also amazing. The first time we ever sat down to write a song together was 'What I Had with You'— Tammy Wynette and then John Conlee had a big hit on it. That one came so easy, and Curly and I were almost like one person when we wrote, we were totally in tune. I wrote several songs with Curly, one of the greatest writers and guys. 'Smooth Sailin'' by T. G. Sheppard is a good one we wrote together when we went to dinner one day and got the idea for that situation, went back and wrote that. All the songs I wrote with Curly—I lived right down the street from him, and he'd come by and pick me up and we'd drive into town, and we'd either write one while we were there or write one while we were driving home. 'Made for Loving You' by Dan Seals was another one Curly Putman and I wrote that has been cut by several people. Dan Seals had a great record on it. Of course, Doug Stone had a number two or three hit with it, and it's one of the few love songs I've ever written, probably because I had a cowriter. I hadn't written very many love songs, and when Curly and I were writing together, we were on, it was such a fluid thing."

Returning to Nashville via the encouragement of Curly Putman and others within his cheerleading section, Sonny Throckmorton would make a triumphant comeback when he topped the charts for the first time a decade into his songwriting career in 1976 when Johnny Rodriguez recorded "Thinkin' of a Rendezvous," bringing him back to Nashville when his style caught on like wildfire with a record 150 songs recorded by Nashville's finest stars and acts within six months! He was still fond of "Thinkin' of a Rendezvous" decades later because "It was my first number one song. I'm not much of a love song writer. I wish I was, it always broke my heart because I wanted to write love songs, but these other kinds of songs came to me, so that's the way it is."

Based on the momentum he was experiencing as a songwriter for other acts, Throckmorton began building his own solo catalog of albums and singles including "Rosie," "Lovin' You, Lovin' Me," "I Wish You Could Have Turned My Head," "Last Cheater's Waltz," "Smooth Sailin'," "Can't You Hear That Whistle Blow," "Friday Night Blues," and "A Girl Like You," pointing to "Waltz" as a song that he recognized had potential "when I first started writing it, but at the time, it was called 'A Strawberry Waltz.' I had that melody, but it didn't have much lyric yet, but I knew it couldn't be 'A Strawberry Waltz' because there had to be a reason he was there, but I had most of the song done before I had that title. A lot of my titles come after I've totally finished the song. Take 'Middle Aged Crazy'—I had that originally as 'He's a little bit crazy, trying to prove he still can,' and right as we were going in to do the demo, I happened to say, 'Middle Age Crazy.'"

He was back in the saddle with a second era of hits that stayed in regular rotation on country radio throughout the rest of the

82   SONGS OF NASHVILLE

1970s with a staggering average of one of his songs appearing in the charts each week. Sonny's prolific nature was on display via hits like "Easy Look" by Charlie Rich, "If We're Not Back in Love by Monday" by Merle Haggard, which peaked at number two on the US Hot Country Songs Chart, "Thank God She's Mine" by Freddie Hart, "I'm Knee Deep in Loving You" by Dave & Sugar, Jerry Lee Lewis's Top 5 rendition of "Middle Aged Crazy," and "Yes Ma'am" and "Fadin' In, Fadin' Out" by Tommy Overstreet. Others included "When Can We Do This Again" and "You Feel Good All Over" by T. G. Sheppard—who also took "Last Cheater's Waltz" to number one, the Top 5 hit "I Had a Lovely Time" by The Kendalls, "It's a Cheating Situation" by Moe Bandy, "I Wish I Was 18 Again" by George Burns, "Temporarily Yours" by Jeanne Pruett, and "The Way I Am," which Merle Haggard took to number two on the charts, recalling that "I wrote that one in about thirty minutes, and it's just the way I was feeling at the time. Songs come a lot of times out of a thought I'm in, and often the music comes with it. But there are times when I get a melody that's really good and I'll have to keep on until I get the lyrics. It all comes together in different ways. I write feelings, that's what I write more than anything. I write about things that are happening to people where there's some emotion there—that's my favorite, when you get into the way people really are, that's my deal."

The Oak Ridge Boys would take another of Throckmorton's classics to the top with "Trying to Love Two Women," an idea he credits to getting "from my neighbor. He told me one day, 'Sonny, if you hear a shooting at my house, you call the law.' And when I said 'Why?' he replied, 'Well, I'm trying to love two women . . .' So, I had actually turned around, went home and started writing that and I had it in about fifteen minutes! It was just obvious: 'Trying to love two women is like a ball and chain . . .' It was a gift. The Oak Ridge Boys had another big hit on 'I Wish You Could Have Turned My Head (And Left My Heart Alone),' and I'd seen a lady walking at

The Way I Am   83

a shopping center in Tennessee, a really good-looking woman. She didn't look at me, she didn't turn her head, she just kept walking, and I thought, 'That's probably good, because every time I'd have turned my head, she'd have broke my heart . . .' So, the song was a continuation of that thought."

Giving country music fans a rare peak inside a typical demo session that preceded any of these songs ever being recorded by the artists who made them chart toppers, Throckmorton recounted a routine at the hit factory that was Tree Publishing: "I had my demo sessions every Monday morning with my new songs at Tree at the studio. I'd just show up with my guitar and I didn't ever know who was going to show up session-players-wise, but they knew if they showed up, they'd get on the demo. Some might be real thin with just a couple players on them, and others with three or four players, and I'd write the licks in my head a lot of times of what they were going to play, but I've also had luck where players in the studio came up with great parts too. You get a great player; they'll give you a great lick. A lot of times, the great players can't keep from playing the great licks for you [*laughs*]!"

As he continued writing his way to being inducted into the Songwriters Hall of Fame in 1985, he penned a new decade of hits like John Conlee's Top 5 hits with "Friday Night Blues" and "She Can't Say That Anymore," "Why Not Me" by The Judds, which Sonny counts as another favorite because, "I wrote that with Harlan Howard and Brent Maher, and I had the melody and the title 'How Bout Me?' and a lot of times, I don't finish songs at first, I just keep singing them and singing them until finally it hits me how to write them, and that was one of them. So when I got with Harlan and Brent, I sang them the melody and Harlan said, 'This should be 'Why Not Me,' and I agreed with him. Harlan was real strong on the lyrics and me on the melody and Brent on the guitar was real strong, I don't think without his guitar melody it would have been half as good as it was." Sonny's hit streak continued as he helped launch a new generation of country music stars via hits like "Stand Up" by Mel McDaniel, and "Made for Lovin' You" by Doug Stone before racking up a coveted George Strait cut with "The Cowboy Rides Away" off of the album *Does Fort Worth Ever Cross Your Mind*, which he remembers "writing with Casey Kelly, and he had the melody, and he said, 'This is driving me crazy,' and played it to me, and as he did, it came to me. I could see a guy riding away on a horse from the situation, so it was his melody, and I came up with the idea and we wrote it from there."

After helping Willie Nelson win the Best Country Solo Performance Grammy in 2019 for "Ride Me Back Home," Sonny still marvels even amid his success with more than a thousand recorded cuts, a Nashville songwriting record, remarking that "I'm amazed that anybody remembers any of this stuff, but I'm just thrilled that I've had a career doing what I like to do." Closing with reflections on his own favorites amid that massive catalog, he proudly focuses in on the late, great "Merle Haggard doing 'The Way I Am.' That was really good, but they all did great jobs on them. I loved all my records, even the artists that I didn't even like, when they cut my song, I instantly became their best fan. So, they're all my babies. They're my creations and so, if they're not my babies, whose are they? I have two songs that were Song of the Year, 'Why Not Me' and 'It's a Cheating Situation,' and I was thrilled both times, how could you not be? It's a great feeling."

Still, at the end of the day, when measuring the meaning behind his songs not in their chart positions or award ceremonies, the greatest satisfaction this legendary songwriter has always taken from his work is in the purer thrill of seeing how they have deeply impacted generations of listeners and been part of the proverbial soundtrack to their lives: "I didn't write to win awards, though. I'd rather emotionally get to your soul with one of my songs and reach you than give me an award."

CHAPTER 7

AVERAGE JOE

. . . .

Colt Ford

"Country-Rap Maverick"—MusicRow magazine

Country rap sounds like an oxymoron about first repeat, but as CMT (originally known as Country Music Television) first captured amid its explosion onto the Nashville mainstream a decade ago, "the genre is exploding across the charts," with a bang powerful enough to capture the *Wall Street Journal*'s attention in a front-page story revealing remarkably that while it "doesn't get much airplay on major radio stations, the all-ages mud-park shows feature dancers that shimmy around chain-link-fence poles cemented onto truck beds, can draw upward of 10,000 fans. They tend to spend freely on CDs and merchandise, from moonshine to mason jars filled with the mud used in a band's music videos." The *Today Show* years later would count Colt Ford among its pioneers, "known within the country world as blending the genre with rap in his music," while *The Tennessean* has affirmed for the historical record that "Nashville resident Colt Ford gets a lot of credit for combining rap and country into a popularized new fusion of genres. . . . There's no denying that his personal brand of country music has struck a chord with Ford's fans." Looking back today, Ford agrees, proud to point out that "I don't think there's any question there was, as far as this whole thing goes, when I first got here, there was nothing that had sounded like what I did. That's just the bottom line."

Carving out his own place in country music history as the first artist, before Jelly Roll blew up a decade later, to have a number one album on Top Country Albums and Top Rap Albums, *Billboard* has admired the success Ford found in developing "a sterling reputation among his fans for coming up with a narrative that they truly identify with," a musical language he explains wasn't designed around some grand plan to make it, but an organic evolution—or revolution, some would argue—of the oral recitation tradition within country music that Ford traces back to its origins:

> Yes, I got my own thing to it, but I didn't set out to create something. I've thought about this for years and years, this kind of I guess hybrid. I never called it "country rap"—I never set out to do that. I wasn't trying to mix country and hip-hop, that was not what I was trying to do. So, if people ask me, I just say I'm a country artist. Nobody said Charlie Daniels was a country rapper when he did "The Devil Went Down to Georgia" or Toby Keith when he did "I Wanna Talk About Me," and you can go to "Hot Rod Lincoln" songs and "Smoke Smoke Smoke (That Cigarette)" by Tex Williams, songs that were before I was even born. So, recitation talking records have been around forever. I mean what do you think Jerry Reed was doing? Now, do I do it my own way with my own thing? Sure I do. I mean, I'm an artist. That's what you should do. A lot of times, Nashville spends way too much time saying "Oh, that works, let me go do that," and I wish it was that easy. I spent a lot of time actually in the music business trying to be something that I really wasn't, and it never completely worked. [I] got close a lot of times, had record deals, finished records that got shelved, and it didn't work. There's part of me that is glad it didn't work because it wouldn't have led me to where I am. I mean, my dad didn't have indoor plumbing till he was eighteen years old. I know

what that's about, he picked cotton, that's what I was
raised on and that's who I am. That authenticity is very
important in my songs.

Beyond memories of his family's lineage, Colt prefers to point
to one of his early hits with Jake Owen on "Back," reminiscing
about his childhood, sharing that "everything in that song is my
life story, it's where it started. That baseball field is a parking lot.
That grave I was standing over was my best friend David, he did
grow up in a wheelchair. He lived right next door to me. We
played hide and go seek; we pushed him. We went [to the] skating
rink, we pushed him. We put him on motorcycles, we put him on
go-karts. It didn't matter to us that he was in a wheelchair, he was
just our buddy. That was real. My son, the day that he wasn't supposed to live. David wasn't supposed to live till he was eighteen.
He died at thirty. [I] knew him my whole life. I was getting ready
to have my son at the time and hadn't picked a name for him and
didn't know what we were going to call him and was bouncing a
bunch of things around. The day I was a pallbearer and that we
buried him, that was the day I found out his middle name was
Reynolds, and that's my son's name."

Before he could be found writing dirt road anthems, Colt
could have first been found growing up playing on the golf course,
playing on tours throughout the 1990s as a semipro golfer. He
even made it onto the *Sports Illustrated* radar, as the magazine
reported that "Ford's country rap didn't find the charts until he
was thirty-nine. . . . For seven or eight years, Ford found himself
on something of a similar path in golf. Though he showed promise
as a junior—Phil Mickelson, Jim Furyk and Charlie Rymer were
among his contemporaries—Jason Brown never found traction after
college and got his first professional start, teeing up in a Powerbilt
Tour event in Florence, SC. Ford still might be in the golf industry
if not for the economic downturn a dozen years ago. A golf travel

88   SONGS OF NASHVILLE

venture with Rymer never got off the ground, and Jason Brown found himself at a crossroads."

Ford knew by then that he wanted to launch his dream to become a Nashville star, but to make his own sound on his own terms. He began to break through his very first album after *Ride Through the Country* showcased a first-of-its-kind formula of Colt recruiting an all-star team of collaborators that cracked the Top 40 of the *Billboard* Top Country Albums Chart, although looking back he jokes that "when I went to kind of put this together, it just kind of came out. The first record, *Ride Through the Country*, was literally written in a week. I didn't necessarily know what I was doing. I just wrote the record, and it just came out that way. I just tried to be completely honest about everything that I knew and everything that was me. Honestly, I felt like I was probably only gonna get to make one record. When we were going in, I thought, 'I'm going to get to make this record. I am going to get to put it out. We have the resources to do all that.' But I really had not looked past to another record. I just tried to plant my flag and say 'This is who I am.'"

Featuring a track listing any established county star would envy, it kicked off with the title track costarring John Michael Montgomery, Joe Diffie, and Ronnie Dunn, who also appeared on the album's second track, "Mr. Goodtime," while the party continued with Jamey Johnson appearing on "Cold Beer," "Never Thought" showcasing Wynonna Judd, and John Anderson on "Waffle House." Ford points to the creation of two of his career-making hits, "Dirt Road Anthem" featuring Brantley Gilbert and "Like Me" featuring Charlie Daniels, as two of his personal favorite teamings on the album to date:

> Charlie Daniels is an absolute hero, man, without question, one of the greatest people I've ever met. I'd give anything if at the end of my career, people refer to me the way that they refer to him and talk about me the way they talk about

him, as somebody who did what he said he was going to do. He showed up when he said, and he played as long as he said he was going to play, he gave back to the community, and he helped people. He supported our country and our soldiers. He flew that flag and that's who Charlie Daniels is. I'll tell you right now, I'd fight a grizzly bear for Charlie Daniels. He's been unbelievably nice to me. I got to stand onstage and play "When the Devil Went Down to Georgia" with him, back and forth trading on one microphone line for line. That's incredible!

Colt would crack the code, so to speak, when he and Brantley Gilbert teamed up as songwriters to write what would become a career-making hit for them both, with *American Songwriter* magazine chronicling the origins of "Dirt Road Anthem," that it was "written by the two in Gilbert's home in Georgia, the first collaboration for the two. Ford would also cowrite 'Country Must Be Country Wide' on Gilbert's *Halfway to Heaven*, along with Mike Dekle . . . inspired by different events, places, and memories in Ford and Gilbert's lives and the dirt road gatherings they grew up around with the ice-cold beer and bonfires." Ford elaborated firsthand about the anthem that has now racked up nearly one billion streams worldwide:

Brantley and I were both working on our albums and we met, and we decided to sit down and write a song together. He's one of the most talented songwriters, honestly, that I've ever written with. He has a gift and he's original and that's cool. He's original and it's authentic, and that's to me what makes someone incredible. We were actually going to write with another friend of ours, Mike [Dekle], who's a veteran songwriter from Athens I've known my whole life who has written "Scarlet Fever" for Kenny Rogers. He goes way back. But I knew him and Brantley knew him, and I went over to pick up Brantley and we were going to lunch, and he said "Hey, man, what do you think about this idea? 'Chillin' on the dirt road . . . This idea would be cool for you,' and we three wrote it from there. It was just a song about what we knew about and what we liked, and then we talked about all the things we liked to do. That guitar riff has turned out to be iconic, and once we started, we were done with "Dirt Road Anthem" in maybe thirty minutes. Who knew that it would be what it is now.

"Ride Through the Country" is another one off that album that is still a lot of people's favorite record. I didn't know that I did anything groundbreaking or anything like that, or changed the music or created this genre, because that was not the intent. Waylon didn't set out to be an outlaw, Waylon just said, "I want to make my music my way. I don't give a shit what y'all wanna do, this is what I wanna do, and that's fine. Y'all do your thing, and I'll go make mine sound the way I want it to sound." It was as simple as that. Now it turned into, "Oh, he's an outlaw . . ." Well, no, he just wanted to do his thing, and made his music his way, and that's really what I did with *Ride Through the Country*.

Colt Ford's *Ride Through the Country* would make history when it became country rap's first platinum album. A benchmark that legitimized the genre commercially for the first time, fittingly charting on *Billboard*'s Top 40 Country Albums, the Top 20 of *Billboard*'s Rap Albums, and in the Top 20 of the Independent Albums Chart simultaneously, driven by singles "Ride Through the Country" and "Cold Beer." The phenomenon that "Dirt Road Anthem" became when Jason Aldean's rendition sold more than four million singles and rocketed to number one on the Hot

Country Songs Chart, giving Ford his first number one hit as a cowriter, helping his next studio album, *Chicken & Biscuits,* debut in the Top 10 of the US Top Country Albums Chart and in the Top 5 of both the US Top Rap Albums and Independent Albums Chart. Popularity and prolificacy dictated a second album release the same year with *Every Chance I Get,* climbing within three spots of number one on *Billboard*'s Top Country Albums Chart, and giving fans these singles: "Country Thang," "She Likes to Ride in Trucks" with Craig Morgan, and "What I Call Home" with the Moonshine Bandits.

Motor Trend magazine at the time reflected on Ford's unique place as a new kind of country music star: "It is not surprising that Colt Ford has taken country music by storm. He has a catchy new genre of music that we consider a mix of country, rock, and hip-hop blended with southern rap lyrics. His tunes are extremely entertaining and hit home, even for those who never really got into the rap scene. Ford has also made his mark on the mud and off-road scene with concerts at major mud events and as host of *Mudslingers* on the Outdoor Channel." Playing his music live at indoor venues, Ford preferred to keep it country, drawing numbers most country stars on the rise would envy as he packed ten thousand fans into a field for a live show over a weekend:

> I knew about places where I work because I've done it as a kid and then you go ride and people get out there but not to the extent of what these things are today. I meant like [I] didn't know. . . . One of the very first ones I played, it wasn't really a mud bog. I would say it was kind of a mud race kind of thing. It was over in South Carolina on this guy's piece of property where he had these lanes cut out and these guys are racing trucks. The stage was literally up in some trees, like some *Jungle Book* shit. It was strapped to the trees with ratchet straps, and it ain't like it's Dale

92 SONGS OF NASHVILLE

Junior and Kevin Harvick driving these trucks, this is Bubba and Earl that are driving them. I don't know how many beers they had, and they got 1,000 horsepower truck and they're going down this little quarter-mile thing. And the people are standing ten feet from it, there's no brick wall, it was like "Wow, one mistake and you could kill thirty people like that." It was insane, I'd never seen anything like that.

So, as the day progressed, people just kept coming and coming. We didn't have a bus or anything like that. Hell, I was driving myself in a Ford SUV, and there was a two-lane road to get in there and after a while, a state trooper shut it down. I mean, there was traffic for miles, you couldn't get in. Even the guy hosting it had no idea how many people were going to show up, and by now the crowd is starting to get rowdy, and like happens a lot, the schedule never is what the schedule says. But there were a lot of kids there and the show was supposed to start at eight o'clock, and they're still racing trucks, so we can't, but the majority of the people were over by us.

I finally told the dude, "We need to do this, we need to play, or I think there's going to be a problem," and I don't want people to think it's me. I'm never that artist who sits back there and says "Oh, let's push it thirty minutes, let's push it thirty minutes. . . ." When it's time to play, I'm ready to do it as soon as I can get out there, you just don't do that, it's not fair to the fans. So, the opening band started their set, and about the third song into the set, the generator craps out, so we had no sound. It wasn't like they had an unbelievable sound company there, it was pretty redneck to start with, and I thought "These people are going to tear this place apart." So, at the time, this kid Chase who worked for me and went on to work for Brantley Gilbert, says, "Well, I've got some sort of amp thing in the back of my car," and basically MacGyver[ed] this thing, taking an extension cord and slicing it and running it into this and that, and he somehow made it work, and we played the show!

With these mud bogs, though, I was playing these places that people have never heard of, and even at that first one I just talked about, there were seven thousand, eight thousand people there in a place that had never had more than four hundred or five hundred. So, that started happening, and it still happens to this day, where they will tell us, "We normally have two thousand people here," and we have to often say, "That's great, but we're probably going to have ten thousand people . . ." and they never believe it, but it happens. We just go out there and do the best we can with it. But I've seen twelve thousand, fifteen thousand people at these shows. It's unreal, that's thirty, forty minutes outside the city. You could put me in the city in those early days in a theater, and we might sell eight hundred tickets. But you put me thirty miles outside in the middle of this field and eight hundred turns into eight thousand.

Within four short years of his debut, Ford had catapulted to the top of the *Billboard* Top Country Albums Chart when his fourth LP, *Declaration of Independence*, peaked at number one in August 2012, remaining there for more than sixty-three weeks. Proud to date of the benchmark achievement for any hardworking country artist, he still beams that "that's as high as it goes, and I think it was like number one in three countries, number two in Australia and Canada! It was just unreal—to me, that's just so humbling. It's nuts, because I realized my part in it, but again, it's not about me. It's about these songs, and I happen to be the guy that gets to stand out there and do it and everybody's cheering Colt Ford and that's unbelievable. But the songs are what made that happen, really, and yeah, I've worked my ass off and I've shook every hand, but I haven't done it to do that. I've done it because that's just who I am as an artist." Driven by another run of hit singles, "Drivin' Round Song" with Jason Aldean, "Ain't Out in the Woods" with Brooks & Dunn, and the Top 40 hit "Back" with Jake Owen, Colt points to this as among his favorites:

> That album started off with "Back" with Jake Owen. Jake and I've been good friends for a long time. Jake was one of the first artists that went into his record label and goes, "Dude, please clear this record for him to put it out at radio. Come on, this is a great record!" which took a lot of balls because he'd already given me his time, been a part of it. But here's a guy who at the time didn't have four number one singles, he wasn't the Jake he is today. This guy that was still trying to get his own thing going to a certain extent, and he flat went in there and told the label, "Hey, check this is out, this song is fantastic. It ain't gonna hurt me being a part of it, and it's not gonna hurt what I'm doing being a part of it."

Winding up the first country rap artist with a CNN headline after "Ford was nominated for an Academy of Country Music Award for vocal event of the year for his performance of his song 'Cold Beer' with Jamey Johnson," he continued to deliver the winning combination of collaborations like "She Likes" with Keith Urban, the Top 40 hit "The High Life" with Chase Rice, and fan favorites "Sip It Slow" with Lee Brice, "Farm Life" with Justin Moore, cracking number two on the *Billboard* Top Country Albums Chart when 2017's *Love Hope Faith* landed as usual in the Top 10 and featured the usual round of heavy hitter guest stars ranging from

Brad Paisley and Toby Keith, to Florida Georgia Line and key members of Lady A. 2019's *We the People* Vol. 1 and 2023's double album *Must Be the Country* treated fans to more of their favorite team-ups with Tracy Lawrence, Brantley Gilbert, Tracy Byrd, and more along Ford's way to more than two million Facebook followers and well over 100 million YouTube views and hundreds of millions of streams of his catalog. Proud of the sound and formula he helped introduce into country music's mainstream, Colt broke the mold by breaking through independently as a solo artist, paving the way for a generation of country rap stars to follow in his footsteps:

> If you look at the timing of that record, based on where Luke's at now, it didn't hurt whatsoever. It didn't hurt Eric Church. It didn't hurt any of those people. Eric's a great friend of mine, he likes what he likes and doesn't make any bones about it, even if it hurts your feelings or whatever. Eric and I have had similar paths from the standpoint that he just kept playing his music his way and the people kept coming, and he kept giving it to them. He's always encouraged me about that, but again, not a one of these guys is just going to do a song because we're friends. They had to like the song. One of my favorite stories with Eric is, right before *Chief* came out and he was right on the verge of going to that next level, and at the time hadn't had radio singles or number one records. There was a lot of radio that wouldn't play Eric Church, they didn't get it for whatever reason, and Eric and I had played some shows, and literally the night before the first-week numbers came out, he texts me and it's a little bit emotional for me, but he said: "Hey, man, I was thinking about you, because I know my numbers on my record are getting ready to come out tomorrow. I just want to remind you that you have hit

songs. I've seen you play in front of me and ten thousand people sing along. I know you're frustrated, and how hard you work, and how honest you are with your music, and I have been where you are and thought about at times quitting, and I didn't have anybody tell me not to. But you have number one songs, don't let them discourage you, keep doing what you're doing, it doesn't matter what the chart says. Tomorrow, I'm going to sell 150,000 units and I've never had a hit song either, so keep doing what you're doing, and music will win in the end." I thought that was really cool that he took time out to tell me that.

If Ford's story isn't already cinematic enough, it comes complete with the fact that he carried on the proud hip-hop tradition of independent labels owned by the very artists they're promoting in the form of Average Joes Entertainment, today the "Motown" of country rap, where Colt quips "we'll take that" before adding the caveat that "we never sat down and said, 'Okay, this is what we're going to do and it's gonna change country music, and all these people will be digging it, and there will be all these artists who do what you do. . . .' We didn't know that, and we'd be lying if we said we weren't, we were both scared to death. I didn't set out to create something, and Average Joes has certainly morphed into a lot of other things, but at first, it was just one lane, straight ahead, and that's all we could do. We didn't have any idea that there would be any other artists like me at all, because we really hadn't seen that. Truthfully, it was a huge risk and gamble, because if I didn't work, that would have been it for Average Joes. We really weren't looking past anything except trying to make this work, we didn't have anything else, we didn't have any other artists, so there was nothing else to do except figure out how to make Colt Ford work. I just wanted to do my music my way, and here it is."

After helping pave the way for the LACs, Tyler Farr, Lenny Cooper, Demun Jones, The Moonshine Bandits, and adding new eras to veteran stars like Bubba Sparxxx and Montgomery Gentry, Ford today feels that his long-term success and mainstay stature as one of country rap's veteran stars has been based on the same foundational philosophy as a songwriter and star he's followed throughout his three-decade career:

> I talk the way I talk on records, the way I'm going to talk to you right now. I don't know any different, so that's the way I did it. I don't want to say a word that I don't know what it means, and I got to get half my fans got to go look it up. That's not how country people talk. It really is about the song anyway. It ain't never been about me or Brantley or Jason or Luke or Carrier or whoever. We will all go away and somebody else will take our place. That's the way it goes. You know what I mean? The songs are what live on, so be humble and thankful and blessed to be able to do what you do. I know I am.

CHAPTER 8

EVERYBODY OUGHTA
SING A SONG

. . . .

Dallas Frazier

"The Oak Ridge Boys gave Frazier his biggest success with their indelible version of 'Elvira,' but legends like Merle Haggard, George Jones, Charley Pride, and Willie Nelson all recorded his songs."—Rolling Stone

For as much as the 1930s took from those who grew up in the Dust Bowl generation, it gave the world some of its most influential country music stars and songwriting catalogs, tracing back to Buck Owens, Merle Haggard, and the late, great Dallas Frazier, whom *People* magazine—upon his death—celebrated as "a legendary and Grammy-nominated country music songwriter." Sitting down for what would be his final interview, Dallas looks back on his humble beginnings coming out of the Dust Bowl and quips, "I don't hardly know anybody that's made it in the music business that wasn't poor boy, I mean just like me. I grew up in the cotton field without in California and all the ones I have known that come out of a background of poverty or hardship, most have appreciated the success. If you look at a song like 'California Cottonfields,' that is autobiographical for sure. We moved from Oklahoma during World War II, and *The Grapes of Wrath*, that's who we were. We picked the cotton, and we lived in a tent for a while. We lived in a boxcar for a while. That's who we were. Years later, I had a real compliment by George Jones. He recorded an album of my songs that was dedicated to me and that's the only one George Jones ever did ever!"

Frazier's story along the way is one that belongs in a book, beginning his career as a child star of sorts after he caught the ear of his earliest mentor in the business, Ferlin Husky, a recording artist and entertainment personality in the early 1950s. *Billboard* would later detail an impressively fast rise where in 1952 at just "twelve years old, he won a talent contest hosted by Husky, [who] signed him to be a featured entertainer in his road show. Husky called up the head of Mercury Records and said he had a boy who wanted to make records. At age fourteen, Frazier was signed to Capitol Records and began issuing teen-themed singles. From 1954 to 1958, the budding songwriter was featured on Cliffie Stone's LA-based television show *Hometown Jamboree* and was a regular on Cousin Herb Henson's country TV show in Bakersfield." Still, even as he performed with Molly Bee and joined other teen stars on the rise like Jean Shepard, Wynn Stewart, Tommy Collins, and more, and though he already had one foot in the business, it never took Dallas out of touch with his humble, working-class roots as he continued to work the same jobs as the everyday man who was already listening to his songs on the radio:

> I was born with a gift, and I was a gifted child. I understood words and alliteration came to me when I was ten or eleven years old. I remember "Tongue-Tied Tenderfoot Day" was the first song I ever wrote. I was just a kid and trying to get started writing and then "Space Command" was my first single released to radio when I was fourteen, but I didn't write that. That was a Capitol Records release, so was "Love Life." My parents weren't really supportive of my musical career. They weren't against it, but they didn't

really know how to do that. The one big thing that kept me from working and really getting out and doing something was that I could not work in an establishment that sold alcohol until I was twenty-one. That eliminated like 99 percent of the live work, and I suffered because of that.

That's how I wrote "Alley Oop," which, originally, I wrote it for myself, with nobody in mind. I was running a suction pipe in a cotton trailer full of cotton, and you move it around, it's telescopic, and you walk around in a big trailer using that pipe to suck the cotton out of the trailer. Long story short, I got to just thinking about "Alley Oop," just playing around with it, and before you know it, I got serious. Then I could start hearing it, I was nineteen, and I started hearing this riff, and it wasn't too long before I had it and put it down on the piano.

When everything's moving, it stimulates creativity. Had I not been in that cotton trailer that day working—and it's hard work too, running that suction pipe around—I wouldn't have written that song, no way. If I'd just been sitting in a house or something, it would never have happened, and I believe that. I don't think songs are just in you and can come out whenever you decide to let them. Some of them are in you and when they show their face, you better write them down because they may never come back to you. That was one of those, and then when Gary Paxton heard it, he loved it, and a couple weeks later cut it on the Hollywood Argyles, and it became my first number one hit as a songwriter in 1957 while still a teenager! I didn't even know the Beach Boys had cut it for a long time either. I was in the studio, though, with Hollywood Argyles when they cut the song.

Everybody Oughta Sing a Song   101

Leaving California for Nashville based on the success of the single and the draw of working full-time as a songwriter and recording artist, Frazier teamed back up with Ferlin Husky for their next decade of even greater success together. He emphasizes his decision as a songwriter with number one hits to stick with independent versus signing with one of Nashville's major publishing houses in 1963, as he reasons it was the right move because "what I've always told everyone, and I know this as a fact, is you've got to be careful who you sign with. You come to town and you're going to sign with a publisher, and there's no way of knowing whether it's good or bad. So, you've got to do as much thinking and find out as much as you can before you sign, because you can wind up signing with a huge company downtown that's comparable to Exxon, and you know what? They really don't need you. You're just a whim, and they don't need you, and sometimes it makes me ask, 'Why do they sign these boys and girls anyway because they're not going to do anything with them …' For example, the guy I signed with after Ferlin, Jim Reeves at Acclaim Music, was hungry, and I was hungry myself as a writer, and he was as a publisher. He had a little $25 a month office down in Madison and I had an old upright piano, and we were partners, and it worked. I'd stay up all night writing them and he'd take them downtown and get them cut. Because if he didn't, he was a poor man with a family and wouldn't make it and the same with me. So, there is some truth to that."

Frazier continued to build a name on the US Hot Country Songs Chart throughout the early 1960s as Dodie Stevens took "Yes-Sir-Ee" and "Why Don't Daddy Live Here Anymore" by Bonnie Owens respectively into the Top 40 in 1963, while in 1964, Ferlin Husky took "Timber I'm Falling" into the Top 20, reminding Dallas of his favorite comic stories to come from his early songwriting career: "Something funny about that, Ferlin talked me temporarily into changing my name to Dalton Timber as a new songwriter in town [laughs]. So, I got my first BMI award under

102   SONGS OF NASHVILLE

the name Dalton Timber! I came back to Dallas after that. That was my first Cadillac [*laughs*]!"

Husky would score a Top 50 hit courtesy of Frazier's songwriting gifts with "Monkey Greases the Wheel" from *Ferlin Husky Sings the Songs of Music City USA* in 1965, along with other charting singles like "Nothing Left to Lose" by Faron Young and "Baby Ain't That Fine" by Gene Pitney and Melba Montgomery. That same year, helping Frazier score his next hit with Charlie Rich's "Mohair Sam" was Ray Baker, one of Acclaim's song pluggers. Frazier would later follow Baker to Blue Crest Music in a new publishing deal in 1965 as his career took off even higher up the charts with his first number one on the country charts with Jack Greene in 1966 with "There Goes My Everything." Reigning atop the charts for seven weeks, Frazier beams with pride, looking back at "how many times that song has been recorded, you'd have to [go] up into the several hundreds! Sharon and I moved to Tennessee on a train in late 1963 and we lived with Ferlin Husky, he was off on the road. He had moved me here to write for him, and so I wrote 'There Goes My Everything' because he was going through a divorce, and I wrote that song about him. That divorce he was going through was the core, the essence. And I had it all finished, when I say it took me about an hour for it to all come together. As I was writing the song, the melody and everything came together quick and it was the first song I wrote when I came to Tennessee, and it's the biggest copyright that I have."

It is one of Frazier's most recorded songs in his catalog and arguably country music history at different points, after Jack Greene's version took home the Country Music Association's Song of the Year honor, Engelbert Humperdinck scored a Top 10 US Hot 100 Singles Chart hit in 1967, and Elvis Presley took it into the Top 10 as a hit, inspiring a smile from Frazier, who proudly points out that "just like for any songwriter, it was fantastic. It was just great. Engelbert Humperdinck, he had the big record in Europe on their charts and everything. He had a monster record, and he was such a good singer, a great singer. But I had five songs recorded by Elvis. 'Mohair Sam' is one of my favorites. That wasn't a big hit, but it was a big song for me. That's one of my favorite songs because when the Beatles invaded America and went out to Hollywood, they met and hung out with Elvis, and he said all he did was play 'Mohair Sam' by Charlie Rich on his juke box [*laughs*]! Peggy Lee and Quincy Jones would go on to cover that too."

Never trading in his ambitions to become a successful recording star in his own right even as so many others were making his songs famous on the charts, Frazier sought to debut those hits in his own name as an artist whenever possible amid his busy songwriting career. Between 1966 and 1971, he released four solo albums, including 1966's *Elvira*, 1967's *Tell It Like It Is* for Capitol Records, 1970's *Singing My Songs*, and 1971's *My Baby Packed Up My Mind and Left Me*. He racked up a number of solo singles during that span, including "Just a Little Bit of You," "Especially for You," "My Woman Up't and Gone," the Top 40 hit "Everybody Ought to Sing a Song," "The Sunshine of My World," "I Hope I Like Mexico Blues," "The Conspiracy of Homer Jones," "California Cotton Fields," "She Wants to Be Good," "The Birthmark Henry Thompson Talks About," "Big Mabel Murphy," and "High Steppin' Mama." While arguably the most popular among those would be "Elvira," revealing that versus being inspired by a woman or heartbreak story, Frazier recalls "that song name came from a street name in East Nashville. My publisher Ray Baker and I were coming from town one night, and we were on Gallatin Road. Back in those days, it was the only road that left Nashville and came out to Madison and Gallatin. Anyway, I was doing a rhythm and blues session for Capital Records and working on a rhythm and blues LP, and we passed by that sign. I just hollered, 'Oh, my God, did you see that?!' because in the first place with *Elvira*, I've always been like a guy that just loved earthy names and when I saw that,

104 SONGS OF NASHVILLE

I thought, 'You know, that's got to be one of the champions right there!' I love it and it wasn't too long till I finished it and entitled my album with the same name."

Frazier's star would continue to ascend as one of the biggest success stories among Nashville Songwriters in the late 1960s as Connie Smith's 1966 smash with "Ain't Had No Lovin'." George Jones would begin his historic run of Frazier-penned hits would have one with "I'm a People,"1967's "If My Heart Had Windows," "I Can't Get There from Here," "Say It's Not You," "Beneath Still Waters," and "Tell Me My Lying Eyes Are Wrong" between 1966 and 1970 alone. Smith followed close on Jones's heels with her own run of Dallas-written chart smashes between the late 1960s and early 1970s, including "Run Away Little Tears," "Where Is My Castle," "I'm Sorry If My Love Got in Your Way," "Just for What I Am," "If It Ain't Love (Let's Leave It Alone)," "Dream Painter," and "Ain't Love a Good Thing," in total setting a record of sorts by recording nearly seventy of Frazier's songs throughout her career, surpassing any other artist. He is proud that both Connie Smith and George Jones thought so much of his songwriting style that "they both recorded entire albums of my songs!"

Frazier was topically talented enough to rise with each new hit to the status of what the *New York Times* championed as "a songwriter of great emotional range," pointing out in their historical analysis that "although his most enduring success came in country music, Mr. Frazier also wrote pop and R&B hits for artists like the country-soul singer Charlie and the Louisiana bluesman Slim Harpo. Mr. Frazier's bread and butter, nevertheless, was country music, where his songs plumbed an array of subjects and emotions, like humor, heartache and his hardscrabble childhood during the Great Depression," pointing to "The *Son of Hickory Holler's* Tramp" by Johnny Darrell and then O. C. Smith—which became a Top 40 hit on both the pop and R&B charts and rocketed all the way to number two on the UK charts—as "definitely another of my

Everybody Oughta Sing a Song   105

favorites. It's not a true story, I'll tell you that much, there's a grain of truth in it. The sound sprung out of that grain."

Frazier singles out "The Most Uncomplicated Goodbye I've Ever Heard" by Henson Cargill, who made it a Top 20 hit, as a song that he cowrote with one of his favorite collaborators, the late Sanger "Whitey" Shafer. In a business where songwriters were often paired together through their publisher scheduling a cowrite, Dallas and Whitey were inseparable throughout the first half of the 1970s. Dallas recalls they first met back "in 1967 when Whitey had just moved to town from Texas. He was a friend of Doodle Owens down in Texas and one thing led to another and I got to meet Whitey, and it wasn't too long before we started writing some things together. The one thing about Whitey that I picked up on right away was his humor. He's one of the funniest guys I ever met in my life, and he pulled it out of me too. I love humor and sometimes we would get together for a writing session and between drinking beer and laughing, not a whole lot got done. We had some laughs; I'll tell you what. We had a good time together when we wrote and got together."

Rather than getting together at an office in Nashville, Frazier fondly recalls the escape both considered their preferred song-writing destination; specifically a cabin set on "a piece of land I owned. I bought and sold several pieces of land in Tennessee, and this particular farm had about eighty acres as I remember and it was very picturesque, and not very far from here, about thirteen or fourteen miles, something like that. It's up in the hills, secluded, and I bought this cabin, and had it moved up there, and it was real nice. Matter of fact, Whitey finished off the inside of it for me, he was good with wood and quite a carpenter. He was a craftsman; he could have done anything he wanted to do. We had a big old upright piano designed for songwriting, no phones allowed, and it had a gate down the hill where you could go up to the cabin, and we put a padlock on the gate: That was a sign that we were up there working. The farm was mostly wooded, and a great place to go out and take a thirty-minute walk on the trails when we'd take a break, just get away from the piano and take a breather. We'd stay up there sometimes two or three days, with a couple of beds we could crash on, and then we'd get right back up and go back at it. I played a little bit of guitar, not much, and Whitey played better than me, a little piano, but we would trade off on the piano. We had different styles; he could do a pop thing or just a plain old Merle Haggard kind of thing."

They created an era of unforgettable hits together that began in 1970 and featured "Lord Is That Me" by Jack Greene, a Top 20 hit, and also several Top 40 hits, including "Darling Days" by Billy Walker, "I'm Sorry If My Love Got in Your Way" and "Dream Painter" by Connie Smith, "Just Because I'm Still in Love With You" by Bobby Wright, "The Love of Your Life" by Penny DeHaven, "The Baptism of Jesse Taylor" by Johnny Russell, "The Rainbow in Daddy's Eyes" by Sammi Smith, "The Way I Lose My Mind" by Carl Smith, and "The Devil Ain't a Lonely Woman's Friend" by Tennessee Ernie Ford. Singling out a few of his personal favorites from their colorful catalog, Dallas leaps right away to "Darling Days," pointing to it as "powerful and just simple, and sometimes a writer doesn't even know how you get ahold of something like that. It just comes, it just flows, it pours out, and it's just so simple and there's no extra fat on it. It's trimmed off and that's the one thing I like to do in my writing is try to trim off as much of the excess as possible and not hurt the song. We would sometimes bat titles around, and he'd say something that really got my attention or vice versa, I'd say something, and he'd reply, 'Oh, Dallas, we need to work on that.' When we sat down to write 'The Baptism of Jesse Taylor,' we were using the name Robert Taylor for a while, and that had to do with this guy who had been scarred somehow or another in war. We worked on that for a while, and we went from that to a guy that knew the Lord, had gotten away

Everybody Oughta Sing a Song 107

from the Lord and then come back to the Lord. My faith showed up in my writing."

Frazier churned out his own era of Top 40 hits with Doodle Owens one-on-one beginning back in 1968 with "San Diego" by Charlie Walker, "She Thinks I'm on That Train" by Henson Cargill, "Raggedy Ann" by Charlie Rich," "True Love Travels on a Gravel Road" by Duane Dee, "What Are Those Things (With Black Wings)" by Charlie Louvin, and "The Conspiracy of Homer Jones" and "I Hope You Like Mexico Blues" by Dallas Frazier. Other hits included "Johnny One Time" by Willie Nelson, "Mama, I Won't Be Wearing a Ring" by Peggy Lee, "If This Is Love" by Jack Greene, and the number one smash hits for Charley Pride including "(I'm So) Afraid of Losing You Again" and "All I Have to Offer You Is Me," noting of the latter chart-topper that "I remember the two big hits of mine and Doodle's that was 'All I Have to Offer You Is Me,' that was Doodle's idea, and '(I'm So) Afraid of Losing You Again' is mine. Doodle was a real talent. If a guy doesn't have it, you just kind of drift away from them. That's just the way that works, you don't have to plan it or anything, it just happens. But Doodle was a fine songwriter, a great songwriter, and he carried his weight when we got together and worked."

Alongside the opportunity to cowrite with one of his country heroes in Doodle Owens, Frazier considered himself equally honored to have the opportunity to get to know country singer-songwriter star Lefty Frizzell through his association with frequent cowriter Whitey Shafer. An influence over Whitey Shafer, Roy Orbison, Willie Nelson, Merle Haggard, and George Jones as well as Dallas, he still beams at his memory of "first meeting Lefty when I was about thirteen years old while working out in California. That's young and it was a big deal to me, just to get to meet Lefty Frizzell, 'The French Man,' and he influenced so many singers, all these guys that sound like Hag, that can be traced back to Lefty. When you talk about everybody that Lefty has influenced, in the first

108   SONGS OF NASHVILLE

place, we could start with Merle Haggard. You can hear Lefty all over Haggard and I say that to Hag's benefit. Merle was a fantastic singer, a great, great singer, but I hear Lefty in him. Haggard's a fantastic singer, great singer, but I hear Lefty in him and it's the same way with me. I remember hearing Lefty singing when I was a kid. I'd go with my dad to this old beer joint called Schweitzer's Corner out in the country, and my dad would play the jukebox over and over: 'Why don't you love me like you used to do, . . .' the Hank Williams songs, and then he played 'Mom and Dad's Waltz' by Lefty Frizzell and I grew up on that stuff, you know. I remember my dad with tears in his eyes, thinking about my mom because she had left him, listening to Lefty. He influenced the whole business, just like they say Jimmy Rogers did. So, Hank Williams and Lefty Frizzell were the two biggest influences in my background. I was very proud when I wrote 'Hank and Lefty Raised My Country Soul.' It's kind of self-explanatory, it's autobiographical because that same beer joint—Schweitzer's Corner—that's where I learned to love old Hank and Lefty."

As songs continued to flow out of him like a fountain, *MusicRow* magazine expanded its legacy coverage by noting that he earned his reputation "as one of the greatest country songwriters in history, the songwriter's string of country successes also continued with Charlie Louvin's 'Will You Visit Me on Sundays' (1968), Jerry Lee Lewis's 'Touching Home' (1971), Ferlin Husky's 'White Fences and Evergreen Trees' (1968), Elvis Presley's 'Where Did They Go Lord' (1971), Nat Stuckey's 'She Wakes Me With a Kiss Every Morning' (1971), Johnny Russell's 'The Baptism of Jesse Taylor' (1974), Roy Head's 'The Door I Used to Close' (1976), Moe Bandy's 'Does Anyone Make Love at Home Anymore' (1976), and Tanya Tucker's 'What's Your Mama's Name.'" Highlighting Tucker's hit as one that almost wrote itself, he recalls that "that was my idea, and 'Peanutt' Montgomery and I wrote it together when we were riding in his car down in Alabama. It's just a story that came out of the blue, as we say, no dramatic starting point. As soon as I got the first idea for the first verse, I could say, 'Well, we're going to the second, third, and fourth and kind of continue this thing as he gets older.' The story changes a little bit as he ages, and Peanutt and I wrote a few things together, and I think that's one of the best ones in my catalog."

Reviewing rock and roll legends who took his hits into crossover success, Frazier proudly points to the Man in Black, fondly recalling that "Johnny Cash cut one of my songs back in 1960, 1961, that was impressive then because he was big in '60. It was a delight, really. Then when Jerry Lee Lewis recorded 'When He Walks On You (Like You Have Walked On Me),' I remember when that idea first came to me. I was just brainstorming, thinking, trying to come up with something. I thought that one of the most touching lines I'd ever written, 'When he walks on you like you have walked on me. . . .' There's nothing greatly poetic about it, it's just raw and it's real."

Billboard recorded another of his favorite memories coming when "Johnny Cash once held a party at his Nashville home in Bob Dylan's honor and invited his favorite songwriters. Dylan asked that Frazier attend and told Frazier that 'Baby Ain't That Fine' was his personal favorite."

Giving the 2020s generation access to a few of his rules of the writing road he applied day in and out in his writing process, Frazier begins by noting that they are universal, "these things I've learned with every writer I've worked with: 1) The power of a certain word. Sometimes you use a certain word, and you know it's not the word, because some words don't sing. That's why you've got to be more than a poet when you're writing, just looking at the words. You're hearing the words, just like you don't want to end a word with 'Shhh' or start a word with 'Shhh,' and that's me now, that's what I think. There's no rules—the only rule is get off your butt and work, that's the only rule for songwriters. 2) I mentioned trimming the fat off of songs. Sometimes songs are filled with things you need to edit and take them out, just leave the bare bones, so to speak, that are essential for your songs. That's kind of hard to get across, because it's a method you do, it comes out of your inner man. There are things I picked up on and I studied them all my life."

It's a measure of how gifted and prolific he was that Dallas Frazier was inducted into the Nashville Songwriters Hall of Fame in 1976 when he was only thirty-six years old. Reasoning the acknowledgment was due by then, Frazier had already become, in their esteemed estimation, "one of the most recorded and successful country songwriters of the 1960s and '70s before he decided to put his songwriting career aside." Dallas reveals, amid pointing out proudly, that "I was the youngest songwriter ever inducted into the Songwriters Hall of Fame. I quit in the end of 1975 to become a full-time minister. Have you ever heard the expression 'Throwing the baby out with the bathwater'? That's kind of what I did with my gifts, my talents, I kind of threw them out. I went through a terrible time with my conscience on what I should do and shouldn't do and what I ought to stop doing and start doing—I just went through a terrible time. I shouldn't have just quit entirely. There were things I needed to quit, for sure. Some things I needed to get away from, but I didn't handle it right. But it's okay. It's turned out alright."

CHAPTER 9

I DID IT MY WAY

. . . .

Clint Black

"There is a magic to creating something that wasn't there before."

C lint Black is one of the most recognizable country music stars in the world, and not only because he could have otherwise been a movie star, even making a cameo in the Mel Gibson–Jodie Foster film *Maverick* back in the 1990s. And that's precisely the word that has defined his success and longevity. Famously bucking Music Row's songwriting system of recording other songwriters' material, Clint Black has long prided himself on writing virtually all his greatest hits, revealing that at the very top of his career, "they basically told me, as soon as they could, that my problem was I insisted on writing the songs, and everywhere I went after that, every major label just insisted that I don't write my songs. So, I never went that route, and I've always made the records I want. I've always been creatively liberated, just by insisting on always making the record I wanted to."

A one-of-a-kind talent in country music history, from head-lining a Super Bowl halftime show to his very own star on the Hollywood Walk of Fame, Clint Black was spotlighted by The Boot (theboot.com) on the thirtieth anniversary of his multiplat-inum debut album, *Killin' Time*: "It's hard for the country star to comprehend that *Killin' Time* has been such an influential body of work for other artists, many of whom are now prominent stars in their own right." Black graduated into stardom as a member of the

112   SONGS OF NASHVILLE

storied "Class of '89," and *The Tennessean* reviewed the history made "by the meteoric rise of Garth Brooks, Alan Jackson, Clint Black, and Travis Tritt—[it] changed the face of one of America's truest art forms, propelling country music to unprecedented commercial success and worldwide popularity."

Shaking his head as he looks back on his one-of-a-kind catalog of songs, Black today reveals that he writes in much the same way he has from the start of his career: "It happens every different kind of way. For instance, with 'Nobody's Home,' I remember I was sharing a house with two other guys in a little section of West Houston, and I was sick with the flu. I remember just barely being able to get out of bed to get a drink of water, and for about three days I was just down with the fever and was pretty much on my own, just sweating it out, sleepin' most of the time. But when I would go get up to get a drink of water or something, I would stop by my desk by the bed and write something down and three days later when I came out of it, all the lyrics were there! I wrote literally nothing else, but that whole song was written and I just picked up the guitar and started to put music to it."

Growing up not surprisingly in a musical home, Clint remembers being surrounded by music: "My mom and dad both had a lot of music playing in the house. My dad taught me to read the liner notes on our 45s, so he would point out, 'This is the singer, this is their songwriter, and this is the producer.' I remember one of the first records he showed me was by Merle Haggard, and it instantly just kind of cemented this habit of mine, of reading the liner notes from then on whenever I got a new record. So, I came to appreciate the singers who wrote their own songs, and songwriters in general and the producers. That really drove me to want to write my own songs and it all started when I was six or seven years old. Then I started harmonica when I was thirteen. I played the drums too, and picked up the guitar at fifteen, and my brother Kevin and I started a band together called the Full House Band. We didn't play big gigs: a chili cook-off booth was one of the early ones, but we were playing right in front of the booth, and people would pass by and try their chili and hear us. I think our PA system was all being plugged into a twin reverb amp!"

Finding that art naturally imitated life as he began playing out more and more around town, Black in particular points to "a pretty decent bar and grill I was playing on Tuesday nights when there weren't very many people there and some gigs at steak and ale restaurants, which really stunk. After that, I got a gig at a happy hour, which inspired 'Winding Down' off *Killin' Time*, because the people there were talking to each other and couldn't care less about me over there playing. For a singer though, I wanted to play places where people came to hear musicians. My first big break came when I was in a music store one day just looking at guitars I couldn't afford, and in walks Shake Russell!"

Seizing the same sort of moment many a hungry artist has when it came walking through the proverbial door, Clint recalls taking a deep breath after "I saw him over looking at guitars and I had one in my hands, so I started playing the introduction to one of his songs, and he said 'Hey,' and we struck up a conversation. Then he bought some guitar strings and left, and I ran after the parking lot to catch him, and said, 'Hey, how does a guy come to open for Shake Russell?' He said, 'Well, you know what, you call this guy,' and it was Shake's road manager. So, when I called him, he had me come out and open for them at a gig the following week, and I did well enough that from that point on, Shake had me open for him at all the places soloists would fit in. So, he really was my entrée into playing bars that were really suitable and more conducive to singing for people who were listening."

After spending years making his bones on the club circuit, playing bigger and bigger gigs in and around Houston, Black linked up with future bandmate and songwriting partner Hayden Nicholas in 1987. A kindred meeting of the musical minds that would lead to

114   SONGS OF NASHVILLE

many of the biggest hits in Black's early career, and perhaps even more important in the meantime, he recalled that "when I'd first met Hayden, I didn't really have any demos, and Hayden had an eight-track recorder in his garage, and we made a deal to demo my songs, and the first one we finished was 'Nobody's Home.' Thankfully, with Hayden, I'd finally found a way to do it affordably with someone who knew how to do it and complemented my skills really well. So, we were able to build these demos and have really strong background vocals. He was a great guitar player too, even back then, and could play bass and I played a lot of drums growing up. So, as a composer and a lyricist, especially, the drums play a critical role where every little part of what the drums were doing I was—and still am—really particular about, because every syllable has to be accounted for. The way the lyrical syllables fall in the groove of the drums can only go counter to that if it really is asking for it. So, all of those little things I was really particular about programming the drum machine and getting just exactly what I wanted out of that. Around then, I started trying to find a new manager with that song and actually went back to my first manager, Sammy, and asked if he'd help me shop it, and he's the one who introduced me to Bill Ham."

Rolling Stone magazine would later rave that "the best thing about *Killin' Time* is Black never sounds like he's trying too hard. Like Merle Haggard, Black understands striking veins of true emotion is the real deal. Neither choirboy nor hellion, he writes and sings about battered hearts, broken dreams and tortured emotions with an unflinching directness," an organic outgrowth Black attributes to the fact that "all of the hits off of *Killin' Time*, including 'A Better Man,' 'Nobody's Home,' and 'Nothing's News' were pretty much those demos I was pre-producing for the album. Hayden was an educated musician and took some writing courses in college while I was strictly by ear, and learned from listening, so we had this balance, and we also were driven to do it. When we wrote together, we could sit in a room together for ten hours, even if we had to stare at the wall, because we knew we were going to get this, and that it had to be gotten. There were things that we did, and I think were different from the nine to fivers, here in Nashville, one being that we would have three to five songs we were writing at a time. So if we sequestered ourselves, or we were just over his garage, we would have three, or four, or five pieces of paper on the table and we'd be working on one song until we just were tired of beating our heads against the wall. We'd say, 'Look, let's jump off this, and move one page over,' and we would start working on that song, which got our heads out of the other one. So, we would dance around and work for a couple of hours and then move over to something else with a completely different style, tempo, chords, melody, and direction, and it would relieve us from the stress of being stuck on this other thing and we'd make some progress."

Pointing to the smash hit that held the number two spot on *Billboard*'s year-end Hot Country Singles chart for 1989, Black is to date proud that "Killin' Time" has stood the test of time with country music fans, crediting its muse to quite literally "the waiting game of, 'I've got my deal, the album is pretty much, basically done and we're still playing for $50 a night, and it seems to be taking forever!' Hayden and I were playing duo gigs and were driving up to one north of Houston one day, just talking about how long it's taking, and I said, 'Well, I just hope it happens soon because this killin' time is killin' me,' and we looked at each other and said, 'That's a song!' I really look at writing a song a lot like an actor fleshing out a scene—you have to understand: What's the point? What's the most profound part of this? What am I supposed to be feeling and what am I saying I'm feeling or showing I'm feeling? So, you take an idea like that and go 'Okay, this killin' time is killin' me,' what's that about? It's not me, 'cause it's not going to make anyone feel much if I'm talking about how I just can't wait for my career to start. So, it needed to be about something with a lot more feeling to it, and

116 SONGS OF NASHVILLE

the most universal subject is love. Love found, love lost, and that's kind of what we did. We figured out that's really what it's got to be about and someone who's waiting for it all to be done, because of the pain of losing love. We really had the song written, except for the last line of the chorus, which is kind of a double line, and so it just went on and on for about a month where we couldn't figure out how to end that chorus. Then we were up at Sammy's lake house—we went there once to write and it hit me, and I looked at Hayden and had this big grin on my face. I knew I'd found the line, and he was going to like it after all our searching, and said, 'I just might find, I'll be killin' time for eternity,' and it was like '*yes*, that's it!'"

Fans would roundly agree, buying up three million copies of Black's debut album. His meteoric rise to stardom at the time was based on the strength of those radio singles, and his sophomore LP, *Put Yourself in My Shoes*, would score four more Top 10 hits on the *Billboard* Hot Country Songs Chart. These included a Top 5 hit with the title track and his next number one smash when Black kicked off 1992 with "Loving Blind" and the number two spot on the US Hot Country Songs chart with "We Tell Ourselves." Singling out "Loving Blind" as one of those magic moments of inspiration where the whole song hit him at once, Clint recalled that "I put my pen to paper and write it straight out. No music in my head, no, nothing, just the tempo of the lyric and meter of that, and I wrote all of that song in fifteen minutes! It was like 'Bam!'—no scratched-out words or anything, it just popped out. I picked up the guitar and figured out what to do with that. When I'm writing, I've kind of learned to not edit as I go and when that happens, just to let it flow out, because you can fix it later."

By the time he was sitting down to write the three Top 10 hits—"We Tell Ourselves," "Burn One Down," and the number one smash, "When My Ship Comes In"—from his third multi-platinum, *The Hard Way* LP, hitting number one for the seventh time in four years, Black remains fond of this dance floor favorite he remembers "writing with my buddy Skip Ewing a couple years before that, maybe even more, and he had a song called 'The Coast of Colorado,' and the song goes: 'When the seas take California and wash up on the great divide, I'll be waitin' for you on the coast of Colorado [*laughs*].' You know, just a fantastic song, and I remember Hayden and I said, 'Let's write a song from after that, where we're gonna sail out of Colorado,' and so that song really sprang out of Skip's song and with both of us being Jimmy Buffett fans, wanted something that really spoke of escapism. One thing you notice about Buffett—and it's the same with Shake Russell, and I told Shake this once—is 'You can write these songs with these great, happy feelings, and I have to write songs when something happens to me. And when something really happy happens I'm too busy celebrating to write a song. When something bad happens, I'm down in this hole, with nothing to do but write about it.' So, I really had to figure out a way to write songs that felt happy, celebratory, and had that escapism of a Margaritaville type of thing. So, we wanted to do that with this idea of being stuck up there with no sun on the Rockies, and that chorus kicks in, 'We're on our way to some place warm. . . .'"

Clint would show his staying power when he scored his eighth straight number one hit on the *Billboard* Hot Country Songs Chart with "A Good Run of Bad Luck," the title track of his fourth studio album, and one of those irresistible concepts that Black recalls knowing right away "we were going to write something from, it was an idea in my notebook, and I remember we had one other song idea Tanya Tucker had told Hayden, 'Y'all should write a song about me,' so we joked with ourselves, 'Tuckered Out,' and that would be it. We ended up snowed in in Toronto, and decided we were gonna write those two songs. I had played many times at Caesar's Palace in Vegas and used to sit down there and play blackjack, and so they knew me, and I called down there and asked for a pit boss. They patched me through to a pit boss, and I said, 'Hey, I'm working on a song, and I need some catchphrases. What term do you guys use for this or that?' One of them was high roller, so I got a little bit out of him, and we made a bubble sheet of all our phrases and terms and how they connected with each other, and created our little road map, and then just went to work on it, and it poured right out. Then we were writing at the same time the other song and we wrote down every country artist's name that could be a noun or a verb or an adjective, and we started writing this story about this guy who's just traveling, and he's worn out from it, and that became 'Good Run of Bad Luck. . . .'"

Reflecting more generally on his songwriting outlook by that point in his career, Clint reveals that "by the time we went in to record *No Time to Kill*, what I was really trying to do was give the songs what they wanted. So, I write a song and I'm hearing and feeling a certain thing about that song in my head, and that's what I want to try to provide that song in terms of a band. For instance, with 'State of Mind,' I wrote the song when I was eighteen, so this arrangement had lived in my head for over a decade." Accompanying this hit and another Top 5 smash, "Burn It Down," to the top of the US Hot Country Songs Chart was the ballad "A Bad Goodbye," a duet with Wynonna Judd. Black instantly knew she was the right voice with whom to deliver the song, so much so that "I remember we were at a TV taping at Opryland shortly before the album was going to come out and I grabbed her and said, 'Come in here,' and we went to some kind of little storage closet. I had my guitar and said, 'Listen to this. Is it something you would be interested in?' When she heard it, she said, 'Hell, yeah!' and that was that. That was the first single that came out before the record, and it sold 170,000 copies in just a couple of weeks before the album hit the stores! So, it was a big song, and it was a great moment on the tour when she came out. I remember thinking, 'This is like *Coal Miner's Daughter*, in the movie when Sissy

Spacek would walk out and you would see all the flashbulbs,' and every night it felt that way. It could have just been some kitschy little, clever little, tongue-in-cheek song but turned out to be a big moment in the show."

When he was pitching his next number one smash, "A Good Run of Bad Luck," to the higher-ups at his record label, Clint remembered surprisingly finding a harder sell was required: "I was shooting the movie *Maverick*, and I told the director Dick Donner, 'I've got a song, "A Good Run of Bad Luck," that might be good for this movie,' and he said, 'Oh, yeah? Send it to me,' and when he heard it, he said, 'Yeah, we definitely want that in there.' Well, at the time, Thom Schuyler was headin' up RCA [RCA Records' Nashville Division], and I just begged him to let them have it for the film, and he said, 'Well, it's gonna be a single, I don't want anything getting in the way of that.' I countered, 'Well, they're not going to release it as a single, it will just go on the soundtrack.' He was really kind of against it, but I kept talking at him about it, and I said, 'Listen, they'll give me any of that movie footage and we'll be able to make a video with me, and James Garner and Mel Gibson and Jody Foster, and on and on. We'll have a really great music video. We gotta do this!' So, he finally said 'Okay,' and it was the first video I directed!"

Black's fifth studio album, *One Emotion*, would become an instant platinum seller on the strength of yet another new run of hit singles including, "Wherever You Go," "Life Gets Away," and "Untanglin' My Mind." He would next rocket to number one with the album's smartly titled single, "Summer's Comin'," which he was happy to have in his arsenal as a surefire hit for the season, and one that he highlights was an obvious single the minute he wrote it: "Sometimes with a song like that, we needed one that feels like fun, started playing a groove and messing around, and Jerry Williams got a drum beat going and he started playing a chord progression. With a song like 'Summer's Comin',' we were

120 SONGS OF NASHVILLE

wanting a song with kind of a Chuck Berry–ish type of thing, and that song was the result."

Clint was already back in the studio recording what would become, in the opinion of The Boot.com, "one of his finest works," starting with the number one smash title track, which the country legend remembers knowing was going to work right away, before offering the caveat that "when I got rolling on a new song, I didn't always know if it was going to work, but I knew always that not everything was gonna work. With 'Nothin' but the Taillights,' I knew that people were gonna like that song. The idea one night when I went to his house about ten o'clock and we wrote for quite a few hours on it. You hear that phrase, and you go, 'Okay, I get where this is going,' and then it was the crafting of it. Working with Steve Wariner is fast and furious, because he's quick with ideas, and that sparks ideas from me. So, we're back and forth, and you just want to be able to write faster on the page. So, we worked on that one for three or four hours, working into the morning, and we were done."

"The Shoes You're Wearing" would grab the other number one single spot off the album and fans too with an invitation they couldn't resist when *People* magazine reported that "on his 110-concert tour to promote his latest album, *Nothin' but the Taillights*, country singer Clint Black has accumulated more than travel miles; he has also collected 41,000 pairs of shoes. The footwear—a charitable tie-in inspired by his single 'The Shoes You're Wearing' has been brought to his concerts by Black's fans and distributed to the needy in cities along his tour route." Following that smash up with another to round out the 1990s with the number two hit "Something That We Do" and the Academy of Country Music Vocal Event of the Year Award with "When I Said I Do," which again took Clint to number one on both the US Hot Country Songs and the US Hot 100 Singles chart, Black once again proudly points to his wife, Lisa Hartman, as its creator and muse: "Our marriage was wonderful, we were so in love, and as time went on, now it goes a little deeper, and you go, 'Man, this is as good as it gets, and then ten years later you have a child,' and there's more down there to feel. I loved producing the string section on that song. I didn't write the arrangements, Steve Dorff wrote those, but Steve and I talked it through, and I told him what I was thinking, and he listened to 'When I Said I Do' over and over and wrote the arrangements. Then I was basically sitting there listening to these fantastic musicians playing symphony music over my track. The first time I did that was with a 101-piece orchestra for my Christmas record, and that was two days of extreme emotions, and then on a song with my wife, it wore me out having that much joy."

Black would offer his contributions to the country Christmas-themed album tradition over *Looking for Christmas* and *Christmas with You* before delivering more hit albums to his legacy fan base with 1998's *D'electrified* and 2004's *Spending Time*, and 2005's *Drinking Songs and Other Logic*. In 2010, Clint claimed a spot on *Billboard* magazine's list of the top twenty-five country artists of the past twenty-five years, continuing to deliver new albums like *Love Songs* in 2007, a record five more greatest-hits albums including *When I Said I Do*, released in an exclusive distribution pact with Cracker Barrel, *The Clint Black Christmas Collection*, *The Long Cool EP*, and the live album *Still Killin' Time*, where he delivered an all-star cast featuring Trace Adkins, Sara Evans, Dierks Bentley, Darius Rucker, Travis Tritt, Steve Wariner, and more, along with 2015's *On Purpose*.

After Clint Black earned his own star on the Hollywood Walk of Fame, the Texas Heritage Songwriters Association reviewed the equally-as-impressive stat that the "overall number of his awards . . . surpasses the number of his hit records, while he has performed for a staggering number of dedicated music fans in concerts through the years." That millions of listeners across his multigenerational fan base still turn out in the 2020s as they have over the past forty years to show Clint Black they still have his back means the most to the singer-songwriter, as their loyalty is rooted in a love of "songs I insisted on writing myself, and to know that I'm really proud of the work I did, it's fantastic for me to have that body of work and know where it came from. It all started with that one song where I can't do a standard and had to write one. Then, 'Okay, now I have to do a whole album,' and that was really daunting. It was hard work and so I like having that catalog. It's like anyone where, if you built a house, you can stand back and look at that house and feel good it's still standing today all these years later!"

CHAPTER 10

RESURRECTION

....

Kinky Friedman

One of Texas music's true musical troubadours, Kinky Friedman has been celebrated in the wake of his passing on June 27, 2024. *USA Today* remembered him fondly as a "rabble rousing man of letters with a penchant for self-mythology and a deep love of animals, whose music and writing was loved by everyone from Bob to Bill Clinton," a depiction that he quips exclusively suited him well as "It was me and Billy Joe Shaver who both thought we were always the snowplow of the 'Outlaw Country' movement."

Revered throughout his fifty-year career as a "folk hero" by *Rolling Stone* magazine, Austin City Limits reported that after Richard Samet Friedman grew up in Texas Hill country on his family's ranch where they operated a summer camp, Echo Hill Ranch, he graduated from the University of Texas at Austin in 1966 with a bachelor's degree in psychology, where he was given his famous nickname "Kinky" by a fellow Tau Delta Phi fraternity member and after "stints with the Peace Corps and in Nashville, Kinky became the quick-witted provocateur of seventies outlaw country. Writing or covering songs ('Get Your Biscuits in the Oven and Your Buns in the Bed,' 'Sold American,' 'They Ain't Making Jews Like Jesus Anymore,' the notorious 'Okie From Muskogee' lampoon, 'Asshole From El Paso') that raised the hackles of the satire-impaired and restricting his audience to connoisseurs with a certain sense of humor." Recalling that he was encouraged to be an individual creatively from the top of his career, "I remember a

124 SONGS OF NASHVILLE

guy at my first record company told me, 'You're an artist, Kinky, you're an artist!' and I managed to be an artist my whole life. That's an accomplishment."

Following his first official recorded single, "Schwinn 24/Beach Party Boo Boo," with his college band King Arthur & the Carrots in 1966, Kinky formed The Texas Jewboys in the early 1970s, scoring his first record deal after Commander Cody turned Vanguard Records—who had discovered Joan Baez—onto Friedman's one-of-a-kind voice, songwriting style, and originality, which he reflected onstage as a performer. *NBC News* reported: "He developed a cult following for his unique, quirky approach to country and Western music. The self-proclaimed 'governor of the heart of Texas' released a robust number of albums starting with 1973's *Sold American*, often considered his foundational record, and in addition to touring with Bob Dylan on his 'Rolling Thunder Revue,' he became the 'first full-blooded Jew' to appear at the Grand Ole Opry."

Parodying anything he saw injustice in within the times he was writing in, *Sold American*'s track listing reflects a protest record of sorts from "We Reserve the Right to Refuse Service to You," to other fan favorites like the title track "Sold American" and "Ride 'Em Jewboy." Friedman proudly points to one of his most humbling reflections of just how powerfully the record resonated with his revelation that none other than South African president Nelson Mandela was a fan at a time when he himself was imprisoned:

> I think sometimes I'm living inside of a Kurt Vonnegut novel, I think it's very strange to make a record in Nashville in 1973 with producer Chuck Glaser of the Glaser brothers, and Chuck at the time said, "Be careful what you do because when you make a record, you never know who's going to be listening." So, the fact that Nelson Mandela was listening in his jail cell and selected that song, he could

have selected "Flying Down the Freeway" or something else, but that one reached him somehow.

I've always been a fan of Mandela's. After he was passed on, I toured South Africa. I found out from Tokyo Sexwale when we did a TV show together over there, Dali Tambo was the host, and Dali's father was Oliver Tambo, a famous civil rights leader there and who was Mandela's mentor. I heard this [from] Tokyo firsthand, who told me, "Kinky, Mandela was a big fan of yours. He was a fan of your music." When he was on Robben Island, which is the end of the road, you don't get off Robben Island, it's like Alcatraz, and these prison guards at first wanted to get rid of him, but somehow he turned them like Jesus could turn people. He went through absolute hell there, working in the quarry, and for some reason, they allowed him to play these smuggled tape cassettes and in the tapes was "Sold America." He had a little pirate radio station in the prison and late at night he would play songs for the other prisoners, and late at night, would sign off with "Ride 'Em Jewboy." So, as Tokyo was telling me this story, he said, "I know this well because I was in the cell next to Mandela for three and a half years. And every night, that was his sign-off, and sometimes he would play the song multiple times." So, you look at the measure of the man—the night he won the election for president, they all cheered "Viva Mandela." They were all his buddies by then. He'd been able to genuinely reach them. Sexwale finally told me, "But don't get a swell head about this, you were never his favorite singer, Dolly Parton was [laughs]!"

Kinky created a catalog of albums throughout the rest of the 1970s that established his legend to come, including 1974's self-titled

126 SONGS OF NASHVILLE

Kinky Friedman LP on ABC Records, which gave the world the classic "They Ain't Makin' Jews Like Jesus Anymore" and 1976's "Lasso from El Paso." Earning a national profile as Willie Nelson took him on the road along with a high-profile opening spot on Bob Dylan's 1975–1976 Rolling Thunder Revue tour alongside Joan Baez, Roger McGuinn, Joni Mitchell, Ronee Blakley, Ramblin' Jack Elliott, and Bob Neuwirth, and featured in the Martin Scorsese–directed documentary. The *Texas Tribune* chronicled his continued rise amid 1977's *Silver Jubilee 1953–1977, Live from the Lone Star Cafe* in 1982, and 1983's *Under the Double Ego* as "he rose to Texas celebrity status for his outsized persona, pithy one-liners, and signature look: curly hair poking out from beneath a black cowboy hat, cigar in hand. He gained the respect of musical titans like Bob Dylan, Willie Nelson, Waylon Jennings, and Kris Kristofferson. In the late 1970s, Friedman played every Sunday night at the Lone Star Cafe in New York City, the storied guests who came to see him, such as actors Robin Williams and John Belushi and other cast members of *Saturday Night Live.*" Kinky's popularity as a pop culture fixture was spotlighted on *Saturday Night Live* when he performed "Dear Abbie" in a salute to friend Abbie Hoffman, an antiwar activist, founder of the "Yippies" (Youth International Party), and member of the Chicago Seven on the run from the US government as a fugitive at the time. Kinky mused that he has relished throughout his career breaking the rules for the right reasons and causes, even if it was at times at his own cost commercially:

> My goals when I was a young man were to be fat, famous, and financially fixed, some I've achieved, and some have eluded me. I've always been very ambivalent about being a "country" singer and anyone who uses the word *ambivalent* should never be a country singer. It's very hard to be funny, I think, in music or anything else. It's a career-killer if people don't take you seriously, that's all there is to it, and

it took me till very recently to realize that. If you have just one funny song, and of course, I'm a serious soul no one takes seriously [*laughs*].

Reaching a place where that realization led him to trade writing songs to writing books for the better part of a quarter century before he famously ran for governor of Texas as an independent candidate in 2006, his literary catalog proved rich for readers via titles that mostly costarred Friedman as a character in hits like *Greenwich Killing Time, A Case of Lone Star, When the Cat's Away, Frequent Flyer, Musical Chairs, Elvis, Jesus and Coca-Cola, Armadillos and Old Lace, God Bless John Wayne, The Love Song of J. Edgar Hoover, Roadkill, Blast from the Past, Spanking Watson, Mile High Club, Steppin' on a Rainbow, Meanwhile Back at the Ranch, Curse of the Missing Puppet Head, The Prisoner of Vandam Street, Ten Little New Yorkers, Kill Two Birds and Get Stoned,* and *The Christmas Pig: A Fable.* Looking back on the literary career that preceded his return to songwriting, he recalls: "That was a lonely, monastic time for me. But I could start with anything, I like very much what [Georges] Simenon said—Inspector Maigret was his character—he said he would start with anything, start with a postcard, that's how much you need. I like to capture what's around me. A critic once said of my books that they 'smelled like New York.'"

Always keeping one boot rooted firmly back home in Texas, he wrote a column for *Texas Monthly* and, as Austin City Limits chronicled "became a national icon when he ran for governor of Texas in 2006, earning 12 percent of the vote—not nearly enough to win, of course, but not too shabby, either." Still, while greatest hits and related legacy compilations of his work were released to satisfy his multigenerational fanbase via *From One Good American to Another, Pearls in the Snow—The Songs of Kinky Friedman, Classic Snatches from Europe, Mayhem Afterthought, The Last of the Jewish Cowboys: Best of, Live from Austin, Texas, Lost and Found: The Famous*

Living Room Tape, 1970, and *The Loneliest Man I've Ever Met*, Kinky found himself sitting there in the 2010s "without having written a new song in nearly forty years, the only one I could remember is 'Loneliest Man I've Ever Met.' When I'm writing a song, it has to come together through just the spiritual void and the unhappiness and everything else, I just try to bring it together." He'd receive the needed nudge to begin his songwriting resurrection again amid such a saddened state when none other than "Willie Nelson called me one night at 3:00 a.m., when I was watching *Matlock*. Willie has been a shade-tree psychologist for me over the years, and he said, 'What are you doing, Kink?' and I told him 'I'm watching *Matlock*,' and he says, 'That's a sure sign of depression. Turn him off, Kinky, and start writing, man, start writing.' For some reason, this inspired me."

Awakening the songwriter again, he soon found himself writing what would become *Resurrection* with the realization that "most people don't even know the song, they think of me as writing 'They Ain't Making Jews Like Jesus Anymore,' and that's not really true anymore." Reflecting on how he felt he'd grown as a songwriter by the time he was writing "those twelve songs in a very short period of time, and I thought they were very high quality, and Willie had asked me to call him when I finished. So, I called him, and I said 'Willie, I've written these twelve songs,' and he said, 'Send them to me, I'd really like to hear them.'"

It turned out, right alongside Nelson, the rest of the world was excited and waiting, with *American Songwriter* magazine for one musing that "if Kinky Friedman had done nothing more than share his daring and defiant brand of outlaw country in the early '70s and merely mined his associations with Bob Dylan and Willie Nelson as part of that celebrity circle, it likely would have been enough to ensure his immortality. . . . Although his album output was relatively sparse during the '90s and early on in the new millennium, he's more than made up for it with new releases [like *Resurrection* that] . . . rank among his best efforts yet. It's noted that the song that starts the album, 'Mandela's Blues,' references the fact that the imprisoned future president of South Africa was an avowed fan of Friedman's music during his years of incarceration. Indeed, it sets the tone for the album overall." Elaborating on the album's poetic opener and equally-as-evocative title track, Kinky begins by sharing his opinion that

> one thing I like very much about *Resurrection* is that these are deep waters, deep thoughts. "Resurrection" was unconsciously written, but just about every person in there is dead, and I didn't start out saying "I see dead people," but they're gone and very close to me. Whether it's my parents, Tom and Min, or Tom Baker, the Baker Man, or all of the women in there just about, so they're all in my phone book that I still use. I don't have any electronic means, but I've got this book and of the names in this book, half are gone, and the song is a tribute to them all.

In a tribute to Kinky Friedman's passing in 2024, the *Austin Chronicle* saluted his final studio album as one that "resets the songwriter altogether. Straightaway, the songs are some of the best he's ever written. Although his voice is more worn and his delivery careful and patient, Larry Campbell's production and arrangements excavate a pathos Kinky's only rarely demonstrated. Whereas sharp humor and shocked satire once formed the foundation for his songs, *Resurrection* delivers a wisdom of experience, loss, mortality. For all the self-reinventions over the decades, he's forged a career out of being Kinky," while NPR paid a nod to his "poignant music" and the *Austin American Statesman* remembered him as "a large and luminous personality that Americana Highways celebrated as a 'revered' contributor to country music." He wound down his conversation with a final reflection on how he hoped his heroic candor and contributions as a songwriter would ultimately land him:

> When I went on this songwriting tear for *Resurrection* and wrote "Jesus in Pajamas," my producer Larry Campbell told me he thought that song relates to him the best of anything I've ever done. When you die and you go to Jesus and realize you've devoted your whole life to promoting yourself, how does that feel? It's very much like when Mark Twain said, "When you get to heaven, don't try to bring your dog in. They won't let you; heaven runs on protocol. If heaven ran on merit, your dog would go in and you would stay outside." May the Lord take a liking to you. . . .

CHAPTER 11

FRIENDS IN LOW PLACES

....

Earl Bud Lee

A rguably any bar in America has the option of hearing "Friends in Low Places," whether the live band or singer-songwriter playing onstage, the old-fashioned dance floor jukebox, or smartphone plugged into a sound system. The song is one of Garth Brooks's biggest and most enduring hits and favorite live staples at stadium concerts around the world where he famously sings a call-and-response a cappella version back and forth with his audiences, with *American Songwriter* magazine recently marking the day "on August 6th in 1990, Garth Brooks released 'Friends in Low Places.' The single went to number one on the *Billboard* Hot Country Songs chart and stayed there for four weeks. More important, it became Brooks' signature song. Later, the superstar would name his Nashville bar and grill after the song. Earl Bud Lee and Dewayne Blackwell wrote the song in 1989 and tapped the little-known Brooks to record a demo for the song!"

Taking fans back inside the song's initial creation with cowriter Dewayne Blackwell, Earl Bud Lee traces the roots of his songwriting style as reflected in the song back to "when I was a kid and my sister and I were washing dishes, and there was a little transistor radio on and suddenly Kris Kristofferson came on, and washing dishes had never been so easy. I was seven or eight years old, and that caught my ear in a big way, and I had no idea that I would write to a cadence like poetry in motion years later with a song like that one. That was my title, I was just being a smart-ass. I was out with some friends having lunch at a place called Tavern on the Row, and

132 SONGS OF NASHVILLE

when the bill came, I realized I didn't have any money, and when someone asked, 'Who's going to pay for this?' I said 'I've got friends in low places....'"

So instantly catchy that the Boot has correctly argued, "Whether or not you know any of his other music, there's a pretty solid chance that you've heard [this one],"and it was a title Lee remembered cowriter Dewayne Blackwell recognized as an instant hit right away, exercising a bit of creative carpe diem that would make country music history in the process:

> Dewayne was with me, and he asked me, "Have you written that yet?" and I said "No, I haven't ..." When you have a title that good, that is the theme, you stay hooked to that foundation while you're writing the rest of the song. From there, repetition is important for emphasis where it's repeated, and then there's that timing and placement of setting when and where it happens. Then when the chorus begins, following that logic again, the musical notes have to fall into place and the words that are chosen, and that's how it came together. Once a song's written, I have to live with it and play it a few times.

> **Garth Brooks to Songfacts.com:** "'Friends in Low Places' was the last demo session I ever did as a singer. . . . The demo was for Bud Lee and Dewayne Blackwell. I sang the session out in Hendersonville, and for the next two weeks, the chorus of the song kept running through my head," he added. "I knew it would be a year and a half before the release of *No Fences* because *Garth Brooks* was just getting ready to be released. I asked Bud Lee and Dewayne if I could hold onto it and, without a blink of an eye, they both said yes. Putting that kind of faith into an unknown artist is unheard of!"

Friends in Low Places   133

Spending four weeks atop the US Hot Country Songs Chart and taking home the Single of the Year Award from both the Country Music Association and the Academy of Country Music, it rocketed Earl Bud Lee into songwriting infamy with a hit that any of his peers would have dreamed of having in their catalog, giving Lee the same joy he's long felt seeing the song inspire its listeners around the world over the past four decades: "It's hard to be unhappy when you have a song in your heart."

He traces his own history as a songwriter past the hits he's written back to a childhood that musically began early, where "I first put my hands on a guitar when I was three, the mandolin I could hold and strum on it, so, they let me play with that. Early on, it would have been my mother and my grandfather influencing me. Kris Kristofferson was another big influence, Larry Gatlin was a huge influence, singing songs like 'I've Done Enough Dying Today.' I really related because it was so simply put."

Lee first landed in Nashville "in 1979 at twenty-three or twenty-four, and I thought this might be a fit for me." He would rack up a staggering catalog of songs recorded by country music's biggest stars along the way to earn his first Grammy nomination for Best Country Song like his first charting hit way back in 1988, "When Karen Comes Around" by Mason Dixon and another Garth Brooks single with "Uptown Down-Home Good Ol' Boy" in 1996 before returning to the top in 1997 with "One Night at a Time" by George Strait. Ranked number six on *Billboard*'s official list of the country music superstar's Top 10 songs, they singled this one out for spending "five weeks atop the charts, this one was George at his romantic best." The dreamy melody captivated listeners when it was released in the spring of 1997, helping lift the *Carrying Your Love with Me* LP all the way to a triple-platinum certification.

Remembering the song being born on "one of those magical days cowriting with Roger Cook," Lee points to the song as an extension of the importance of forming the right collaborative connections with other Nashville Songwriters for musical moments like these that might emerge during a cowrite, recalling here that "I had met [him] years ago when I first moved to town, and that day, Roger brought in that title. I was initially leery of that title because there were so many different angles to come at it from, how it could go, but Roger had a direction in his mind, and we wrote it from there. Then Eddie Kilgallon showed up at the end and put some keyboard parts on it that were really instrumental to the feel of the song." Recognizing it as an instant hit, the powers within George Strait's universe recorded it "within a week of us writing it! We wrote the song, and Roger went in and did the demo, then the publisher got it to Strait right away. So, it was written in one week and demoed in one week, and the next week, George Strait heard it and went in and cut it."

He kept country radio entertained with other hits like "Why" by Tracy Byrd, "Look Out Yonder" by the Randy Rogers Band, "Starlight, Starbright" by legendary country pioneer Loretta Lynn, "The Way It Is" by Shawn Camp, and "Keep On Lovin' You" by Rob Mayes. Earl points to another of his proudest songwriting accomplishments—Blake Shelton's number one smash "Who Are You When I'm Not Looking." Cowritten with John Wayne Wiggins, the double-platinum single that Lee considers from his compositional point of view to be a natural by-product of his sensibilities developed as he grew up primarily around women: "My mama was a girl, my sister was a girl, my aunts were girls, my nieces and cousins were girls, and every girl I've ever known, it's like 'Do you break things when you get mad?' Yes. 'Do you eat a box of chocolates 'cause you're feelin' bad?' Yes. 'Do you call up your mama when all else fails ya?' Yes. So, those are all yes answers except, 'Who are you when I'm not around?' John and I were out to lunch one day at the Mojo Grill and both started talking about what we realized was the same song idea."

Knowing they were onto something big, cowriter John Wiggins shared that once they'd finished writing it, he knew they needed to get right into the studio, recounting to the Boot how it developed from there: "I wanted to demo the song, but I just felt like something was missing. It didn't have that little release in it—that 'I wanna know, I wanna know, I wanna know . . .' part. It wasn't 'releasing,' we say in songwriter terms; this tense lyric all the way through was a question, and it never really resolved or made you exhale, so to speak. I told Bud I wanted to put it on a demo session, but that it's not releasing, and that maybe we could think about it that night before recording it. I knew it was a good song, even without any kind of release, but it just felt like it needed to exhale. And then we came up with that 'I wanna know, I wanna know, I wanna know. . . .' Without that, I don't think it would've been recorded. It answers the question: Who are you when I'm not looking? I wanna know."

Still going strong these days after five decades in the business of songwriting and performing, Earl Bud Lee feels he's matured to the point in his craft where "I can do anything with a song; I can paint you pictures. I love being able to take something that makes no sense and make sense of it in my songwriting." Closing with his own personal philosophy on the craft that has helped him stay on track, Lee begins with perhaps the most basic one: "I like to stay current and be relevant. My second rule is to be patient, and rule number three is keep the faith. As long as my intentions are good and I'm projecting that good, positive energy, good always eventually wins and does even better than I could have dreamed." Having fulfilled the dream every aspiring Nashville Songwriter has of rising to the top with songs that stand the test of time, these sound like a few solid rules of the songwriting road worth following.

CHAPTER 12

PEACEFUL, EASY FEELING

. . . .

Jack Tempchin

Jack Tempchin is perhaps most famous in pop country music circles for penning the Eagles' monster hit "Peaceful Easy Feeling," an authentic celebration of the band's country music roots that continues to be a fan favorite fifty years after its release. Tempchin as a songsmith reveals that he first began writing his own because "I wasn't really able to do a good job on anybody else's [*laughs*]! Over the next few years, I start playing in the coffeehouses and it gave me a good experience as a performer because most of the time there was nobody in the audience, there'd be three or four people. So, I got very comfortable onstage after a while." It was here that a fateful meeting with future Eagles cofounder Glenn Frey would forever change the stage that Tempchin's songs were being heard on:

> By about 1970, I was running what we call the Hot Nights, where anyone could come in and sit in and play, and I was hosting those at three or four coffeehouses in town, making about $20 each night and that's how I was making my living. There was one place called the Candy Company, and Jackson Browne came to play there, and also Glenn Frey and J. D. Souther all came to play there, so I met those guys before they ever did their first albums or anything.
>
> A few years later, I was visiting Jackson Browne and Glenn Frey up in Silver Lake and staying at Jackson's, and Glenn was there when I played a new song I'd written called

"Peaceful Easy Feeling," and he asked, "What's that?" He taped it on a cassette and took it to the rehearsal for his new band, the Eagles, that was only eight days old. They'd just been playing with Linda Ronstadt, got off the road and decided to form their own band. So, he brought back the next day a version they had worked up and that's kind of how all that connected.

For me, a song doesn't usually start with a lyric or a melody, it begins with a central idea and goes from there. I actually began writing the lyrics to "Peaceful Easy Feeling" on the back of a concert poster after a concert and then finished it back in San Diego. I was trying to take the beauty of these different girls I saw and pour them into the song. I just looked at the lines in the verses, and chopped away all the stuff that's no good. Even when I've got a song that seems to have the three verses, the chorus, and the bridge, and it's all done, I still go circle all the lines that I don't think are quite as good that I want to make better, and that's the most difficult part of the writing process because you've got a line in the middle of the song that you're trying to replace. It's got to fit with everything that came before and everything that's coming after, and so I focused in and really tried to do that. When I wrote "Peaceful Easy Feeling," I had no idea about writing a hit song, I'd never had anything like that. I just wrote them for me. But when it came out on the radio, it was just the thrill of a lifetime, and it even is when I still hear it today.

Putting not only the Eagles on the map but Tempchin as a songwriter as he scored his first publishing deal and record deals in the wake of the song's Top 40 success, the songwriter would see even greater success in 1974 when the Eagles released their anthemic rendition of "Already Gone." Recalling he cowrote the song with Robb Strandlund, becoming one of the Eagles' live favorites and an AM and FM radio regular, Tempchin still shakes his head looking back at the legs and longevity the song would have in the decades to come: "I wrote that song in 1970 with my friend in twenty minutes at a place in San Diego called The Back Door before a show and that was it! Glenn heard it and liked it, but it never came up about the Eagles doing it. Then about four years later, Glenn called me and said, 'Hey, you know that country song? I think that would make a great rock song,' so, they went in and recorded it right after that. He called me from the studio and held the phone up and let me hear it. That song was written very simply, just three chords repeating in the same order over and over, but the Eagles modulated it at the end. But it's the simplest song a person could ever learn. I wrote most of the lyrics, but Robb wrote the middle verse, including 'You can see the stars and still not see the light . . .' The third verse I actually wrote about a publisher who wasn't paying me, the guy might owe me $25 for this song I'd written or that, which was a fortune to me at the time. So, after a year of writing letters to the guy, I sort of had an epiphany that I was going to trust everybody until they let me down and then cross them off my list and move on. But I was not going to let it make me bitter or encumber me, so I made a decision to move on and that was influencing that song's last verse. It was at heart about the freedom of adjustment after you adjust your mind, like 'I'm going to move on and not let this bother me. . . .' It's such a freeing feeling."

Tempchin's earliest songwriting successes with the Eagles led him to record his first studio album in 1976 with the Funky Kings, penning his second charting hit with "Slow Dancing," which, in a reflection of Jack's natural sensibilities as both a pop and country writer, became a Top 10 pop single for Johnny Rivers as "Swayin' to the Music (Slow Dancing)" and then a country Top 10 hit for Johnny Duncan. Tempchin released his first self-titled solo album

Peaceful, Easy Feeling   139

in 1978 featuring highlight solo cuts like "Stingaree," "She Belonged to You," "Fifteen Days Under the Hood," "Lifetime Friend," "Golden Life," "Tijuana," "Pick Up Truck," and "Walkaway." It was another fateful call from Glenn Frey in 1981 after the Eagles had broken up that would launch Jack's next decade of success in the 1980s all over pop radio and MTV cowriting "Smuggler's Blues," an unofficial theme song of sorts for the wildly popular television show *Miami Vice* and "You Belong to the City," along with other charting singles like "Party Town," "The One You Love," "Don't Give Up," "Sexy Girl," "True Love," "Livin' Right," and "Soul Searching." Focusing in on the writing of two decade-defining hits within "Smuggler's Blues" and "You Belong to the City," Tempchin reveals that the inspiration for these FM radio staples began with random chance via a flight Glenn Frey was on:

Glenn was flying first class by then, and he explained to me he wore a suit because you never knew who was going to sit next to you. Well, on one of those flights, Michael Mann happened to sit down next to him, and as they began talking during the flight, Mann told Glenn, "I'm going to be doing a show called *Miami Vice*," and wanted a song for an episode where Tubbs goes to New York City and is walking the streets. So, that's what we had to go on, and we were over at my house writing and Glenn was sitting there strumming some E Minor chord, and one of us said 'You belong to the city . . .' and we knew we were onto something. We went back and forth with the lyrics. My favorite line I came up with was "Livin' in a river of darkness beneath the neon light." At the time, the Linn drum machine was just newly on the market, and I had one, it wasn't even the 9000, it was an older model like the 1A. I had this little room at my house in Hollywood with that drum machine and some keyboards and a little box machine with four bass sounds in it, and it was all hooked up to MIDI. So, when we wrote the song, Glenn tapped out that beat on the drum machine and from there, we tapped out three different patterns for the three different parts of the song and sequenced them in there. Then he played the bass on a keyboard and chose the bass sounds from that little box with four sounds I had. Then he played the piano part on the keyboard and was just an unbelievable arranger, because he came up with it all right there. He played the signature saxophone riff onto the same keyboard, and then when he brought him into the real recording session, told him exactly what to play based off our demo from that day. Along with cowriting the song, I got credit for producing because I engineered the stuff onto this MIDI Recorder I had.

When we turned to writing "Smuggler's Blues," which was featured on the official *Miami Vice* soundtrack and became a big single and video hit for Glenn, as the two longtime cowriters began framing the lyrics out around the song's drug trafficking/lifestyle theme as portrayed on the show, Jack begins by explaining in credit to Frey that "I learned a lot from him about using imagery rather than description, and with that one as a great example, it was about starting to tell a story and give the listener some pictures to look at in their mind, and have those pictures tell instead of describing your feelings. So, Glenn's really good at having a narrative that goes from one place to another and flows, and we were helped out on that one because Glenn and Irving Azoff had purchased the rights to a book called *Snow Blind* about the cocaine trade. So, we wrote it through the drug dealer's point of view. I also had a friend who was flying dope from Mexico to San

Diego all the time, so we pulled from stories he'd tell me of people involved in the drug trade. I think it took us two days to write that song. Musically, I told him, "I wanna make this a blues thing with some slide guitar on it," and had an 8-track in my house. We started working on the music from there together and then he took it into a proper studio and cut what you hear on the record."

Alongside his smash successes with Glenn Frey, Tempchin would pen other country hits like "Someone You Used to Know" by George Jones, and "White Shoes" by Emmylou Harris. Others included "Somebody Trying to Tell You Something" by Tanya Tucker, "To Feel That Way at All" by Patty Loveless, and "Your Tattoo" by Sammy Kershaw; he would continue releasing solo albums like 1994's *After the Rain*, 1995's *Lonely Midnight*, his own 1997 *Best Of* album based on his hit catalog, 2000's *Live on Hwy 101*, *Staying Home* in 2004, *Songs* in 2007, *Live at Tales from the Tavern* in 2012, 2015's *Learning to Dance*, 2016's *One More Song*, 2019's *One More Time with Feeling*, and 2024's *More of Less*. Remaining as philosophical as he has always been about his songs' place out there in the hearts of so many millions of listeners who consider them very much a part of the proverbial "soundtrack of their lives," he closes with a musing that seems relevant to any songwriter dreaming of the same success:

I'm just thrilled to have them go out and be a part of people's lives. It's what everybody dreams about. If you're going to be a writer, the dream of every songwriter, of course, is to have a hit song, but the real dream is to have a classic song, a song that people just keep playing year after year. There's an art and a magic to writing a song where people can hear it the way you record it, or maybe later an artist or band will play it a little differently or change it for the time, but it has to start with some kind of a classic song. There's no greater feeling that comes than from when I write a song, and the key is to keep doing it every day, whether it's a bad song or a mediocre one or a classic one, they all take the same effort. So, if I get an idea, I just put it into a song and don't over-worry about it. You have to be free to just let it flow.

CHAPTER 13

KING OF THE JUKE JOINT

. . . .

Wayne "The Train" Hancock

The undisputed King of the Juke Joint, Wayne "The Train" Hancock is a bit of a Music Row outlier, with the *Austin Chronicle* in a deeper dive describing his sound as "hardly slam-and-spit power chords and has no roots in CBGB's speed noise (country bluegrass blues). He'd sooner kick back his Stetson and slip on a pair of two-tone fifties foot boats than slouch around in leather and a pair of ripped denims. But punk is 75 percent attitude, and Dallas-native Hancock's got that by the freight carload. Listen to Hancock talk and realize there's no love lost between him and Nashville." Still, his prolific output of albums and almost-constant touring in support of those albums has earned Wayne "The Train" his place in the spotlight with countless fan favorites counting in the tens of millions of streams on Spotify alone over a wildly colorful catalog that features "You Don't Have to Cry," "Wild, Free and Reckless," "That's What Daddy Wants," "Juke Joint Jumping," "Brand New Cadillac," "Thunderstorms and Neon Signs," and "Flatland Boogie." Others include "Miller, Jack and Mad Dog," "Slinging Rhythm," "Knocked Out Rhythm," "Gonna Be Some Trouble Tonight," "Cold Lonesome Wind," "Ride," "Drinkin' Blues," "Shootin' Stars from Texas," "Viper of Melody," "Jump the Blues," "Killed Them Both," "87 Southbound," "Your Love and His Blood," "Hillbilly Hill Country Gal," "Tulsa," "Long Road Home," "Man of the Road," and "Life on the Road."

Writing nonstop while on the road touring his songs, Wayne points to his new trusty van as proof of his dedication to that path:

144 SONGS OF NASHVILLE

"My old one had 550,000 miles on it, and my new one has 40,000 already! My aim with every show is to play my songs and make the same sound in the bar that I made on all my records: good music without having a whole lot of sound gear or anything to go with it. For example, I don't have any drums in my set. Just the sound of the bass, the guy slapping, and me and my rhythm guitar at the same time. It's almost like the sound Hank Williams had on a lot of his records with just him and the bass you just let chop, and I don't know how he got that sound, but I loved it. My father, Robert Leslie Hancock, when I was about eleven or twelve years old, started to teach me guitar in '75. I grew up on the road with my father, he was a jack-of-all-trades man, the guy did everything. Besides teaching music, he really loved mathematics. We moved at one point from Texas to Idaho where he was a horse ranger for a couple of years, and I remember riding with him in the truck where we crossed the country a couple of times. So, he bred that into me, my dad, just the general love of being on the road. I love the highway, I love motels, I love to drive, so I think that's where all that comes from. I think he would be proud about what I'm doing with music."

Gazing back on the inspiration for one of his most enduring live favorites, "Shootin' Stars from Texas," Wayne fondly recalls it as "another memory from childhood. Sometimes a title will come first, and that was the case with that song. I didn't want to let Hank Williams down, and when I was old enough, I went out there searching for the myth. 'Thunderstorms and Neon Signs' was one on the other hand where the song came first, then the title. I was actually in Austin at a friend's house out on this porch when there was this huge, great big lightning storm coming in from the west. I was out on the porch to see if I could see the lightning, and I couldn't see the lighting because of the light from the city. It was right on top of you, that's why I wrote that song. I wanted to be out there someplace where I could sit back and watch the storm go over, but unfortunately, I was in Austin."

Revealing the lineage of his famous stage name, Wayne remembers first being crowned "The Train" thanks to his "ferocious way of playing the guitar, and I play for two, sometimes three hours a night, it depends on the crowd and if we're doing good. But it's all energy and the crowd can feel it, they feed off it. That's how I've kept doing this for thirty years. One time I remember somebody from Germany came up to me and said, 'Oh, you're Wayne the Train. We've heard of you,' so, it turned out to be a good nickname! [*laughs*]"

Able to sustain his sets with a constantly flowing river of new music, Hancock is proud to keep up with its current creatively because "all my songs come to me within ten or fifteen minutes. I get an idea in my head and I'm thinking of the music and the words at the same time, and I can picture any instrument I want. I can actually hear it in my mind, any kind of solo or instrument, like the violin or trumpet and how it would sound. So that when the song is completed, it really is completed. My stuff comes from the experiences of just being out on the road, just walking in places from town to town and seeing life from that side of it. It's also given me a pretty good edge on songwriting as well. Taught me a lot about life too, man. Take 'Juke Joint Jumping,' for example: I was wanting to write about the places I was playing and kind of summing it up. Even when I was playing those places back in '91, '92, they were on their way out—if they were on the endangered species list that's when I played them. Most of them, I don't even think any of those places exist anymore, and not all juke joints are what you'd call 'honky tonks.' '87 Southbound' was another road song I wrote after I broke down. I was running out of highway and trying to drive over to San Antonio, and I'm living out of my car at the time. I threw a rod on an old '70 Ford Explorer, and just took my cowboy hat and my guitar and walked home. I stopped off at a bar to play a couple songs and get a drink, and a lot of my songs are about being a troubadour. Some of my best love songs [were] written when I had nobody at all, you know? Every girl I've ever written a love song about, they're long gone. . . ."

Seeing songwriting as the medicine to many listeners' life woes, at the end of any show, Wayne hopes his fans feel like "my songs have kind of a moral to them. I do think about people listening to my music, and I've had people come up to me over the years and tell me that they listen and that kept them from maybe putting the gun in their mouth. I just always tell people to stay true to themselves, do your own music. There are still people who ask, 'When are you gonna make it?' I tell them I've already made it. I play music and get paid to do it. I'm really happy."

CHAPTER 14

LOST IN A SONG

. . . .

Willy "Tea" Taylor

When *Saving Country Music* published its Essential Albums of 2023 list, it expectedly featured names like Rodney Crowell, Ashley McBryde, Zach Bryan, Luke Combs, Old Crow Medicine Show, Jon Pardi, Chris Stapleton, and in arguably their coolest indie cred ranking, Willy Tea Taylor, crossing their fingers that *The Great Western Hangover* would become "his breakout from a cult following to more widespread critical acclaim, and a bridge to his back catalog for those that discover him through it. Willy Tea Taylor's music is about healing. It's about refusing to pass judgment, and willing to give forgiveness and understanding to all. It's medicine as music."

Reflecting back to the beginning of his journey reaching that cult following with his music, Willy remembers: "I was twenty-two when I wrote my first song, and I felt like it had some kind of magic behind it, like a spell of some sort. I look at writing a song like a piece of art, like a painting that I worked on." Growing up in the "Cowboy Capitol of the World," Oakdale, California, Taylor found his way to music following a baseball injury, hitting the road with his band Good Luck Thrift Store Outfit, featuring Chris Doud, drummer Aaron Burtch, bass and vocals Taylor Webster, and multi-instrumentalists Matt Cordano and Chandler Pratt. He began his journey from there, amassing a catalog of one-of-a-kind songs and albums that feature *Born and Raised*, *Color This Album*, *4 Strings*, *Damn Good Dog*, *Knuckleball Prime*, and the aforementioned *Great Western Hangover*, along with band albums *Old Excuses*, *The Ghost of Good Manners*, and

148 SONGS OF NASHVILLE

the self-titled *Good Luck Thrift Store Outlet*. When Taylor takes a break from performing to reminisce on writing a few of his favorite songs, he begins with "Wrong Way to Run," recalling that "we had a songwriting club that me and my friend Vandenavond started, and we had this game where we sang every week on some kind of theme that would pop up. That weekend my son was running around this little garden, and he must have been about seven years old or something like that. He said, 'Dad, I started running the wrong way . . .' and I thought 'That's deep, Son. I love it.' So, that just kind of made me think, 'What's the right way to run.' Then it's like admitting 'I ran the wrong way there,' and just kind of redemption in it and forgiving yourself."

An equal fan of the title track to his *Knuckleball Prime* album, Willy marvels at the songwriter's gift to play with metaphor in his recollections of reaching back into his own baseball past to inform the song that followed, reasoning that "knuckleball pitchers tend to be just phenomenal when they hit their late thirties and early forties. That's when, like, they have to get trickier to still get that youth and skill. Old age and treachery kind of come in and that's where the knuckleball drives, and I just love that even a knuckleball pitcher doesn't know when he's gonna throw it. Either it's not gonna spin or he doesn't know what it's going to do. It's such a beautiful thing! Then I was talking to my friend Nathan Moore out of Virginia, another amazing songwriter. My label wanted me to cowrite with somebody, you know, they were insistent about it. I never really did that before, and so we just kind of wrote the melody and let the words play on it, and that's how that one was born."

He counts "Nothing Ever Dies" as another personal favorite, especially as it was a song born out of art imitating life, the way the best country music can be. Willy shares that "a friend of mine was telling us how, when a family member dies, the way they prepare them for death, and it's just a tradition in their family. So, for instance, when both of his parents passed, he watched the guy comb their hair and prepare them for death. And I just always thought how beautiful that is. Then just a few weeks later, he was telling me the story of the night in the Sierra Nevada mountains when his wife got in a head-on collision and died instantly. It was a terrible wreck, and afterward, how they strongly urged him not to even look at her. But he went in, and he washed her body. Hearing about her death, it still moves me just how powerful that is. That thought still haunts me in the most beautiful way. So, that's kind of where that song came out."

Taylor's popularity among fans of his songwriting is nowhere more evident than on YouTube, where his independently released projects like *The Gondola Sessions* have garnered views into the millions along with other viral hits like *The Tomboy Sessions, The Depression Sessions, The Blackwing Sessions,* and *The Tiny Porch Sessions*—all recorded while on the road making his living as a performing artist. Willy candidly confronts the challenges of making a living as a working songwriter:

> I love to travel around and sing and meet people, and when I don't, I'm no good. I got the itchy feet. Maybe it'll stop one day, but the hard part is being lonely for my kids. My eleven-year-old daughter, we miss each other. My son's twenty-one and he's a musician, so he understands, I mean, as much as they can. I can't speak for them. They know that it's me and that it's just what I do. If I'm gonna do something, I'm gonna do what's calling me. I used to be a carpenter and when I ran into old friends who asked what I was up to, I said, "I'm a carpenter, I've also been writing songs," and now I say, "I'm a songwriter and sometimes I do carpentry [*laughs*]!" That I can write a song, and it goes out into the world, and you follow the vibration, it's just an incredible thing. I feel so blessed.

Colt Ford (Photo credit: Average Joes Ent)

Buddy Cannon
(Photo credit: Jake Brown)

Dallas Frazier
(Photo credit: Jake Brown)

Clint Black
(Photo credit: Kevin Mazur)

Jack Tempchin
(Photo credit: Jake Brown)

Earl Bud Lee
(Photo credit: Jake Brown)

Rock Killough
(Photo credit: Rock Killough Estate)

Jim Weatherly
(Photo credit: Jim Weatherly Estate)

Kinky Friedman
(Photo credit: Trevor Paulhus)

Tim Dubois
(Photo credit: Oklahoma Hall of Fame)

Willy "Tea" Taylor
(Photo credit: Willy Tea Taylor FB)

Wayne "The Train" Hancock
(Photo credit: Atomic Music Group)

Bobby Braddock
(Photo credit: Bobby Braddock)

Sonny Throckmorton
(Photo credit: Sonny Throckmorton)

Vince Gill
(Photo credit: vincegill.com)

CHAPTER 15

MIDNIGHT PLANE TO HOUSTON

. . . .

Jim Weatherly

"Midnight Train to Georgia" by Gladys Knight and the Pips is one of those songs that haunts the landscape, whether driving through the night or drinking alone. It envelopes the listener in its longing, playing over and over in the mind long after the first line in the way only music's greatest hits can. This one has the perfect title, tailor-made for the number one spot it overtook in August 1973 on the *Billboard* Hot 100 Singles, US R&B Charts, and Cashbox Top 100 Singles Spot, before earning the Grammy for Best R&B Vocal Performance by a Duo, Group, or Chorus and being inducted into the Grammy Hall of Fame in 1999, along with being ranked by the Record Industry Association of America's 365 Songs of the Century ahead of John Lennon's "Imagine." One not well-known fact that songwriter Jim Weatherly reveals is that "it started out as a song called 'Midnight Plane to Houston.' I was playing flag football in LA with a bunch of guys, and Lee Majors played on our team, and Lee had just started dating Farrah Fawcett. She had just moved to LA. I called his house one day, and she answered the phone, and during the course of the conversation she said she was packing her clothes, and she was going to take a midnight plane to Houston to visit her folks. So, it just sounded like a song title to me."

That's the sort of natural ear a songwriter needs to recognize a song idea when it's singing out to them. Weatherly reveals another behind-the-scenes fact about the legendary anthem's creation, namely that writing the song with an R&B singer like

Midnight Plane to Houston 155

Gladys Knight in mind influenced the results. Initially Weatherly approached the song envisioning "Glen Campbell singing it. At the time, he was having a lot of success with cities or states or whatever in his titles, so I wrote it as a song that I felt would kind of fit that mode. That song had a lot of holes in it. The lyrics weren't smashed up against each other like a lot of songs, so there was a lot of space. When I wrote 'Midnight Plane to Houston,' it just kind of fell out after that conversation with Farrah Fawcett, and it's just the way it came, so I think one reason that Gladys latched on to some of my songs was because of the space in-between that allowed her to express her own emotions in the song. It gave her some room to back-phrase or front-phrase, and then it also gave room for the background voices, the Pips, to sing lines before or after or whatever. And I thought about what it was she heard in those songs, and I'm glad she did. I thought they were good songs, but I never expected them to be cut R&B. I really thought they were country-pop kind of things. So, I believe one of the reasons she liked them was because of the space involved."

Weatherly recounts how the song ended up on his own 1972 solo album, *Weatherly*, under the original title before it made its way into the hands of producer Tony Camillo: "I recorded it on my first album that way, and then, my publisher got a call from Sonny Limbo in Atlanta who wanted to cut the song on Sissy Houston, who is Whitney's mom. I guess they had been kind of toying with the idea of changing the title to 'Midnight Train to Georgia,' and Sonny said he would like a more R&B-sounding title and asked if he could record it under that name. And we said, 'Yeah, go ahead, you just can't change the writer or the publisher,' and I think we had already pitched the song to Gladys as 'Midnight Plane to Houston,' and they wanted to change the title too. It was pretty obvious to them, being from Atlanta and everything."

Weatherly is proud of a pattern he's established throughout his career where "I write songs that, if they get cut, and if they

156   SONGS OF NASHVILLE

become hits, they will sound just as fresh thirty years from now. Good examples were the songs that Gladys Knight cut that were hits—they're reaching people today, just the same way they did when they were first hits. *American Idol* used 'Midnight Train' for about five years in a row, and Jennifer Hudson sang 'Neither One of Us' on *American Idol*, so when you've got an outlet like that, and they go back and reach for the old songs, there's just more emotion in them. They can put their heart and soul into those kinds of songs. If you sing a pop song today, for the most part, it goes in one ear and out the other, you don't get the artist's emotion of it, and I think that has to do with the way the song was written."

While he explains that "I always considered myself a country songwriter, I think there was a lot of R&B influence in my songs. It wasn't something I did intentionally, it just happened to be the way I wrote, and I thought really when I was writing some of my early songs that I was writing country songs. I formed a band when I was in junior high, and just kind of started songs at that point, at about thirteen years old when I first started writing, and just copied what was on the radio, that kind of thing. Back then, it was right after Elvis just became big, so there was a lot of Chuck Berry and Fats Domino and Johnnie & Joe. I used to listen to a lot of R&B."

At the same time, when he wasn't playing in a band, he was making them on the football field, with CNN reporting that "Weatherly played on the University of Mississippi football team in an undefeated 1962 season, a Southeastern Conference championship and a national championship. The next year, he was the starting quarterback when the Rebels repeated as Southeastern Conference champs. After college, he decided to pursue music instead of football," and he points to that decision as the most consequential career call he ever made:

I turned down pro football to write songs, I was drafted by the Boston Patriots in the NFL right out of college. I played quarterback at Ole Miss, and it didn't even enter my mind to play pro football. I had my rock group in college, and we were traveling, and I didn't think about it, it's just where my heart was. By the early '70s, I had gotten with a publisher in LA who'd gotten me a record deal, so I was writing songs for me to record them, but I was writing for other people to record as well. When I recorded them, they had what they called a 'cosmopolitan country' feel at that time, which had a country attitude to them, but they were really polished, and I didn't have any kind of pop crossover in mind, I just was writing songs and hoping somebody somewhere would like them.

I used to, in the early stages of my career, they came simultaneously, that I would just start playing a guitar and kind of humming and singing, and I remember when I wrote "Neither One of Us," I actually sat down and took a guitar and sang the first verse to the song, and I didn't have an idea, a melody, a lyric, I just picked up the guitar and sang it like it had always been there, it was just there. And when that first verse just fell out, it really wasn't hard to complete the song, because I remember when I heard myself say, "Neither one of us wants to be the first to say goodbye," I thought "Good gracious, this sounds like a real song, you know?" So, it didn't take me long to finish it.

After fronting Jim Weatherly and the Vegas and then The Gordian Knot and signing his first record deal with Verve Records in 1968, he next signed to RCA as a solo artist. Releasing his first three solo albums including the aforementioned *Weatherly* in 1972 and *A Gentler Time* and the eponymous *Jim Weatherly* in 1973. On

158   SONGS OF NASHVILLE

1974's *The Songs of Jim Weatherly,* he broke through on radio with his first solo hits, "The Need to Be," which became a Top 20 pop hit and reached number six on the US Hot Country Songs Chart—covered the same year by Ray Price—and "I'll Still Love You," another Top 10 hit on the country chart. Pointing to the composition of these hits as an extension of his instincts as a songwriter that guide him when he's writing, he explains

> my way of writing comes more from the gut, from the heart, from the emotion of the song. I don't sit there and say, "Okay, I've said this and this and this, now I need to say this." I don't do that, I just kind of let that song roll on. I just kind of wrote whatever fell out, and sometimes they were like that, and sometimes they were more country-rock oriented, and sometimes they were pop. For instance, "The Need to Be" was actually written for a woman, but I had a hit on it, and there's a line in there that actually leans obviously more toward a woman than it would a man, and it says, "There's the need to be something more than just a reflection of a man, I can't survive in someone's shadow, I need my own spot to stand." Well, that's obviously a female-oriented line, the idea of the song is "I am what I am, and I have the need to be," but when I sing it, I was thinking a lot in terms of my dad: There's a need to be something more than just a reflection of my father. I can't survive in his shadow; I need to make my own way. But if you just hear the song, you first think of the lyric as being female oriented. "The Need to Be" was a real pop song, Gladys cut it too, and I had a number eleven pop record on my own with that, and it was straight pop, so I did write some songs that were straight pop like that. But back in those days, people listened to songs, not for what genre it fit, but whether or not it was a

Midnight Plane to Houston 159

great song, and then they would just adapt it to whatever way they wanted to take it.

Keeping his own prolific release schedule up throughout the rest of the 1970s, Jim released *Magnolias & Misfits* in 1975, *Pictures and Rhymes* and *The People Some Choose to Love* in 1976, along with a run of Top 40 Country Singles Chart hits like "It Must Have Been the Rain," "All That Keeps Me Going," "Smooth Sailin'," "Gift from Missouri," "Safe in the Arms of Love" in 1980, and "The Love That Went Away" in 1981. Over the decades that followed, his catalog of songs would be recorded by stars like Kenny Rogers, Neil Diamond, Glenn Campbell, Kenny Chesney, and Garth Brooks to name just a few, with the Nashville Songwriters Hall of Fame rounding out coverage of that legacy when "Weatherly was named the NSAI's Songwriter of the Year and ASCAP's Country Songwriter of the Year in 1974, the same year that Glen Campbell's recording of Weatherly's 'Where Shadows Never Fall' won a Dove Award. Weatherly's songs were often recorded by country artists, and he moved to Nashville in 1985. He's penned country hits for Charley Pride, Bryan White, Ray Price (who has recorded more than fifty of Weatherly's songs), Bob Luman, Bill Anderson, Earl Thomas Conley, and others, and his songs have been recorded by a diverse array of artists including Neil Dean Martin, the Indigo Girls, Vince Gill, Hall & Oates, the Temptations, Etta James, Steve Wariner, and the Manhattans."

Whenever Jim Weatherly has written throughout his catalog, he has followed a guiding creative light of "always trying to write universal songs with a universal concept, with something that maybe I had never heard before. For instance, if I had a title or something I'd never heard, and then I would try to write it where it was done in a way that I'd never heard it done. That was a conscious thing, but I always had it in my mind to write a universal song, and it worked real well for me at that time because my songs have been cut pop, R&B, country, jazz, reggae, gospel, they've been cut in every style. Today, it's rare when that kind of opportunity comes along." When passing along sage words on the mysterious art of songwriting, Weatherly keeps it real when speaking on his commercial successes in that craft, offering that "if you want to be a songwriter that makes money, you have to write for your generation. You have to write what radio will play, and what kids want to hear, and what record companies can sell. I think if you're a great songwriter, you're going to find your own path. If you're not a great songwriter, you can read all the books in the world, and it won't help you. That's the way I look at it. I'm very fortunate that I've had some hits that have sustained me for a long period of time, which has allowed me to continue to write the kind of song that I write. What means the most to me is when I perform it, maybe there's some people out there who say 'Wow, that really touched me.'" Mission accomplished. RIP.

CHAPTER 16

OKLAHOMA SWING

Tim DuBois

Tim DuBois is a Music Row legend. His influence, as *American Songwriter* magazine has highlighted, can be felt "through the halls of the Vanderbilt University Owen Graduate School of Management, where DuBois has been a professor of late. A hit songwriter, producer, artist manager, and former head of both Arista Nashville and Universal Records South—there's not much Tim DuBois hasn't tackled" since hooking his first number one hit as a songwriter way back in 1981 when he and Woods Newton cowrote the chart-topper "Midnight Hauler" by Razzy Bailey. He'd hit a grand slam thereafter, establishing himself overnight as a Nashville Songwriter after Alabama took "Love in the First Degree" to the top and then country music legend Jerry Reed followed up with the smash hit "She Got the Goldmine (I Got the Shaft)."

Smiling when he looks back on his early hit streak, he remembers feeling on fire after "I got very lucky in that, within that first twelve months being here in Nashville, between 'Midnight Hauler' and 'Love in the First Degree' by Alabama and then 'She Got the Gold Mine (I Got the Shaft)', I had three number one hits. With 'Love in the First Degree,' I was standing at the corner of 12th and Wedgewood on a summer day waiting to turn left and the guy on the radio said somebody was found guilty of murder in the first degree. When you have your songwriter ears on, why, you just think in those terms, and I just saw a good idea. So, that very day, I walked into the writers house at House of Gold, and my good friend Jim Hunt was in the kitchen getting a cup of coffee, and said, 'Are you writing with anybody?' and I said 'Nope' and we went upstairs and wrote that song, all of it—except for two lines in the second verse—that morning. So, I walked into the room just with that idea, I didn't have anything further, and the idea of 'Love in the First Degree' as opposed to 'Murder in the First Degree' was enough of a hook to get started on. Jim was a great melody person, and we worked well together because of that. I'm more of a lyricist. So, I took the song home and finished up, brought it back in the next day finished. For me, the biggest part of my writing starts from an idea generation that is a lyrical idea and then eventually grows into lyrics and music. I just kind of start with an idea that I think has a hook. 'Midnight Hauler' and 'Love in the First Degree' and 'She Got the Goldmine' were all three hooks that just kind of came to me from odd places."

Tracing his path from playing in college bands in Texas to how it eventually led him to Nashville, DuBois recalls that "in 1974, I went back to Oklahoma State to work on a PhD in accounting, and I made my first trip to Nashville, bringing songs out here in 1975. By 1977, I was making regular trips out here and got a chance to take a teaching job at what used to be UT-Nashville, which was an adult education division of the University of Tennessee. So, I came here in what was a two-year leave of absence from the PhD program, and I'm still on leave forty-something years later [*laughs*]!"

His big break came after "a gentleman by the name of John Ragsdale took an interest in me on that first trip out here. He was working for MCA Music, and on subsequent trips, we continued to work together. I brought him a song that became my first Top 40 country hit, a song called 'A Good Old Fashioned Saturday Night (West Texas Ballroom Brawl),' which he'd suggested we rewrite into 'A Good Old Fashioned Saturday Night Honky Tonk Ballroom Brawl,' which was recorded by Vernon Oxford. I was still a PhD candidate at Oklahoma State at that time, so that was in '76, but getting to hear that song on the radio, if I wasn't already hooked, why I was totally hooked after that. When I moved out here in '77, I got a few more album cuts, had a single with 'I'm a Good Friend of Mine' by Wood Newton, who became one of my cowriters through the years. Then I got a Charlie Rich cut, which was just an album cut, but I continued to write and cowrite, and when my two-year leave of absence was up, I had gotten a few more songs cut, but not enough to feed a family of four, which I was at that time."

Knowing instinctively he didn't want to abandon his dream, Tim knew the clock was ticking, "but instead of going home, I asked for another year to stay, and in that next year, I got signed to my first writer's deal with Bob Montgomery and House of Gold Music. Bob Montgomery had a song we'd written called 'Midnight Hauler' by Razzy Bailey, which wound up being my first number one hit. I used to drive back and forth between Stillwater, Texas, and Tulsa while I was in school at Oklahoma State on Highway 51, and one night, I was going home after teaching and this 18-wheeler just blew past me. It was one of those two-lane highways, and he passed me, and it was obvious it was in a hurry going somewhere. On the back of his truck, it said 'A Midnight Hauler.' So, I don't know who it was, but I owe him a great debt, because I got behind him and followed him on into Stillwater. I figured he would get a ticket before me and be my lead person. So, I started that song in the car and ended up writing the song on the rest of that trip about a truck driver who's trying to get home to his baby. By the time the song was a hit, I was still teaching and had moved over to Vanderbilt to teach at the Owen Graduate School of Management. So, even after that first number one hit, I didn't let go of my day job, I continued to teach and song-write at the same time."

One of Tim DuBois's signature hits would arrive with country music legend Jerry Reed's "She Got the Goldmine (I Got the Shaft)," which CountryUniverse.net marked as part of Reed's "1982 hot streak [which] keeps going with yet another classic single from a Hall of Fame artist. Jerry Reed's biggest hits have always bordered on novelty, but the pain in this one is too palpable for it to be reduced to a comedy track. Future Arista Nashville honcho Tim DuBois penned this divorce track, which is one of the best country records ever made about the subject. Reed's inherent wit makes him the perfect artist for delivering this particular lyric." Thankfully, its muse wasn't an autobiographical one for Tim, who remembers feeling inspired to write the song after "John Ragsdale said to me one time, 'Yeah, my first marriage was kind of like a goldmine, only problem was, when we split up, she got all the gold and all I got was the shaft.' And that had always stuck with me and was the idea for that song there."

DuBois still today points to his years writing and producing number one hits for Restless Heart as among his finest Music Row moments. Beginning a hot streak of Top 10 hits for the band in 1985 with "Let the Heartache Ride" and then "(Back to the) Heartbreak Kid," the group's first Top 10 hit before rocketing to number three with "Big Dreams in a Small Town" and then all the way to number one with "Bluest Eyes in Texas," crediting the latter smash to "Van Stephenson, who brought that idea to the table. There were a group of us that wrote together at House of Gold that wrote by far the majority of the early Restless Heart stuff. Van was a really key part of that, Van and Dave Robbins, both of whom went on to be a part of Blackhawk. But Van had a very Don Henley type voice, and he and Dave and I were all Harmony Group nuts, and so a lot of that stuff was written very specifically with the vocal arrangements in mind from the beginning, and they were demoed to sound like Restless Heart. Again, it was Van's idea, and we just jumped on it, and just started with very, very visually painting a picture, which was one of the things we were really trying to do lyrically with a lot of their stuff."

Aided greatly by the hit songs they already had sitting in their back pocket, Tim became a scientist of the band's sound

Oklahoma Swing 165

in that "producing the band you write for, almost all the songs I wrote for Restless Heart were written with a specific thought in mind as to what the group could be. In fact, the songs existed before the band did, so it was a backward way of how it happened in that, there were four or five of us—myself, Van Stephenson, Dave Robbins, Jeff Silbar, and Sam Lorber, who wrote together on a fairly regular basis. We were writing material that would have been suitable for Alabama had Alabama continued down a more pop route. It was aimed at the rock side of what was going on in country at that point in time, and actually was out of frustration of me not being able to get those songs cut, the idea to put together the band Restless Heart came about. So, with songs like 'Big Dreams in a Small Town,' we all three had small-town upbringings, and once we had the idea, it was another one of those songs that was very visual."

DuBois details a songwriting routine he had down pat by then: "Sometimes I wouldn't have an idea yet and the idea would come from listening to the track. Other times, I'd take the track and a specific idea, and I wrote a lot of that stuff, the lyrics to it, pretty much by myself, because I'd get a musical idea, we'd put a track down, and then I would just work on it by myself. A lot of it was done in the car. I don't know why, but I write better in the car than I do almost anywhere else. I can write a lyric to a rhythm and not even have to have a melody in mind. 'Back to the Heartbreak Kid' was a funny one. That was me and Van by ourselves. I walked into the writers house over at House of Gold one morning, and Van was sitting there by himself playing that intro lick that's on the song on the guitar, and I said 'Hey, I like that,' and he said 'I don't feel it, let's go fishing . . .' So, I said, 'No, man, I like that lick, let's find something to do with that lick,' and he said 'Nah, I'm just not into it.' And I said, 'We're not going fishing until we write something to that lick,' because I had the boat. So, we came up with that hook and wrote the song in about an hour and a half, and it turned out to be a better song than the day ended up being a fishing day. But we wrote the song and went fishing all in the same day [*laughs*]!"

Arguably one of Tim DuBois's most celebrated later-career songwriting alliances came via his work writing with Vince Gill on early career hits like "Oklahoma Swing" and "When I Call Your Name," when the Oklahoma Hall of Fame, in inducting Tim into its ranks, noted impressively that the latter smash became the Country Music Association's Song of the Year. Reflecting on the significance of his compositional collaboration with Gill: "Vince and I actually sat down to write 'Oklahoma Swing' as a duet for Vince and Reba, and if you listen to the lyric, it's very definitely aimed at Reba—'There's a redhead from my hometown that loves to let her hair down'—it was written with that idea in mind and trying to write something swinging. We wrote 'When I Call Your Name' in one day. Vince decided he wanted to play golf the next day and canceled the writing appointment. And it rained, so I called him up and said 'Hey, since it rained, do you want to work again?' I went over to his house, and he had that idea, and we actually wrote it in one sitting over three or four hours. It was so much about that incredibly haunting melody that he had, and trying to paint the picture with words, and it ended up being a huge song for his career. His first number one song, and the song that kind of brought him out into the mainstream."

CHAPTER 17

COTTON BELT MUSIC

....

Rock Killough

Rock Killough is one of those songwriters that other songwriters like to play writer rounds and festival stages with, the sort of songwriter who didn't need Nashville, even though Nashville was a stronger songwriting town when he was added to its legendary lineage. Rock looks back today on a career he's proud to say he played his way: "Within a year of arriving in Nashville, I got a deal with Epic Records. They gave me money to make a country record, and I just took it and went and recorded what I do. After that, I decided it would be best for me to go back to where I come from and make my deal in a smaller pond, and that's what I did, and I've done well. I couldn't be happier with my life."

His compositional contributions, as Gulf Coast Media has highlighted, have been made famous by "a few musicians you might have heard of, like the Oak Ridge Boys, Sammy Kershaw, Randy Travis, Waylon Jennings, Hank Williams Jr., Merle Haggard, Latimore, Jerry Jeff Walker, 4 Runner, Hank Snow, David Frizzell, Larry Cordle, and Coon Elder Band. All read his songs and liked them enough to record them." His greatest hits feature "The House at the End of the Road," "The Lord'll Provide," "Old Nashville Cowboy," "Where Can I Surrender," "Alibis," "Still Loving You," "Absence of Love," "Going Home," "Wish I Had a Bottle," "Hank Williams Is the King," "Take Jesus as Your Lawyer," "You Only Cry When It Hurts Me," and "Rolling the Dice of Life." Others included "Rusty Plow," "Stand in Your Own Light," "You Gotta

168 SONGS OF NASHVILLE

Be Tough as Hell to Get Old," and in looking back on his life in songwriting, he points first to the importance of his musical roots:

> I grew up in a time when there was no FM dial, everything was on the AM, and AM stations were not programmed stations, so there would be an hour of gospel, an hour of country/bluegrass, and then an hour of big band, and an hour of torch singers. And my family was musical, but my mother was really musical, and while she was doing housework, she kept the radio on all the time, and that's what I got. When Hank Williams did his show on WMGY in Montgomery, we'd listen to it every day, and the Grand Ole Opry at night, and WCKY in Cincinnati. We went to church every day, and as a matter of fact, I sang in a trio with my mother and father, starting when I was eight years old. I learned to play guitar around ten years old, and that's when I first discovered Chet Atkins, and I could not stop playing that stuff!

> I'm a romantic, and a big fan of the Old South, and the South of my generation, it was big to own a cotton gin, and I got to be around cotton a lot in different ways, and I identified with it. With what I'm talking about, my music reflects the heartland of my area, which is the Cotton Belt. If you look at a map of it, it touches on black music and blues and gospel, as well as country. I grew up on a big farm fourteen miles east of Greenville, Alabama—that's big dirt country—and my father was a farmer, and part of his farming operation was harvesting cotton. And I wanted to get away from that farm as fast as I could, and I did. I graduated from high school in 1960 and went straight into the Army two months later.

Cotton Belt Music 169

After serving his country and attending Auburn University, Rock and his true calling found each other when "I was about twenty-five and thank God songwriting came around, because all I wanted to do before that was be a guitar player in a band and sing backup. But when songwriting came down, it came down at a time after I'd been in the Army and was back home playing in college bands and found out I was not good enough to be a lead guitar player in a band. At that point, I stopped trying to be a lead guitar player and started writing songs, and thank God, because I could have never made it as a guitar player. The first song I ever wrote was called 'Another One of These Days.'"

Mentored by legendary Nashville songwriting titan Hank Cochran, he still marvels at the serendipity of his discovery story. "Before I got to Nashville, I was playing in a lounge in Sarasota, Florida, and because of a storm, Hank Cochran pulled his boat into the Bay to wait out the storm, and that lounge I was playing in was basically a lounge for a large, exclusive restaurant, and his people came in, were waiting to eat and listened for a bit. Then they went to eat and when they came back on their way out, listened for a bit more, and asked me if I wrote all the songs I played, and offered for me to play some for Hank. When I did, basically what he said was, 'I'm going to be in Nashville on June 26, and I'll be at the end of the pier on my boat. I want you to be standing there when I get there,' and I was. Within three, four weeks, he called one day and told me he was sending his cousin and aide down to Tree Publishing with me to sign and for them to sign me up, so they did. Now, I did have to sleep in my car a lot when I first got to Nashville, because I didn't have any place to live and didn't know a soul, but I was taken care of and treated wonderfully and met all of my heroes. It was great to be in the same building with them."

Recounting a bit of his heyday coming up under Hank Cochran's wing, Rock says, "Hank brought me to town in June

1976, and all the big writers who were in town came to see him out on this big yacht he had out on Old Hickory Lake, and they had a big party there. I was so astonished being there among those people that I proceeded to retire and get drunk, which is what I did. Well, I passed out and went to bed way before the party stopped, and about three o'clock in the morning, I got up and found me a bottle of water, and sat down by a window, and across the way, I saw this car pull in. Then this guy got out of it and stumbled down the hill and he was drunk, but it was amazing because he walked on down to the end of the dock, got up on the boat, put his arm up on the window, looked at me, and said, 'Is Hank here?' I replied, 'Yeah, but you know, he's asleep,' then Whitey asked, 'Well, who are you?' That was my introduction to Whitey Shafer! I've actually written a couple songs with him. One was 'We're Going to See Willie Tonight,' which we wrote in a hotel room in Texas while we were waiting for him to hit the stage. We had the guitars out, laughing, drinking, having a good time and a lyric would come out, he'd do one, then I'd do one, 'We're going to see Willie tonight!' Whitey was quick."

As he forged forward in his own writing career, Rock proudly points to one of his favorite cowrites with fellow songwriter Larry T. Wilson on what became one of Killough's most celebrated songs, "The House at the End of the Road," reminiscing on his childhood when he first began doing so as he remembers: "I want to write a song about where I grew up, and I grew up at the house at the end of the road. Larry and I had a successful cowriting relationship for maybe four or five songs. We played in a band together for a long, long time, fifteen, twenty years, and he was writing songs, I was writing songs, and one day he came to me with a story. He said he was outside hunting once in January when it was really cold, and got out there before the sunrise, and was in his stand and the sun came up, and he was on a clear-cut. Okay, in this part of the country, from Birmingham on down, it's basically a huge pine forest, and the way it works is every twelve years, they'll come in and thin and take one tree from every row out. Then a few years later, they'll come back in and cut the whole thing and put telephone poles out there. So, he told me he was sitting on one side of this clear-cut, which was about a quarter-mile wide, and as the sun came up, and as he looked across the clear-cut, all that was left standing was this old live oak tree, and while he was down there, he got this feeling like someone's watching you, and his hair stood up. This tree was a monster, he said. It would take maybe three or four people with stretched hands to fit around it, and there, carved in the side, was a big heart and inside the heart were carved these words: 'Carter loves Angel, 1893,' and when he told me that story, I loved that romantic notion, and took his story and wrote most of it. Before too long, we had the song pretty much done. It's a piano song, and when he left, I went to work on it and came out like it is. That's my chorus, and songs are much more interesting to me melodically than my guitar songs are, with a couple exceptions. Once again, I'm a romantic, I like melody and sadness, I like those old sad songs. That's what I grew up listening to, all that blues people sang was sad. . . . After that, we wrote another one called 'Too Far Gone to Leave,' which Sam Kershaw recorded."

Killough spotlights "Old Nashville Cowboy" as a potent example of the magic way songs can arrive out of a simple story that he quips is "another sad one, about being at 'the end of the line,' so to speak. As a matter of fact, that's what the last line of the song says, 'Them old Nashville cowboys will sing for a dime, and hard times are cheap at the end of the line. . . .' Jerry Jeff Walker cut that. My friend Billy McClure told me about a time he'd been down on Broadway a long time ago when Broadway was not like it is today, and behind Union Station, there was a big, huge shed where people waited to get on the trains. It was snowing, and during the winter at night, that's where all the homeless people stayed. There was some kind of unspoken agreement between the owner and the authorities that they'd be left alone if they went in there, and he saw an old man walking up that hill wearing an old coat with patches on the elbows, you could see a

172 SONGS OF NASHVILLE

wine bottle stuck in his back pocket, and he had an old guitar with string tied to it over his shoulder, and I said, 'That's an old Nashville cowboy,' and *boom*, there it was! It was snowing that same day, the biggest snowstorm we'd have in Nashville for a long, long time. It was maybe twelve, fifteen inches, and Billy couldn't get his car out of my driveway. So, he spent the night, we threw wood on the fireplace, sat up and wrote that song."

As Rock's unique songwriting talent caught the ear of country's biggest bands and recording stars, the Oak Ridge Boys would make "The Absence of Love" one of the live staples for years and a fan favorite. Killough revealed that versus being written on Music Row or backstage at a show: "I wrote that song in jail in 1989 after I'd been arrested for pot possession in Alabama. While I was there serving my time, there wasn't a lot of activities in a small jail south of Alabama, and I managed to get out of population to where I got a private room, so I didn't have to bunk with other people. My job was to work in the kitchen, and every job that needed to be done the cook couldn't do, I did. It was good, and I'd get through with that working from about 5:00 in the morning till 4:00 in the afternoon, and from 6:00 p.m. on, I'd go get a shower and then sit around in complete boredom. There was no cable TV, just boredom, and I hadn't written anything in maybe five, six years. My career has been one of extreme production and then extreme nonproduction [*laughs*], and [I] hadn't played my guitar in four or five years. I asked the sheriff if I could have it, and he brought it up to me. It took me about four or five weeks to get to figure out where I was heading in my playing. I was sitting in the kitchen one day and it had hard tile and a good reverb system, and I was just pickin' along and all of a sudden, God opened my heart and started pouring lyrics in. That jail was packed; there were forty-nine of us in there, so that's where it started. I wrote 'Still Loving You' while I was locked up in that jail too, which is about my second wife, and unless you have some kind of agreement, it's hard to keep a marriage going if you're not there. So, our dissolution was traumatic to me, I hated it, I didn't want it. In fact, she was the love of my life. By then, I'd already been remarried for three or four years when I got put in jail, and no matter what you think about jail, it's an extremely lonely and trying time for someone who had never been in there before. So, I started thinking about everything we'd been through, and that song came out."

Johnny Rodriguez would have a big single with "Alibis," which Rock points to as a natural offshoot of being a performing songwriter courtesy of the sorts of inspiration that can come in the moment of pulling from the muse in the air around you, sharing his memory of being "down playing in residence at a place in Florida, maybe three or four months, and the owner and his wife were having problems. One day these people came in, four people in a group, and the men were dressed in suits and ties, but the women were dressed in cocktail attire, pretty dresses cut above the knee, and one of them was a startling woman in a black cocktail dress and she had stark white hair. Whiter than sheet paper, and I'd never seen anything like that before in my life, and she was young. So, one thing led to another—after coming back two or three times with her friend, she came over and asked me one time to go for a hamburger one day. Then one thing really led to another and the next thing you know, I'm really embroiled in this deal, and didn't even know she was married until it was too late. So, when I left there and moved to Nashville, she came, and we got married. For five years, we had the most marvelous time, and eventually dissolved."

A vagabond and journeyman songwriter in the classic sense of the word, Rock's favorite place to write many times has been while "on the road. I get a lot of lyric ideas there. When you're in a car, riding for hours and hours, it gives you a chance to think. I keep a pen and pad on the seat next to me, and any time I get an idea, I pull off and write it down. Sometimes a song idea comes one way, sometimes it comes another, a lot of times it comes from me sitting down and noodling on my guitar." When he passes along final words of wisdom on the subject of songwriting from his rich chest of gems, Rock closes with the notion that honesty will always shine through the genre's most timeless songs:

> I've written about being in love as much as I've written about being out of love. "Where Can I Surrender," for one example, has I think a timelessness about it, and I think "Still Lovin' You" does, and of course, I think "House at the End of the Road" is timeless. I think the greatest country songs come from writers who have lived the life they're writing about. I think it's supremely important, the most important thing of all is to write about real deals in people's lives, their hardships and loves. Most songwriters aren't trained, they're coming in off the street and writing a song because they feel a certain way. Hank Cochran used to tell me, "Write what you know about and don't worry about what people think about it." The way I look at the whole thing is I want everybody to do the best they can with the best they got. The younger songwriters today are doing what they know to do, and I did what I knew to do. I have been accepted broadly by my peers; I haven't been accepted by the general public. But if you know all the writers who happen to know me, ask them. . . . I am honored that I've what I consider to be great writers know my name. I never felt like I qualified, but here I am walking the halls with Curly Putman, Bobby Braddock, Hank Cochran, and the songs I wrote then are still here all these years later, and people still want to hear them, that's about all a songwriter can ask for.

CHAPTER 18

HERE IN THE REAL WORLD

Mark Irwin

The Bluebird Cafe is a legendary institution in Nashville, a stage where many of country music's biggest songwriters got their start, and one where once you've been accepted by your peers, most become lifelong members, appearing in writers rounds years after they were unknowns starting out there. For a young writer new to town, during the 1970s, '80s, and '90s, landing a waitering or bartending job at Bluebird was not only a networking paradise for that writer, but also an opportunity to become a student of the craft, listening night after night to the best writers in the world debuting new songs, playing hits and telling the stories behind their creation, and if you were lucky, maybe even getting an opportunity to play one of your own for those established writers. Leading to many a foot in the cowriting and publishing door throughout the decades, this was precisely the lucky opportunity that came knocking when then-unknown Mark Irwin stuck his head in to inquire about a bar-back job upon arriving to town back in 1989

with $1,500 in my pocket. I moved out to Nashville because I understood that songwriting was a career that you could focus on in Nashville. Being a New York Jew, there was nothing more alien to me than coming down to Tennessee. So, when I got down here, I was really lucky to get a job at the Bluebird Cafe like my second or third day in town. Back then, they were still serving lunch, so I got to go in there and just be a bar-back and dishwasher and worked my way up to bartender. So, I was then there every night, and got to hear all these great songwriters, and got to network. The Bluebird Cafe, particularly in the 1980s and '90s, was just a real songwriter mecca, and the lady who owned it at the time, Amy Kurland, was just known for being a songwriter's best friend, and would give struggling newcomers a chance to get up onstage and perform their songs, as well as established, well-known writers.

At that time, everybody who was focusing on country music writing and performing would just all be there, so, for instance, my first night working there as a bartender, Don Schlitz—who wrote "The Gambler"—played, and I got to talk to him for a few minutes in the kitchen area before he went on, not really even knowing who he was. Then when he went on and performed, and it was like "Wow," and just eye opening, and we became friends through that. So, I think I was exposed and got to have relationships with songwriters who were at a higher level than me at the time because of my employment at the Bluebird. They were always willing to sit around and talk, either after hours or beforehand, and so that was kind of my way of networking, and I was getting paid for it at the same time, getting exposed to some of the greatest writers working in town back then.

Mark's focus on getting to know, perform, and cowrite with his fellow up-and-coming songwriters led to several pivotal relationships that would help launch him up the charts to his first Top 5 hit, including his first publishing deal and a charmed cowrite session with a newly signed and still unknown country singer named Alan Jackson, both of which Irwin argued were a direct consequence of "getting out there and networking as much as get up there and play your songs. Hopefully, you'll hear somebody where something connects in you, and you might discover a cowriting partner. So, through that, I made a few friends, and one of them told me about this new upstart publishing company called Ten Ten Music Group that was taking interviews with songwriters, so I started bringing them songs, and they started liking more and more of what I was bringing in. They didn't sign me to a publishing deal right away but started demoing some of my songs that they liked, where we did single-song contracts, and they would start pitching them, and we just developed a relationship that way. At the same time, they were also managing a couple of acts, Holly Dunn and this new guy named Alan Jackson—who didn't have a record deal yet, so they were going around town trying to get Alan a deal for probably three years. So, they hooked us up to write, and we had dinner over at the owners' house, Barry and Jewell Coburn, and got together the next day to write, and wrote two songs, one of them being 'Here in the Real World' and the other being the one Chely Wright cut a while back called 'Till I Was Loved by You.' Those are the only two songs we ever wrote, and they both did pretty well." Taking fans inside the room for the writing of what became both his and Jackson's first hit single, and the title track of the country singer's debut LP, the two-million selling *Here in the Real World*, Mark began by crediting Jackson with

coming in when Alan had those first two lines. I remember when we first sat down, it was that point when you're looking at each other that first blank half hour of a writing appointment when you're trying to figure out what you want to write. And Alan just said, "You know, I have these two lines, and I don't know what to do with them," and he just blurted out: "Cowboys don't cry, heroes don't die," and I'm a big movie buff, and I don't know, it just kind of clicked to me that it was a song about movies. So, really, once we realized that and came up with the whole concept of "In the movies, everything's great, but here in the real world. . . ." Once we realized that concept and that that's what we were writing, the song really fell out. I don't want to sound tootsie, but the song really wrote itself in about forty-five minutes, once we zeroed in on what we were writing. I didn't have that idea or title beforehand, so it took Alan saying those two lines that a light went off in my head and it just kind of poured out.

In the meantime, I had a song recorded by Holly Dunn but then it didn't make the album, didn't come out, and as much as it was heartbreaking at the time, looking back now, I was kind of exposed through that process to the reality that, "Okay, even getting your song cut, as thrilling as it is, that's not the end of the story. . . ." So, even though the Holly Dunn cut didn't make the album, meanwhile an older song of mine I'd written before I'd started working with Ten Ten, a Christmas song I had written with a couple of friends, got recorded by Randy Travis and put on a Christmas album he was releasing. He was pretty hot at the time, so that was pretty thrilling, and then the song I'd written with Alan got demoed. Actually, a guy on Warner Bros. cut it before Alan did, but he got dropped before his album ever came out, then Alan got his record deal, cut the song, it became a hit, and it just seemed to steamroll from there. There's nothing like being on the ground floor of the next big thing.

Over the next twenty years, Mark would revisit chart success many times over, allowing him to write cuts for the biggest country stars of the day like Tim McGraw and Martina McBride, as well as legends like Jimmy Buffett, who made Irwin cowrite not only a single, but also the title of his 2008 "Bama Breeze" tour. Taking fans back to the roots of what he considers to be among "my favorites," Mark explains that "this is a song that me, Josh Kear, and a guy named Chris Thompkins wrote, and that it was recorded by Jimmy Buffett was really thrilling. The story behind that one is it's truly the name of a club Chris used to play at in Muscle Shoals, and he had the first verse and idea behind it. He used to play at this place, and it burned down, so he just laid out that first verse, and me and Josh just jumped on it and made up a story. But it was really kind of true, from Chris's experiences, and we just felt like either Jimmy Buffett—which seemed like an impossibility at the time—or maybe Kenny Chesney would cut it, because he was really at the peak of doing kind of those beachy Buffett-style songs. It was passed on by Chesney, and I figured it was dead, but then somehow the song got to Mac McAnally—who was producing Jimmy Buffett at the time—and one thing led to another. I didn't know anything about it, but Josh and Chris kind of heard about it as it was happening, and I got a call one day that Buffett had cut the song! It was just amazing."

Hank Williams Jr.'s decision to record "That's How They Do It in Dixie" would mark another highlight for the songwriter in the category of collaborating with country legends. Grateful to date for the cut, when he and his cowriters rolled up their sleeves and got down to the business of writing the song, while Irwin remembered "we were trying to write something commercial," the song took a unique change in direction for all three writers: "If you listen to a lot of other songs of mine or Josh or Chris's, it's really not like a lot of other songs we've written, it's a lot more redneck than we usually write, for lack of a better word. That was another one I wrote with Josh Kear and Chris Thompkins, and Josh is from East Tennessee and Chris is from Alabama, and I'm sure that song started from Chris's point of view, and we just ended up writing it with him.

It sounded to us like what was getting cut on the radio more and more. I love the song, I think there's some great images in there, and we really tried to create different images that at the time you hadn't really seen in a song before, so there's a line about going skinny-dipping, a belly button dangles, all that stuff. So, we really tried to come up with some unique pictures and images in it. Once you write the song and publish and demo it, and your publisher starts pitching it, you have no control over any of that stuff. Jamie Johnson, believe it or not, sang the demo, and it got pitched to Hank's producer, and he loved it. Being the subject matter of it, Big & Rich and Gretchen [Wilson] were really hot at the time and always gave a nod to Hank, so I have to give a nod to Doug Johnson, who was at Curb [Records] at the time, he's the one who engineered all that. Getting that cut was really fortunate. When we heard about that, we were thrilled."

Though it's the hits that have kept the lights on for Irwin and his family over the past twenty years and afforded him the opportunity so many songwriters dream of—getting up every day to go write for a living—not surprisingly, many of his favorite cuts "are songs that haven't been recorded, a lot of them, and I have a couple that have been recorded but haven't come out yet. One of my favorites, of course, is 'Bama Breeze' because I love the way it was written and that Jimmy Buffett of course cut it. 'Real World,' that was twenty-five, twenty-seven years ago, and I'm just now at the point where if I'm in my car and it's on the radio, where I can turn my car off and get out before it's over. That of course is always going to be special to me, and my Christmas song, because it's the first time I ever had a cut that came out. I spend a lot of time every year trying to get that song cut again because I think it's really special."

In 2013, that creative fire fueled Irwin back up to the top of the charts twice, scoring a smash hit cowriting Tim McGraw's duet with Taylor Swift, "Highway Don't Care," and a number two hit with "Redneck Crazy" by Tyler Farr. These successes he was grateful for amid the current climate within the broader record industry where sales revenues have shrunk dramatically over the past twenty years, leading to smaller royalty checks for artists and writers alike. Mark Irwin offers the closing advice to the next generation of writers arriving in Nashville by the day—to keep their eyes and ears wide open to the fact that

> the business isn't like it was in the 1990s, when country was doing that boom, selling millions of records. You could make a good living and be a hot commodity as a writer just getting album cuts. Nowadays, the only way for a writer *really* to make a good chunk of money is trying to get singles, because album sales just aren't what they used to be. Every once in a while, you get lucky with an artist who sells one or two million records, but that's gotten to be less and less as the years have gone on. Now, it's really just trying to write singles, and that's how I've changed, because back in the day, I was just trying to write great songs, and I figured if you had a great song, somebody was going to love it and want to sing it. That worked for a while, but now I'm trying to look at it like "What does Chesney need that he hasn't done before that can sound like a single?" So, I'm really trying to focus on the artists and trying to get something that sounds like it could work as a single, but yet is something fresh for a particular artist. I still have that desire.

CHAPTER 19

MURDER ON MUSIC ROW

Larry Cordle

"Murder on Music Row" sounds like the name of a true crime podcast, not a country radio smash, but that's precisely what songwriter Larry Cordle and cowriter Larry Shell created together before George Strait and Alan Jackson recorded a duet that took home the Country Music Association's award for Vocal Event of the Year "and the CMA's Song of the Year award!" Cordle proudly pulls the curtain back on the memory of cowriting the song with "my best friend Larry, who I've written many songs with. We wrote 'Mama Don't Forget to Pray for Me' and 'Daddy Was a Navy Man.' I'd been on the road with my bluegrass band—Lonesome Standard Time—and Glen Duncan and I had quit working in '95, and I had been off the road. My daughter was little, so I wanted to spend some more time at home anyway. Then in 1999, she was a little bit older, I got to really hankering to do that again and to cut a new album. I already had the songs picked out, and I'd already quit writing, and Larry called me and said, 'Bud, I've got an idea, a great song idea for me and you.' I said, 'What is it?' but truthfully, I kind of wasn't very interested in it, because I already had the songs picked out. Next, he said, 'It's called 'Murder on Music Row,' and I said, 'Oh, my God, is it about killing country music?' And he said, 'Yeah, that's exactly what it's about.'"

Knowing instantly they were onto something special, Cordle remembered an inspired cowrite followed where, he found, once "we were down at the office we shared together on 18th Avenue a few days later, we wrote that song in a couple of hours! I recorded it on a little cassette tape and thought that was the end of it. I recorded it for my album with Lonesome Standard Time and then played a show at the Bluebird Cafe with Jerry Salley, Rebecca Lynn Howard, and Carl Jackson, and I decided to play 'Murder on Music Row,' just to see how the crowd responded. Well, when I got to the title of the song, the roof comes off that place! People were sitting there listening to every word of it, I could tell that. I didn't know what that meant, and when it got to the payoff on the thing, it was just bedlam."

The kind of reaction any songwriter welcomes when debuting a new song for a live crowd, Larry marked the moment because, "I'd never really been involved in anything like that before! So, I finished the song, we finished the night, and life goes on. Then I was rehearsing for these sides to do this bluegrass album, and next I play live at the Station Inn and the same thing happens. So, we cut that album in two nights, and when we're in the studio the last night of the session, I told the boys, 'Let's put this on here because, if nothing else, I need a demo for it anyway.' So, we put it on there and then I took the mix to Larry for him to listen to, and we start having the conversation, 'Well, maybe we should take this thing around.' He said, 'I want to, just get me that cut and bring it up here.' I'm thinking about taking this thing over to Carl P. Mayfield. He had a show at 103.5 WKDF and was kind of the anti-commercial country guy in the morning. You had Gerry House and the other guys, but Carl played the old stuff, and he had Waylon on in the mornings and stuff. So, I go get some crime scene tape from these guys over at the Longhorn—these cops I'd run into—and we make this big gaudy package up. We don't put any names or any phone numbers or anything about it. We just put the song on a disc and take it over there and leave it in Carl P.'s inbox. Well, when he came in, he plays this thing and the first morning he played it, this friend of mine that I write with every once in a while, Kim Fox, called me at like 6:00, 6:30 a.m. and said, 'Oh, my God, they're playing your song on WKDF!' Carl P. told me that he played it every thirty minutes until

184 SONGS OF NASHVILLE

he was off. The phones, they couldn't answer the calls. So, I guess Erv Woolsey heard this thing on the way to work and called George Strait and tells him he's found this song, and that was it." "Murder at Music Row" was awarded Song of the Year at the International Bluegrass Music Awards.

Cordle's unique pedigree as a songwriter traces back throughout his entire career as a performer in his own right as front man of Larry Cordle and Lonesome Standard Time. National Public Radio in a profile would report about his earliest successes that "Cordle became one of Nashville's most respected songwriters, beginning when his childhood friend Ricky Skaggs recorded his song 'Highway 40 Blues.' Since then, Cordle's music has appeared on projects that have sold more than 55 million records by artists such as Alison Krauss [and] Garth Brooks," proudly pointing to his solo role writing the number one hit on the US Hot Country Songs Chart for Skaggs as he recorded the band's debut for Sugar Hill Records in 1992 as part of Larry Cordle, Glen Duncan, and Lonesome Standard Time; *Murder on Music Row* and *Songs from the Work Bench* respectively for Shell Point Records in 2000 and 2003; Lonesome Skynyrd Time: A Bluegrass Tribute to Lynyrd Skynyrd for CMH Records followed in 2004; and the *All-Star Duets* album for Mighty Cord Records in 2014. Counting his collaboration with Ricky Skaggs as among his personal favorite renditions of another artist recording one of his early songs, Cordle recalled surprising the future country superstar with the song after he'd first written it:

> Ricky was working for Emmylou Harris by then and I remember I said, "Ricky, I've got all these songs, and I'm not leaning on you to do anything here but, people tell me they are good. Would you be interested in hearing these things at all?" And he said "Yeah," so I go to his house, and he has this little cassette tape recorder and we recorded maybe twelve songs. I don't know the exact number, but in those songs

were "Highway 40 Blues." I believe "Two Highways" was in there too that Alison Krauss has a big record on. Ricky told me after hearing it that if he ever got a big record deal that he was going to do some of these songs. And I thought, "That would be great," but it still sounded pretty far-fetched to me. Then Ricky records this thing in '82 on an album called *Highways and Heartaches,* and they actually had three singles before they released "Highway 40 Blues."

In fact, he came though Lexington and I was working in Winchester, and I got off one night. Ricky came through and was doing a show and wanted to borrow fifty bucks off me; I gave him what money I had. I don't even think I had fifty bucks. He gave me the cassette tape that had the "Highway 40 Blues" roughs on it and told me it was going to be on that album. So, time went on and it became a number one record! I still hadn't moved to Nashville because I didn't know exactly what to do. But Ricky made a deal with Welk Music—Lawrence Welk's company—and then sometime when I was on the road with him in '84, he asked me if I wanted to move here. I said, "Well, what do you want me to do, like, make up songs?" And he said, "Yeah!" and I was in!

Cordle's solo album catalog has remained just as prolific, with *Took Down and Put Up* released in 2007, Pud Marcum's *Hanging* in 2011, *Give Me Jesus* in 2017, *Tales from East Kentucky* in 2018, and *Where the Trees Know My Name* in 2021, with *Bluegrass Today* (a news website) admiring within its review of his most recent release that "at 75 years of age, Larry Cordle is still stringing together hit after hit in bluegrass music, and after a quick listen, it seems certain that his latest, releasing today, will continue this trend."

Over the rest of the 1980s, he would lay the groundwork for that legacy to take shape with country chart hits like "Honky Tonk

186   SONGS OF NASHVILLE

Crowd" by John Anderson, "Heartbreak Hurricane" for Ricky Skaggs, "Hollywood Squares" for George Strait, "You Can't Take It with You When You Go" by Gene Watson, "Mama Don't Forget to Pray for Me" by Diamond Rio, "Lonesome Standard Time" by Kathy Mattea, "Country in My Genes" by Loretta Lynn, "Lonesome Dove" by Trisha Yearwood, and Garth Brooks's "Against the Grain" off of the history-making *Ropin' the Wind*, which Cordle closes by inviting fans inside to look at his cowriting process in action:

> I think cowriting in general is a trick, because part of the deal of cowriting is showing up. Now, this is just me—but with songwriting—to be in the game and be a player in the game requires focus. What happens is: You may not feel like writing tomorrow, but as I look at this calendar and I've got Leslie Satcher or I've got Jim Rushing or I've got Carl Jackson or I've got some of these people on there, I may not have anything. I may be bone dry. I may not feel like going, but you may go and something fruitful may come out of going to work. That's why you go to work, hopefully you've just got a great idea that you can just do—but that just doesn't happen every day. Just the act of going, your partner may have something that you're really interested in. So, I don't know if that's a "trick," but I'm not a very technical person when it comes to writing songs. I trust my gut; I take the lessons that I've learned just by observing very seriously. You can't do this every day, but you know, you're trying for every line to beat the one you just wrote and you're trying to write something that comes from your heart that might connect with other people's hearts. That's as simple as I know how to put it. I love this life. It's been such a blessing to me, and I think, I think it's what God intended for me to do.

CHAPTER 20

AMERICANA'S AMBASSADOR

···

Jim Lauderdale

"Revered Americana singer-songwriter Jim Lauderdale has elevated the practice of politely deflecting praise to an art."
—Guitar Player *magazine*

"Influential country artist." —*The Boot*

Not every country songwriter can lay claim to helping invent a subgenre, but Jim Lauderdale rightfully can. *Rolling Stone* has correctly crowned him both "Americana's King" and "Godfather," and National Public Radio, in a deeper analysis, reported that "Lauderdale is rightfully considered one of the kings of Americana music. He's a songwriter's songwriter, having written for George Strait, Loveless, Vince, George Jones, and countless others. He's sung on records for Dwight Yoakam and Lucinda Williams. He has toured with Johnny Cash, Merle Haggard, and Nick Lowe. He's one of the hardest working musicians in Nashville, recording and releasing thirty albums since his debut album in 1991. In 2016, the Americana Music Association handed him a lifetime achievement award."

In bringing his influence full circle, *Texas Monthly* captured a prized moment for any songwriter when George Strait presented Jim "with the Wagonmaster Award—a lifetime achievement award named after Porter Wagoner—at the Americana Honors and Awards show in Nashville." Pointing back in time to a major breakthrough moment in his own beginnings as a songwriter, Jim remembered its arrival "when I started kind of hearing the banjo more and more and just really loved it, like the 'Beverly Hillbillies Theme' [also known as 'The Ballad of Jed Clampett'] and then Bonnie and Clyde hearing 'Foggy Mountain Breakdown.' There are certain songs in bluegrass, for instance, that kind of have this IT factor that drives people wild like 'Orange Blossom,' 'Special Ruby,' and 'Rocky Top.' There are just these things that somehow, no pun intended, touch a chord in people. Then I started playing banjo when I was fifteen, and I would entertain my folks and friends."

Spotlighting the first moment he ever went past playing other songwriters' music and took his first real stab at composing his own, Lauderdale credits his parents' belief in his obviously special talent and passion for music as an important belief that helped his own confidence grow: "Around the same age, my folks let me go with some college students to this huge bluegrass festival called the Union Grove Fiddlers Convention. They had a fiddler contest, and these guys that I met said, 'Hey, if we get up there and do a song and enter the contest, we get our money back,' which was I think $5 to get into this festival. So, we got together and started jamming around and I start singing and came up with this kind of improvised lyric. We did not win, obviously, but that was very exciting. Then I didn't do anything until the summer before college, and I was visiting some folks who are like my surrogate grandparents in Troutman, North Carolina, where I lived until I was five. I had been working on this kind of old-timey bluegrass-y thing called 'I'm Chopping Wood' and, basically, I just had the chorus and a couple of verses and that was really my first song."

After graduating from the North Carolina School of the Arts, Lauderdale wound up heading to the songwriting mecca of Nashville in 1979, where he recorded his first original music "in Earl Scruggs's basement working with this mandolin player, Roland White, who was my hero. Marty Stuart even played lead acoustic guitar on a bunch of it. After I made that record with Roland,

I thought, 'I made it!' We just called it *Roland White and Jim Lauderdale*, and it was kind of half bluegrass, half without banjo, and we did a few Delmore Brothers songs, things like that, and a Shell Silverstein song. I sent cassettes out to the bluegrass labels."

While waiting to hear back from record labels, Lauderdale's ever-expanding network of collaborators took him north to the Big Apple after "a friend of mine named John Nester told me about this famous country bar in New York City where he got me a gig playing in-between the house band's sets. The first night I was playing there, they were using a pedal steel guitar player named Larry Campbell, who also played electric guitar and fiddle, and I vowed 'Someday, I'm going to play with this guy.' Then I met another fiddle player named Larry Packer who was in this group Cat Mother and The All Night Newsboys that Jimi Hendrix produced a record on and hired him to play twin fiddles with me at some shows. Next, I got a gig at a place called City Limits where this drummer named Hank Beanie would front a band and just kind of call people that day, 'What are you doing tonight? Can you come in?' and he would throw together these bands for pickup gigs. I met this woman named Kathleen Wynn who was a great singer through one of those shows, and she and I started a bluegrass band after that called Charged Particles. Then, by day, I had a job working for *Rolling Stone* magazine as a messenger."

Amid his live gigging, Lauderdale naturally found his songwriting repertoire expanding: "I started writing more and more in New York, and with these country gigs and bluegrass gigs I would do, I'd throw in a few originals and slowly started building up my catalog. I was always playing my songs live whenever I could and, through that, met a bass player named Tony Garnier, who now plays with Bob Dylan, who loaned me a bunch of Johnny Bush and Ray Price records. I hadn't really delved into that before, and it really opened up a country side of things for me. I met Steve Satterwhite through Tony, and he had a little studio, and a piano player named Stephen

190 SONGS OF NASHVILLE

Gaboury as the engineer and I would spend every penny, other than rent, I had left over on doing demos. During this time, too, I got in this play called *Cotton Patch Gospel* that Harry Chapin wrote the music for, and it was a one-man show. This guy Tom Key was the actor playing all these different parts, and on off nights, there was this bluegrass band I play banjo and some guitar for. So, my day job then shifted to doing this off-Broadway show, and I'd still do gigs at night, but I had my daytime to write."

Finding that the music naturally drew him out on the road, Jim settled into a roving musical routine that would follow his entire career: "Eventually that show traveled to Atlanta and Dallas. A very important person I met during this time in 1980 was Buddy Miller, and through him I met John Leventhal. Eventually, I got into this other play, a country-ish musical called *Pump Boys and Dinettes* based in Cleveland, Ohio. So, I do these shows for several months and go back to New York and do more demos while I was living in Cleveland. Then that went to Chicago, and I'd fly to New York on Sunday evenings and do demos Monday and then fly back to Chicago. I'd met Dwight Yoakam when he was playing a gig in Chicago, took a demo with songs including 'Stay Out of My Arms' and 'What I've Done in New York,' and I went out to Dwight and asked, 'Can I give you some songs?' and he said, 'Give it to my producer over here, Pete Anderson.' Throughout all of that, John Leventhal became kind of more of a key guy to these demos. I was hoping for a record deal, and I was kind of finding my sound."

Traveling next to Los Angeles with *Pump Boys and Dinettes*, Lauderdale found himself in the proverbial right place at the right time: "That very first night I was in LA, when I went with Eddie Bathhouse to a bar where this band called Top Jimmy & The Rhythm Pigs was playing and began sitting in with them. I invited Pete Anderson to come, and he eventually became my first producer, and met another guy there named John Ciambotti, who played bass on Elvis Costello's first record with a group called Clover, and he became my manager. Eventually, after many rejections from Nashville labels, I got an offer with Epic Records—not in Nashville and so, we had recorded three songs. 'Stay Out of My Arms' was one of them. With everything Pete was hearing, he said, 'You've got seven smash hits on this.'"

Lauderdale would finally see his first charting success as a songwriter in 1988 when his single "Stay Out of My Arms" hit number eighty-six on the US Hot Country Singles Chart, the creative product of "a lady that I liked, a lot. She was pretty devout, and I just thought, 'You need to stay away from me because I'm not going to be good for you.' So, she was the muse. After getting rejected by all these record labels, I had finally signed a record deal with Epic for the record I made with Pete Anderson. At one point during the later 1980s, I had traveled back to New York and was staying with John Leventhal in his little apartment in the East Village. We wrote another song, and he demoed, and it was just like, 'Wow, this guy's just got this incredible tone and everything's so tasteful.' One day we were working, and I played him something I'd mumbled into my tape recorder, 'I found a new planet, that only I can see . . .' and he said, 'Wait a minute,' and we sat down and wrote this song called 'Planet of Love.'"

Marveling years later at the sheer size of Lauderdale's songwriting catalog, *American Songwriter* magazine mused that "if Jim Lauderdale never recorded another note ever again—a most unlikely scenario given his prodigious output—he would still boast a catalog that would be the envy of any other artist, regardless of genre. Known for releasing multiple albums in the space of a single year—sometimes up to three concurrent efforts at a time—he boasts a catalog that's averaged at least one album for every year of a more than thirty-year career." The first would arrive in 1988 with *Point of No Return* and his second in 1991 with *Planet of Love* after the aforementioned self-titled single became the title of Jim's first solo album, released on Reprise Records, which while scoring

192 SONGS OF NASHVILLE

no major breakthrough hits, would land Lauderdale his first publishing deal:

> At first, I really felt like with that record, "Man, we'll release 'Where the Sidewalk Ends,' then we'll release 'King of Broken Hearts,' then after those are hits, we'll release 'Planet of Love' and that is really gonna kick the doors in!" and it didn't happen. That was crushing, but in the meantime, too, I signed a publishing deal, which was very important, with an independent company called Blue Water Music and eight out of those ten songs ended up being recorded by other people! The first two totally changed my fate after I got a call from my song plugger whose name is Pat McMurray, and she said "Well, Tony Brown from MCA recorded 'Where the Sidewalk Ends' and 'King of Broken Hearts' yesterday with George Strait for this new movie that George is gonna be in!" Then when that happened, other producers start coming to Blue Water looking for my stuff.

Finally finding a friend in his songwriting successes, George Strait would continue to record Lauderdale's songs throughout the early and mid-1990s following "The King of Broken Hearts" and "Where the Sidewalk Ends" from the *Pure Country* soundtrack, "I Wasn't Fooling Around" and "Stay Out of My Arms" on 1993's *Easy Come, Easy Go* LP, "Nobody Has to Get Hurt" and "What Am I Waiting For" off of 1994's multiplatinum *Lead On*, "Do the Right Thing" from 1996's *Blue Clear Sky* LP, the Top 5 hit "We Shouldn't Be Doing This" off of 1998's *One Step at a Time* LP, and "One of You" and "What Do You Say to That," another Top 5 smash, from 1999's *Always Never the Same* LP. Reflecting on his staggering first decade of songwriting success with George Strait, Jim begins by pointing at one of his early favorites:

"We Really Shouldn't Be Doing This" was a song I wrote as I was working on a record called *Whisper*, a country record for RCA. My last, there was another record after that, but that was my last major label deal. I had a great deal at this place, the Union Station Hotel, which used to be an old train station, for a small, one-bedroom kind of apartment, with no kitchen and my bedroom window faced the train tracks and I could hear the trains. So, I was there one time, and I was working on my record and "We Really Shouldn't Be Doing This" just starts talking to me and I demoed it. Then I remembered George Strait was recording at Ocean Way Studios, and I went by Ocean Way and left it with the engineer who in turn left it on the console, and they recorded it!

With George Strait, I've got either fourteen or fifteen, so he's cut the most of anybody among a lot of people that have recorded my songs. So, every time I would get with a cowriter where we'd hear "Strait's going in next week," it was always "Let's write something," and there were many times where my cowriter and I would go: "This is a smash hit for George. This is the one undeniable hit, this is George," and then, nothing. Then there were those that I kind of least expected. With "What Do You Say to That," I was writing with Melba Montgomery, and she had that title and it just kind of came out and then I ended up putting that on my *Whisper* album. I thought, "Okay, well, this is unmistakably country, unapologetically traditional country," and knew that Joe Galante, the head of the label, really loved that song and believed in it. He ran it up the flagpole with radio. That was my fourth major label deal, and I was over forty. I told Joe when he signed me, I said, "Look, they're taking a shot. This is a real gamble for you, but at least give me two records," and he did. I really appreciate that. *Whisper* didn't do anything as an album but George Strait recording that song.

Now, with one of the most recent cuts I had with George, a song I wrote with Odie Blackmon. It's on an album that Odie and I wrote, gosh, over ten years ago now. I kind of tongue-in-cheek called it *Country Super Hits Vol. I*, and kind of as a funny nod to these K-tel records. I thought, "Look, subliminally, some musician and some country superstar's band is gonna go, 'Hey, you gotta hear track four,' and then they hear it, they cut it, and nothing got cut until that song ten years later. This one was called "Two More Wishes." I told my song plugger then as the years went by, I eventually went to Bug Music, which got bought by Windswept, but merged with Windswept Pacific, which got bought by BMG, which is where I am now. When George was going in, I told my song plugger Chris Oglesby, I said, "How about this one, that one, this one. . . ." So, "Two More Wishes" was on that list and luckily George recorded it.

With "Twang," that was the first time I wrote with two people having a three-way cowrite, what were two very talented writers, Jimmy Ritchie and Kendell Marvel. I got to Jimmy Ritchie's place. Naturally ten minutes late, maybe more because when I got in there, they said, "Hey, we're all ready on the one. Let's play it." It was called "Twang." Now my initial reaction all of a sudden was, "Nobody's ever gonna cut a song called 'Twang,'" because country radio, they kind of moved on from the twangy, it was almost like if you were twangy, that was a detriment. So, what happened was they played a verse and a chorus and then I said, "Oh, hey, how about at the end of the chorus you go, 'I need a little twang, twang, twang, twang, twang,'" and they liked it. Then I helped with the lyrics on the second verse. So, that was really cool in that first session—we wrote two hit songs and then got another George Strait cut!"

Fortunately, Jim found that as he continued to pursue his path as a recording artist, it organically crossed with those of the Music Row record-making machine continually on the hunt for new material for country's top artists to record as Lauderdale cranked out an impressive first era of solo albums. They featured a who's who of early fellow up-and-coming session players and performers as his first album had, from Shawn Colvin to heroes like Rodney Crowell and Larry Campbell on the debut, and on 1994's *Pretty Close to the Truth* and 1995's *Every Second Counts* on Atlantic, 1996's *Persimmons* LP on Rounder Records, 1998's *Whisper* on BNA, and back-to-back albums in 1999 for Rebel Records and RCA respectively—*I Feel Like Singing Today* and *Onward Through It All*. Whether conscious of it or not at the time, he was helping to lay the foundation with each new studio album as a co-inventor of the new musical genre that followed known as Americana.

Reaching number one as a songwriter for the first time in 1995 when Mark Chesnutt took "Gonna Get a Life" all the way to the top, Lauderdale continued to enjoy other 1990s songwriting success when Patty Loveless's rendition of "Halfway Down" hit number six and made "You Don't Seem to Miss Me" a Top 20 hit via a duet with country music legend George Jones. Beyond the charts, his solo catalog continued to expand with 2001's *The Other Sessions* LP for Dual tone Records, along with 2001's *The Hummingbirds* and *Lost in the Lonely Pines*, a collaboration with iconic bluegrass artist Ralph Stanley & The Clinch Mountain Boys that so impressed listeners that Lauderdale wound up taking home his first Grammy win for

196 SONGS OF NASHVILLE

Best Bluegrass Album, a surreal moment that he still welcomed "by the early 2000s, where for all the trials and tribulations you go through with these labels, the Grammys start to take notice. I'd been at this twenty, twenty-plus years at this point, and it shows the advice that the perseverance that's required to do this for a living. So, to win that award with Ralph was mind-blowing!"

Jim considers George Jones's rendition of "You Don't Seem to Miss Me" as a highlight, carrying on his tradition of duets, this one with Patty Loveless, and notably one of his last Top 20 singles before he passed. He invited fans inside its writing via his memory that "I wrote that during my stays in the desert. My friend, former bass player, engineer, and coproducer Dusty Wakeman, had this place called the Rimrock Ranch, which was some cabins up in Yucca Valley above a place called Pioneertown, California, which is a place I still go to once a year to do a gig at Pappy and Harriet's Pioneertown Palace. It's great bar. Then I go up and write for a couple of days. So, I was there and wrote 'You Don't Seem to Miss Me' after Victoria Williams, a great singer-songwriter and I were talking, and I was asking her how she met someone and she said they'd gone on a date and then she said, 'And then I dated him for eight years. It didn't seem like he missed me.' And so I said, 'I've got an idea, let's write it.' Then it was kind of like 'Tulsa Time' with Danny Flowers. He got this song idea, and he tried to get one of his bandmates and he's playing with Don Williams, 'Hey, can we write this?' and then it didn't happen. So, I changed things around, it became, 'You Don't Seem to Miss Me.' I was at a pitch session for Patty Loveless—she and her husband, Emory Gordy Jr. Her producer wanted to invite writers to play stuff for them for an upcoming album for Patty. So, when I got in there, I brought my guitar and I brought some songs, CDs, and lyric sheets and it's like, 'How about this one?' and then they'd say, 'Oh, yeah, yeah, we've heard that one . . .' and 'They played that one for us . . .' I was thinking to myself, 'This is embarrassing. I don't have anything. Well, I'll play the song I'm gonna record for my record for RCA.' I didn't tell him that, but I played it and then the next day I heard, 'They want to cut that song you played.' So, then I told Joe Galante, 'Joe, I got a problem here. Patty Loveless wants to cut 'You Don't Seem to Miss Me,' and he said, 'Let her do it.' So, when she did that with George Jones, who was like, as I mentioned earlier, one of my favorites. I've cried many times hearing that song."

Hitting the 2000s with *The Wind at His Back*, Lauderdale's prolific output of solo material is dizzying and has amassed more than thirty albums, including 2001's *The Other Sessions*, *The Hummingbirds* and *Lost in the Lonesome Pines* in 2002, *Wait 'til Spring* in 2003, *Headed for the Hills* in 2004, *Bluegrass* in 2006, *Country Super Hits Vol. 1*, *The Bluegrass Diaries* in 2007, *Honey Songs* in 2008, *Could We Get Any Closer* in 2009, and *Patchwork River* in 2010. His next decade kicked off with *Reason and Rhyme* in 2011, *Carolina Moonrise* and *Buddy and Jim* in 2012, *Old Time Angels*, *Black Roses*, and *Blue Moon Junction* in 2013, *I'm a Song* in 2014, *Soul Searching* in 2015, *This Changes Everything* in 2016, *London Southern* in 2017, *Time Flies* and *Jim Lauderdale and Roland White* in 2018, *From Another World* in 2019, *When Carolina Comes Home Again* in 2020, *Hope* in 2021, *Game Changer* in 2022, and *The Long and Lonesome Letting Go* in 2023.

Taking his legions of longtime fans inside the writing room for how a typical songwriting session unfolds when a new idea hits him, Jim begins by revealing that "as the song idea starts coming, the melody or the title, it becomes this kind of zone. It has to be and so it's kind of this magical thing, that's like this feeling. I think when you write with somebody else, the interesting thing is how two people or three people can come up with something within a short period of time that could possibly even change their lives. That just by being with that person or people you come up with something that is remarkable. Then going into the studio and recording

198 SONGS OF NASHVILLE

it and then having it come together. Where you think you dig it, but you're not quite sure if it's gonna fly. Then when you get the other musicians and they are such a huge part of records, that is a very magical thing. Then finishing it is just very gratifying, and going out onstage to perform through the years with different songs, it's interesting how place to place some people request the same song that somebody requested the night before. Then when other people cover your songs it's continually fascinating. For instance, John Mayer cut a song called 'When the Devil Starts Crying' and then Solomon Burke cut 'It Seems Like You're Going to Take Me Back.'"

Today in the 2020s, five decades after he first began strumming his guitar and singing his songs for a world clearly ready to listen, the *Nashville Scene* recently declared him "one of Americana's Most Recognizable Figures." Looking ahead even as he's spent time here looking back, Jim Lauderdale muses for all his success and status becoming an Americana and bluegrass legend over the past fifty years, he gives advice from the footing of an aspiring songwriter in imparting his closing reflections and words of wisdom:

> I still feel like a new artist. As far as the challenges you face, I don't feel established. I feel like, "Hey, I've still got a long way to go." In order to kind of reach these goals, you might never reach them. It's so difficult; it's a really tough business. It's competitive in the way that is just because there's so many people here, so many really great recording artists and writers. So, I mean that it's competitive in the sense that you've got to be on your game. You've got to deliver if you're a recording artist with your recordings, at your stage performances, or as a writer with these songs that stand out. I think in my early days I felt competition and jealousy in another way with recording artists. It's like, "How come? Why is this song a hit and mine's not?" and "Why is this guy having hits and selling tons of records and

I'm getting dropped. It's just not fair . . ." I got beyond that after a while and now I'm able to enjoy, just enjoy music.

Whenever I talk to young writers that I meet, the first thing I tell them is: You have to really have to write. You have to do it. That's because of all the rejection and heartache, you have to just want it, you have to have ambition. But on the other hand, I think sometimes when you're starting out, you feel like you've got to prove to people how much you want it. I don't think that's actually necessary. I think you just have to do the work and then present that world and deliver the goods, but not wear people out. I think that that makes people more receptive. After all, you can only challenge yourself.

CHAPTER 21

LOOKIN' FOR LOVE IN ALL THE WRONG PLACES

Wanda Mallette

When a song winds up on the radio, it's a thrill for any songwriter, a hit music video is an added excitement, but winding up the theme song for a John Travolta movie is a whole other level of euphoria—especially if you're a grade-school teacher from Southern Mississippi. That's exactly what happened to a songwriter named Wanda L. Mallette, a late bloomer whose success serves as proof that songwriting has no age limits: "I was thirty-three when I wrote my first song, and I started writing and never stopped, and I was just compelled to write. I think to teach children, I had to learn to get to the very heart of a concept, take it down to bare bones, and get it across to second graders, and I think we do the same thing when we write a song: We have to take a complicated idea and put it into an acceptable story form, and give it a nice melody and make it pleasing to the ear, and have musical movements, all in three minutes or so. And we hope to communicate that deep message that we originally had thought of."

Still, Wanda's love for working with children would prove fertile ground as source material for what would become one of the biggest country hits of all time, "Looking for Love in All the Wrong Places." Though the song would eventually become targeted lyrically toward an adult listening audience, Wanda remembered being inspired to write the song in the first place

> while I was observing my second-grade class, and when
> I wrote the first version of "Looking for Love," which I

wrote on my own, I was looking for a universal idea for a song, and I realized that among the children, the ones that were acting out were the ones who most wanted my attention. I thought about that a lot, I remember one child in particular who was from a real troubled background, and he would just act out and throw his books around, and then come and throw his arms around me and tell me how much he loved me. I thought, "Wow, that's the same thing grown-ups do when they really want love, they do the wrong things, and try to get the wrong people to love them," so the light bulb went off, and I thought "Hey, everybody does that, the children are our teachers, but everybody does it," and segued into the title, which I thought was very catchy, "Looking for Love in All the Wrong Places," and that's where it was born.

I wrote a song with the idea, and it was originally more of a spiritual song, like looking for God's love and self-love, instead of looking for love from other people. That partially comes from growing up in a dysfunctional family. And when I say, "Looking for God," I'm talking about the thing that made Jesus turn to his murderers really and say "Father, forgive them for they know not what they do." I think we all have to get to that point at some time in our lives where we can just forgive everything and just get past our egos and hearts and wounds, so it was a very, very spiritual version.

Knowing she needed to take a chance if the song was ever going to get off paper and on to record for anyone to hear it at all, let alone the world of waiting ears that eventually would, she took a chance with "my first six songs and my last $600, and went to [Chuck Ryan's] studio in Long Beach, and was demoing those first

202 SONGS OF NASHVILLE

six songs when Patti Ryan walked in and that's the first time I'd seen her. She'd been playing around the Gulf Coast performing for a long time, and we both just gelled. We both loved to shop, and we both loved to talk about deep subjects, we love art and architecture, and of course we love to write songs. So, we actually laughed and shopped our way into that collaboration [*laughs*]. Well, when I played the song for her, she wanted to help me rewrite it and make it more of a commercial song, but when Patti and I first started writing, we were just having fun. I don't even think we had a plan for what to do with our work, but after rewriting 'Looking for Love' with her, it did turn out to be a much more commercial song. She really liked the idea, and as I said, I was really a storyteller and Patti was a player more so than I, and we rewrote the song rather fast because we were very quick cowriters. Patti was actually driving to Hattiesburg, and came back with that upbeat chorus melody, so I have to give her credit for that chorus melody. She sang it to me, and I rewrote some of the chorus lyrics in the swimming pool with my children. So, in the end, we wrote a country song that was a love song and had spiritual connotations to an upbeat tempo, and we made the decision to give it a happy ending, so, what more can you want [*laughs*]?"

Eager to get their song's demo out to publishers, they landed a deal with Combine Music in the late 1970s and did what every newly signed songwriter should while waiting to hear about one of their songs being shopped: *Keep writing.* The most therapeutic way to keep busy during the torture for many writers, and the smartest way to have more songs to present if one takes off or doesn't so you have backups, Wanda and her writing partner Patti Ryan did just that, recalling that "before we got the call that we had a song in a movie, Patti and I had just continued to write even as nobody was cutting our song. During that time, we wrote 'Just Another Woman in Love,' which became a number one for Anne Murray after 'Looking for Love,' and that was actually Patti's song idea.

Lookin' for Love in All the Wrong Places 203

She had that idea and a little bit of melody, and asked me in on it, and I was very heavy on the lyrics, and also contributed to melody. Before that, Helen Reddy had already had 'I Am Woman' and the women's lib movement was going strong, and Patti and I are very strong, independent, outspoken women, but we wanted to write a song about a very strong woman who could hold her own out there in the workforce—because so many families had two working parents. I was a working mother, and we wanted to write a song that was soft and sexy but also told about a very strong woman who'd gone out in the business world. I can remember when we got to the chorus, I said, 'Let's get soft and sexy, real soft and sexy, to contrast to the first verse,' and then when we got to the second verse, we kind of didn't know what to do! So, when we started discussing that, I said, 'Let's just get sexier,' and we did, and we turned on the whole world for a little while [*laughs*]."

After a while of waiting, Mallette began to worry—and with reason. "That song had been pitched around Nashville for well over a year and turned down by every viable act, and we couldn't buy a cut on it," she said, leading her publishing company to make one last-ditch effort to get the song placed, making a Hail Mary pass that landed the song "in a cardboard box by Combine Music and sent to Paramount Studios, I understand, kind of as an afterthought, and sent to Johnny Dee. Johnny later told me he went through about twelve songs he didn't like before he listened to 'Looking for Love,' and told them to take the box away and that that was the song he was going to sing in the movie. Then there was haggling over the publishing rights between Combine and Paramount, and they were threatening to take it out of the movie. In the meantime, John Travolta had come to love 'Looking for Love' and said it was his favorite song, and we understand that was instrumental in making sure it was not only in the movie, but also used in the end as a theme song, so, thank you, John! When the film first came out, Combine had told us, 'Don't expect anything big because it's not going to be a single,' but Patti and I went to see the movie in Biloxi and there were two teenage girls sitting in the row in front of us, and they were so excited and one of them kept telling the other one, 'It's coming up, it's coming up, just wait till you hear this!' She had already seen the movie, and of course what she was talking about was 'Looking for Love,' and I knew at that point how special it was. These two little teenage girls were so excited and just loved it so much, but I didn't really know how big it was until my brother had driven all the way from California, and called me and said, 'Wanda, do you realize you're a writer on the biggest song in the nation? I heard "Looking for Love" on one radio station or another all the way across the country driving here,' and that just totally amazed me. Then when I started listening to the radio, every time I heard it, I would have to pull over and cry."

Feeling that the song's success was a fulfillment of a vision she'd had all along about its potential appeal, Wanda honed in on one particularly special moment of affirmation. "One year before we got the call about the movie, I had a dream and it was about a person in a movie leaning against a bar with a beer in his hand, and they panned from his belt buckle up to his hat, and when I was sitting in the premier of *Urban Cowboy*, that scene came on and I started crying. I felt like this was meant to be, so in a sense, you could say I felt like it was written for the movie, and on some spiritual sense, I believe it was. I think that was the universe letting me know this was meant to be, and that might sound a little hokey, but I do strongly believe in things like that. I remember as I was crying because it was just overwhelming and so moving, I looked down the row of seats and Andy Warhol was sitting there staring at me as I was sitting in my little cowgirl outfit crying, and I thought 'This is too cool. Andy Warhol is watching me cry and wondering why.'"

CHAPTER 22

A BRIDGE THAT JUST WON'T BURN

. . . .

Jim McBride

I t's not uncommon in country music for stars to find songwriters whose songs they love so much they always put them on hold when new ones become available. Take Dean Dillon and George Strait for one popular example. Another creative fusion that burst into a star-making one for both songwriter and country star came with Alan Jackson and Jim McBride's collaboration. *Billboard* put their unique songwriting relationship in country music in historical perspective: "The two may not have been an exclusive writing team in the vein of John Lennon and Paul McCartney or George and Ira Gershwin, but Jackson and McBride were still a dynamic duo. They cowrote two of Jackson's signature songs, 'Chattahoochee' and 'Chasin' That Neon Rainbow,' collected five Top 20 country singles as cowriters and shared composer credits on fourteen titles among Jackson's first five studio albums. Released between 1990–1996, each of those projects went multiplatinum, with RIAA certifications representing nineteen million total units sold. . . . Jackson entered the Nashville Songwriters Hall in 2011. They may not write together anymore, but each is still key to the other's career."

Their storied career writing together began with Jackson's first album, *Here in the Real World*, with "She Don't Get the Blues," "Short Sweet Ride," and the number two smash, "Chasin' That Neon Rainbow," which McBride remembers instantly knowing was perfect for Jackson "the first time I sat down with Alan to write. I'd seen Alan at the office, with boots and a cowboy hat on, and I thought 'He looks like a country star,' and I didn't even know his name, but

206 SONGS OF NASHVILLE

he got my phone number, called me up one day and asked 'Would you be willing to write with me? I've seen you there at the office a couple times.' By then I knew who he was, so I told him, 'Yeah, let's get together and see if it's going to work.' So, we got together in this room where Kris Kristofferson used to write at the office, and he plays me this song called 'Home' that was on his first album and later on a single, and I played him a song called 'Dixie Boy' about my life growing up that Alabama had recorded. He's from Georgia, I'm from Alabama, so we thought alike and were both fans of Vern Gosdin and George Jones, loved the same kind of music, and I think we realized who and what we were. I'd first gotten the song idea driving back to Nashville late one night, probably 2:00 in the morning, when this idea popped in my head, 'chasing the neon rainbow, living the honky tonk dream . . .' So, I pulled over and wrote it down, and when I got home, put it in my notebook. I kind of knew what it was about, but I had never played in coffeehouses or been in a band, so hadn't really ever lived that life. So, he's telling me his story about traveling in that old Dodge van he had and not making any money by the time he bought gas and paid the band, driving to Arkansas and Florida and all this. I told him, 'I think I have a title,' pulled out that title, and we decided to write it. So, we just basically wrote his story, and there's a little bit of mine in there too. I always said that writing with Alan was like writing with myself."

The four-million-selling follow-up, *Don't Rock the Jukebox*, would feature the US Hot Country Songs chart topper "Someday," which Jim recounts as a mirror of the real-life struggles he watched Jackson himself go through as a singer-songwriter dealing with the same routine rejections that every undiscovered star does before they make it, sharing his firsthand memory: "When we first started writing together, we wrote 'Someday' in the building where his manager's office was, and at that point, it was Barry, Jewell, and Blue the dog, and Alan and I would be in the back room writing. He had no career yet at that point, and we'd come out and take a break from writing and Alan would ask, 'Anybody call back yet?' and Barry would say 'No, not yet, not yet. . . .' So, to see it go from that to where it went was pretty amazing, but we wrote the song about that."

By the time it wound up on the six-million-selling *A Lot About Livin' (And a Little 'bout Love)* LP "Chattahoochee" represented to McBride a favorite example of how he knew when he had a perfect new song idea for Jackson: "At this point, I had two notebooks. I had an Alan Jackson notebook, and I had another notebook of ideas, and if it was something I thought Alan would like, I wrote it in his notebook. And if it was something I thought wasn't for him, I'd write the idea in the other notebook. With 'Chattahoochee' specifically, I had a house out in Green Hills, and I had a little office upstairs, and I would sit up there in the morning and try to come up with ideas and then go into the office, maybe after lunch, and see what was going on. During lunch that day, I had a magazine from Exxon, and there was a story in there about the Chattahoochee River, and I read that and got an atlas out and saw how close Alan lived to the river. So, I started fiddling with it and came up with the first two lines and the melody. Then I got on the road with Alan, showed that to him, and he immediately said, 'Sing that for me again.' As I sang them, he came up with the next two lines on the spot, and we wrote that over a two- to three-day period on the road."

Measuring the song's stature within Jackson's massive catalog of hits, *Atlanta* magazine reported: "The tune was released as a single on May 15, 1993—accompanied by a video of Jackson waterskiing in boots and a cowboy hat. It spent four weeks at number one on the *Billboard* Hot Country charts, won CMA Song of the Year and ASCAP Song of the Year, and is still so ubiquitous that people of all ages continue to yell-sing it from their boats some thirty years later." The dynamic duo would pen other popular cuts off the album like "Tropical Depression," "If It Ain't One Thing (It's You)," and

208   SONGS OF NASHVILLE

the Top 5 hit "(Who Says) You Can't Have It All," revealing that the song almost didn't wind up on the album at all:

> We wrote that during that same early era we wrote "(Who Says) You Can't Have It All" in that Ten Ten building on 16th Avenue. I was at Tree and he was at Warner Brothers at that point, and after we wrote it, we did a demo for it, and Max Barnes heard it over at Tree and ran into George Jones, and George asked "You got anything for me, Max?" and he said, "No, George, I really don't, but I heard a song this morning you need to hear." So, George went over to hear the song, and when they played it for him, he went in and cut it, and to be quite honest, it was done before Alan and I knew about it. When Alan's manager found out about it, he was very upset, because Alan was going to cut that song on the next album. At that point, Alan and George were kind of friends, and he asked George if he'd give it up, and he said, "Yes."

McBride and Jackson would collaborate on his five-million-selling *Who I Am* album on "Hole in the Wall," "If I Had You," "Buicks to the Moon," and "A House with No Curtains" on the three-time platinum *Everything I Love*, pointing to the Top 20 hit as one that first crashed his musical mind: "I was driving down Woodmont Avenue and like a lot of places that have big houses, Belle Meade, and I'd see these houses with no curtains, and thought to myself, 'I'd hate to live in a house with no curtains,' and then my next thought was, 'But I'd love to write a song about it!' So, I showed Alan that idea, and we ran with it."

Topping off his first decade of success as a Music Row hit writer when another of his musical heroes made one of his compositions their own, Jim draws a distinction between his decade of hits cowritten with Alan Jackson from the time Jackson was still

A Bridge That Just Won't Burn 209

unsigned and his admission that "I never had much luck writing for a particular artist, it just seemed to never really work out for me, but I badly wanted a George Jones cut. It was 1981 or 1982, and Keith Stegall and I sat down one day and said, 'Let's write a song about George,' and the first line of the song says, 'They think I'm a legend.' The song was called 'I'm a Survivor' and once it got to George, I couldn't believe it, but he was actually going to go in and cut it! Then on the day of the session, Billy Sherrill called the office and said, 'George won't say that "legend" word, is it okay if he says, "They think I'm somebody"?' And, of course, Keith and I said 'Sure!' and he recorded it. Then at some point, Waylon's brother cut that song on Johnny Paycheck and Johnny didn't have a problem singing 'They say I'm a legend . . .' [*laughs*]. They advertised that album on TV, and it sold quite a few albums, but just to have a George Jones cut. . . ."

Among the countless BMI Country Awards and Academy of Country Music Award trophies for Single and Album of the Year or CMA Single of the Year nods, Jim McBride holds his induction into the Nashville Songwriters Hall of Fame as among his proudest moments. In offering closing advice to aspiring songwriters looking to wind up in the same royal annals one day, Jim begins with the recommendation to be realistic—even if you write a hit by yourself, it still takes a team to get a hit to the top of the charts:

I've run into some brash young songwriters who swear, "I'm never giving up half of my publishing!" and I'm like "Yes, then you'll never get a deal." That's not how it works. You will give up half of your publishing if you want a writing deal. Later on in my writing career, I started giving my publishing company my ASCAP, because I got a bigger draw. That money was in my hands already, because of waiting three or six months to see what your check's going to be, that's a hard way to live. When I first moved to Nashville, even if you got a hit, it was still seven to nine months before you started seeing any money, from anybody! Banks wouldn't even loan you money, even if you had a Conway Twitty hit. Even when you get a copublishing deal, they still get a quarter of the publishing, so either way, you have to play the game if you want to get a publishing deal. If they think you're going to be an artist, they might cut you some slack on the publishing, for instance, Alan Jackson had half of his publishing starting out because he set out to be an artist. So, he had a 50/50 deal with Glen Campbell, but if you're a songwriter and you want a publishing deal, you'll do what they ask you to do.

CHAPTER 23

GENTLE ON MY MIND

· ·

Carl Jackson

"Grammy-winning producer; hit songwriter; celebrated musician and vocalist; tireless mentor and trusted friend. Carl Jackson has been called all these over his fifty-year career!" according to PBS. Jackson is a bluegrass legend as a banjo and guitar instrumentalist who is equally celebrated as a Nashville Songwriter. Practically born into the business, he remembers first finding his gift with stringed instruments before he was even ten years old: "My uncle taught me a few things on guitar and the way I finished up first learning how to play was listening to records. I just worked at it constantly, I loved to play, I always wanted to play music or baseball, and music won!"

Landing his first professional gig as a performing musician with Jim & Jesse and the Virginia Boys "when I was twelve years old, my dad took me to one of their shows in a little town in Mississippi, and they were playing in an old, little schoolhouse. It was on a Saturday night, and I remember I didn't really want to go; I wanted to stay home and listen to an Ole Miss football game, but once I got there, I loved it. During the intermission of their show, my dad just walked me backstage because there really wasn't a lot of security, struck up a conversation with one of the band, told them I played, and they wanted to listen to me play. So, I played something for them, and after the intermission, next thing I know, they put me up onstage with them!"

Knowing he was standing right where he was supposed to be, Jackson found himself at the proverbial "right place at the right time" as he watched in amazement "after the show as my dad continued conversing with them. My mom and dad were so supportive, it was such a blessing. So, my dad, who was acting as my manager I guess you'd say at that age, told them, 'Hey, if you guys are ever in need of a banjo player, please keep us in mind.' So, they took our number and told us they'd keep me in mind, and a couple of years later, when I turned fourteen, next thing you know we're getting a call where they wanted to know if my mom and dad would let me go on the road with them . . . and they did! They were absolutely wonderful people, still today some of the finest guys I know."

Finding his earliest musical mentors in band leaders Jim and Jesse, Carl was an eager student as "Jim and Jesse both took me under their wing and were so kind. But on the road, there was no drinking, no drugs, just music. They showed me so much, from how they reacted to fans, where they always had time, even if we were at a restaurant or whatever, and I saw how that made people really love them. That's the first place I learned that and then of course later on playing with Glen Campbell. Right after Jim and Jesse, I played with a gospel group called the Sullivan Family for a little while, traveled with them for almost a year playing guitar and some banjo."

Jackson's ticket into country music and songwriting fame, following his teenage stint playing with Jim and Jesse and the Virginia Boys and the Sullivan family, would arrive when he formed a short-lived bluegrass band called the Country Store, who would in turn provide his serendipitous introduction to future mentor Campbell. Jackson shares the fateful formation of the Country Store: "Back in 1973, I joined that group with my good friend Keith Whitley on guitar, Jimmy Gaudreau on mandolin, Bill Rawlings on bass, and myself on banjo. I had talked previously with Keith and Jimmy about forming a group, and one day got a call from Jimmy and so I decided that would be a great idea. I went up to Columbus, Ohio, met with the boys, and we went into a studio, turned the tape

Gentle on My Mind   213

machine on and recorded five or six things. I think we played one gig and then Keith and I saw Glen Campbell was going to be playing at the Ohio State Fair, and we both were really big fans. Glen was the biggest thing in country right then. Well, after the show on our way back to the car, we had to walk right past the backstage area, and I glanced over and saw Larry McNeely standing behind the rope. He had played banjo with Roy Acuff at the same time I was playing with Jim and Jesse, and was now playing guitar for Glen. We'd never met but I knew who he was. I didn't know he knew who I was, but when I walked over, shook out my hand and told him how much I enjoyed the show and loved his playing, he replied, 'Carl Jackson, what in the world are you doing here?!'"

In a reflection of how his playing reputation already preceded him, Jackson took the opportunity to fill his buddy in: "I introduced him to Keith and told him the whole story, and he invited us to come by the bar the next day, and so when I went back over there, we got our banjos out and were trading some tunes back and forth, and I remember Larry kept asking me to play certain things, lots of standards, then asks me to play some more difficult stuff, and then he asked me if I could play guitar, and then asked me out of the blue, 'Do you want this job?' My first reaction was to ask him, 'What do you mean?' and he said, 'I'm tired of traveling, and have been looking for someone to take my place, and you could do it.' So, I replied, 'Sure!' and he left me alone for a minute, then brought us into the next trailer over from his, and when we walked in, there sat Glen Campbell! He was a hero to me, and he proceeds to put me through the same routine of questions Larry had. At the time, on guitar, I could play all of Glen's songs, all his solos and everything. He had me play for him, and next thing, he looks over at me after I was finished and asked, 'How much would you like to make?' Me being an eighteen-year-old silly kid said, 'Oh, a million bucks, man [*laughs*]!' and next thing I know, I was in the band! Glen told me, 'Go home and get your things together, you got the job,'

214 SONGS OF NASHVILLE

and this was right before I turned nineteen years old. It was like a self-fulfilling prophecy."

MusicRow magazine would capture a portrait of the pair's unique relationship in country music history. "Carl Jackson has been acknowledged in so many ways for his remarkable talents that it has already become impossible to encapsulate his 'legendary' body of work without leaving out some pretty significant moments. Campbell was thirty-six in 1972, when he hired an eighteen-year-old Jackson to perform with him onstage. Campbell watched as Jackson concentrated heavily on his vocal and songwriting chops, as well as his musicianship, developing talents from playing banjo to producing." Taking fans back inside the first steps Glen took toward that end, "not long after I started playing with Glen, he said 'Man, we should do an album,' so we did and went in the studio, and he got me my first record deal on Capitol Records. We went in and did this instrumental album with his band backing me up and him playing guitar, it was called *Carl Jackson: Banjo Player*. That one actually did real well, especially overseas. My first original songs were banjo instrumentals, and I loved Jerry Reed and when I first decided I wanted to start writing songs with lyrics, I didn't take myself real seriously, just wrote what was in my heart that came out with the pen. All through my career, I've never really tried to sit down and write a 'bluegrass' song, I've always just tried to write the best songs I could. I've had songs recorded with a country feel and a bluegrass feel."

Coming up under Glen Campbell's wing as a songwriter, Jackson remembered as he handed in his second solo album, *Old Friends*, in 1977 that "I think Capitol thought they were going to get another instrumental album but in that time in-between the first and second albums, I had decided I was going to be much more of a songwriter. I had been focusing on it and finally got the nerve to play some songs for Glen, and he said, 'Man, these are really good! Why don't you record these?' So, that's how that album happened,

Gentle on My Mind 215

and when I really got more serious about songwriting. The way that Glen made a difference in my songwriting was just with his encouragement, he signed me as a songwriter, and I never really considered myself one, but here all of a sudden, my hero, Glen Campbell, wanted to sign me to a publishing deal. That really made a difference and gave me a lot of confidence."

During his stint playing in Glen Campbell's band for twelve years between 1972 and 1984, Carl would continue building his career and catalog, releasing albums including 1981's *Banjo Man: A Tribute to Earl Scruggs*, *Mississippi Homecoming*, and *Songs of the South*, spotlighting among its soundtrack one of his still-personal favorites with "a song I'd written about Keith Whitley, and I called 'Jesse and Me.' At the time, Keith was married to Kathy, and she and I went out to sit in the audience and watch a show he was playing with J. D., and while he was onstage, he was wearing a shirt that had a little, short, built-in collar on it, and I thought it was so cool and asked, 'Kathy, where did he get that shirt?' She told me he'd gone and seen this movie called *The Long Rider*, and Stacy Keach was playing Jesse James and wearing a shirt like that in the movie, and ever since Keith had seen the movie, 'He thinks he's Jesse James,' and that's where I got the title. So, I decided to write a song about Keith and me and how we were both pursuing our dreams. I called him 'Jesse' in the song, and he called me 'Rebel' in real life, which was my nickname."

Scoring his first US Hot Country Songs charting single in 1984 with "All That's Left for Me," Jackson would rocket into the Top 20 in 1985 with "(Love Always) Letter to Home" before Carl returned to the charts that same year with "Dixie Train"—a hit he still considers a great privilege to have cowritten with the late, great Jim Weatherly: "Jim was a great friend of mine. I had a deal on Columbia, and we got together and decided we wanted to write a nice, up-tempo thing. Jim had that title and wrote that; Jim and I wrote quite frequently back then. 'When Shadows Fall' is another

216   SONGS OF NASHVILLE

one we wrote together where sometimes a title can just inspire you, you don't have to have a story behind it to write the song. We're both believers and just decided to write a gospel song, and it worked out and won a Dove Award!"

Jackson would continue racking up Top 40 hits as his songwriting career rolled on with "Breakin' New Ground" by Wild Rose and "Put Yourself in My Place" by Pam Tillis and as the end of the 1980s approached, *Bluegrass Today* reported that "Jackson, a seven-time IMBA [International Bluegrass Music Association], three-time Grammy, and two-time Dove Award [who has] penned such crowd favorites as *Erase the Miles* and *I'm Not Over You*, among numerous others, . . . has found that his young grandson's favorite is 'Little Mountain Church House.' The sixty-nine-year-old has developed a unique bond with the ten-month-old." Writing the song for his own performance, Carl reveals that, at the time, he was thinking instead "of Dolly Parton. Ricky Skaggs at the time was getting ready to produce an album on her. I was writing for Ricky at the time, and he asked me to write something for Dolly's album. So, Dolly, being the mountain girl that she is, I just got this idea in my head about a gospel song about that little mountain church house that Dolly probably attended when she was a kid. That's how the idea came about, and then I went to the hospital to visit my friend Jim Rushing and told him about this and what he thought of this idea, and he loved it. So, we decided we'd get together after he got out and write it and we did. Then when we played it for Ricky, he liked it so much that he decided to cut it himself with the Nitty Gritty Dirt Band, and I think it's been recorded well over a hundred times."

Jackson would reach another milestone in 1992 when he took home his first Grammy for an album he recorded with John Starling and the Nash Ramblers, *Spring Training*, chuckling at the extemporaneous invitation and inspiration arriving after "John Starling, who I'd never met before, asked me to come do a show with him on a radio show, and we really enjoyed playing and singing together. So, afterward we started talking and one of us said, 'Hey, man, let's do a record together!' I know it sounds crazy, but I said, 'Okay, let's do one, but if we do one, let's win a Grammy! Let's do it right . . . [*laughs*].' So, we both were huge baseball fans, and went in and recorded this record with . . . I think there's five or six of my songs that I wrote on there, and then for the cover, we decided we were going to wear our baseball uniforms, so, that's how the title happened. Emmylou Harris was on the record with us too, which was a real treat."

Vince Gill had taken a liking by then to Jackson's songwriting style, and reached out to the songwriter with another invitation he couldn't resist. After "Vince came over to my office there on Music Row and when he came in that day, he said 'Man, we need to write something real up-tempo for my new album. . . .' Vince and I had never written together before when we got together, and I had the title 'No Future in the Past' written down in my notebook. When I started going through titles, he liked that one. We always joke with each other that we wrote that to see who could sing the highest. That day, we sat there and wrote on it for a couple hours, and then went to the West End Cooker, got something to eat, came back and wrote for another hour, and had it done. It went on to win the CMA Record of the Year 1993."

Jackson beams with equivalent pride looking back on scoring the title cut from Garth Brooks's breakout fourteen-million-selling number one Top US *Billboard* 200 and Top Country Albums Chart on *Ropin' in the Wind* with "Against the Grain," remembering the song having legs after the idea first popped up when "myself, Larry Cordle, Glen Duncan, and Bruce Bouton had been offered a deal on Capitol Records as a group, and Larry and Bruce and I got together to write a song for our project. I told you I normally write lyrics first, but this is one of the few times that I had actually written this melody, with those two modulations in it and everything, and that whole modulation sequence ahead of time, I

218   SONGS OF NASHVILLE

had that already, and I had the title 'Against the Grain.' And when Bruce and Larry came in that day, I threw it out there and played them that melody and they liked it. Once we started writing on the song, we wrote the first verse together, then I came home that same day and wrote the second verse by myself, and then Larry and I got together and wrote the third verse. How it got to Garth was our deal fell apart, and we didn't sign that deal. Bryan Kennedy was pitching songs for Ricky Scaggs over at Polygram, and of course Garth went in to record and Bryan was then looking for songs for Garth, who was a big John Wayne fan, and Bryan knew that, so he took it in, and Garth fell in love with the song, cut it and it became the first song on *Ropin' in the Wind*!"

Jackson's storied career would continue to have many future chapters to come, featuring highlights like winning his second Grammy for producing *Livin', Lovin', Losin'—Songs of the Louvin Brothers* and taking home the 2003 Grammy winner for Country Album of the Year, and in 2011, being honored by the state of Mississippi with an official Country Music Trail Marker in his hometown of Louisville and then being inducted into the Mississippi Musicians Hall of Fame. Producing hero and mentor Glen Campbell's final studio album, *Adios*, remains among his highest honors, singling out a song he wrote specifically for Campbell to perform on the project in tribute to everything the country legend had done for him and meant to him throughout a dream-come-true career Carl insists today he'd never have lived out without Campbell:

> When we got around to producing that album, there was a song called "Arkansas Farm Boy" that I specifically wrote about Glen Campbell, every word of it's true. I wrote it on a plane to Australia, and Glenn had told me about the story of the $5 gift card that led to a fortune, and how his granddaddy taught him to play in the pines, and that gave

me the idea for the song. The title "Arkansas Farm Boy" just popped in my head because Glen was from Delight, Arkansas, and he was a farm boy, one of twelve kids, and so I wrote the song, played it for Glen, he loved it, and we actually went in and did a version of it that never was released. Then when we got around to doing the *Adios* album, right after his last goodbye tour, it was such an honor that Glen wanted to do that song, because when I brought it up and we talked about it, he had Alzheimer's, and couldn't remember lyrics, but it was really wild because he remembered a good bit of that song. He hadn't forgotten the melodies at all, and I was so honored that after all that time, he still loved that song, and it got nominated for a Grammy. I'm so proud of that song, it's Glen Campbell's song, and he's family to me.

Jim Lauderdale
(Photo credit: Beck Fisher)

Larry Gatlin
(Photo credit: Jake Brown)

Carl Jackson
(Photo credit: Tracy May)

Randy Brooks
(Photo credit: Randy Brooks)

Jim McBride (Photo credit: Spirit Music Group)

Jody (left) and Jeff Stevens (Photo credit: Jake Brown)

Mark Irwin
(Photo credit: Smack Songs)

Drew Parker
(Photo credit: Make Wake Artists)

Will Weatherly
(Photo credit: CS Swanbeck)

Steve Moakler
(Photo credit: Micah McNair)

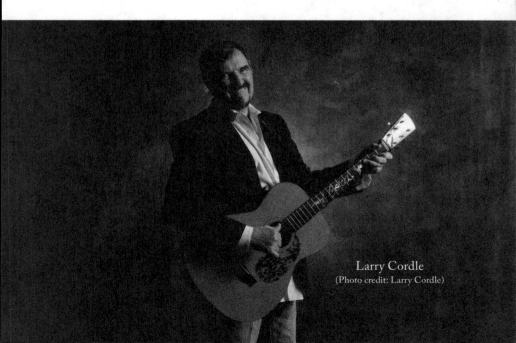

Larry Cordle
(Photo credit: Larry Cordle)

Wanda Mallette
(Photo credit: Wanda Mallette)

Don Cook
(Photo credit: Jake Brown)

John Thompson
(Photo credit: John Thompson FB)

Matt Rogers
(Photo credit: Matt Rogers)

CHAPTER 24

GRANDMA GOT RUN OVER BY A REINDEER

Randy Brooks

Every country star has a Christmas album, and Nashville Songwriters love rolling their sleeves up each year as the season approaches to come up with new twists on traditional holiday tropes, but one Christmas-themed song has proven timeless despite being played around the world on the radio over the past five decades—"Grandma Got Run Over by a Reindeer." *CBS News* has correctly spotlighted it as "one of the most popular Christmas songs ever composed."

Randy Brooks traces the roots of his comedic brand as one of the world's finest songwriting satirists back to a natural love of comedy that he remembers first arriving when "I discovered the Marx Brothers when I was ten years old, *A Night in Casablanca*, and I remember saying to myself, 'This is funny,' and I still watch them every chance I get. That was an influence on me in terms of humor. Then there was a radio show that used to piece together the hit songs of the day and tell a funny story, and I fell for Sheb Wooley's 'Purple People Eater,' Pat Boone, that might sound weird now, but I really loved his pop stuff on radio too, and Ray Stevens. A few years ago, Ray decided to record 'Grandma Got Run Over by a Reindeer' for one of his albums, and I thought 'Wow, this is great, it's come full circle for me!'"

Remembering he was drawn to songwriting just as early once he began playing guitar as a kid, Randy found that "my first songwriting attempts came with putting my own words to somebody else's melody in high school, and it was always humorous stuff. Then in high school, my brother and I along with another friend had a folk trio that played on local TV and even got to go to New York, so I was used to getting in front of people." Moving to Nashville when he was just eighteen years old, versus confirming it was in pursuit of his dream of becoming a professional songwriter, instead, Brooks confesses that "I went to Vanderbilt because it was the only college that didn't require me to write an essay. But once I was living in Nashville, I bought a reel-to-reel tape machine. I recorded demos in my apartment, and I'd go around cold-calling publishers on Music Row. After a couple of rejections, I thought, 'Well, I might as well give this up.'"

Not giving up on his dream of becoming a professional performer, Randy stuck to his guns, finding his niche and natural place onstage during "a summer job I had down in Dallas during my last two years at Vandy while working as a singing waiter at a dinner theater. There were eight of us on the waiting staff, and after we got through serving drinks, we'd go do a musical show before the play came on, singing mostly folk music. But our closing song was written by one of the guys in the group, and it got a great response, and I got to thinking, 'Well, that's a whole different thing than writing for the record industry. If I could just write for this theater,' so I wrote one called 'Getting Near the End' and we started performing my song."

Finding audiences loved the wit woven within his satiric style of songwriting, soon enough the house band took notice and "started inviting me to sit in with them and do a novelty song every once in a while. They were a Dallas-based band called Young Country, and I eventually wound up joining the group. The first song I wrote for the group was called 'Nudeness Is Rudeness,' about the era of miniskirts and see-through blouses. Then I wrote another one called 'The Garbage Monster Took My Love Away,' and what I always strove for in songs was punch lines, like every other line to try and get a laugh from people. So in the band I was playing with,

226   SONGS OF NASHVILLE

being folk and harmony oriented, we did a lot of Linda Ronstadt, Michael Martin Murphy, John Denver, and once I began writing these novelty songs for a feature spot I got once every hour. Back then in Texas, every restaurant worth its salt had a cocktail lounge with a stage for bands, and people didn't mind having a wait for a table because they were being entertained, and that's what I did about Dallas, Houston, and Austin. The thrill was getting that laugh and applause at the end of the song. It's instant love; it's great."

As the band grew in popularity in and around Texas, that audience expanded out West to a fateful set of live dates at a Hyatt Hotel lounge in Reno, Nevada, where holiday musical history would be made. Brooks recalls as if it were yesterday that "I was playing at The Hyatt on the North Shore of Lake Tahoe, and the band would drive out there from Texas and do a three-week stint. I'd never met Elmo & Patsy Shropshire, who were high energy comedy fun when they played as Elmo and Patsy. So our run ended on December 15, 1978, and they were next band to start. We were supposed to be on our way back to Texas but when we went out to leave, our band van's breaks had frozen. So we checked back into the hotel for one more night and went to the lounge to hear them. Someone told them that Young Country, the band that had preceded them, were there and they kindly invited us up to sit in with them and do some bluegrass songs that we all knew together. That was the plan, but it just so happened a casino employee who was in the lounge on a night off sent up a request on a napkin for 'Grandma Got Run Over by a Reindeer,' being familiar with me doing it. So they said, 'Go ahead,' I sang it, and right at the side of the stage, they said 'Hey, we've got a tape recorder in the dressing room, that's our kind of song. Would you come record it, we'd like to learn it,' and I was absolutely thrilled that anyone who wasn't in a group I was in wanted to sing one of my songs. I thought that was just the highest praise, so I've actually got a picture of us in the dressing room that night right after they'd recorded the song."

Grandma Got Run Over by a Reindeer   227

Taking the generations of fans who grew up with the song as part of the soundtrack of their holiday memories back inside his own of creating the song, he remembers having some grand vision: "This was initially just an exercise in parody one night when I was sitting home by myself. I got in bed with my guitar and my cowriter Johnny Walker Black and wrote the chorus and first verse. Then I thought, 'That sounds okay, if it still sounds good to me in the morning, I'll continue,' fell asleep, and in the morning, it was still very much on my mind, so while I was in the shower, I wrote verses 2 and 3 and that was it. I think sometimes the best and most successful ones come that way, you don't have to give birth, they just come out."

Crediting the late, great Merle Haggard as a roundabout inspiration and influence on the legendary song's creation, Brooks reveals that "Merle Haggard had a song on his very first Christmas album called *Grandma's Christmas Card* and it was not a sung song, it was a recitation, and grandma was an artist and every year the family waited anxiously for the arrival of the cards so they could put it up on the mantel with all the other Christmas decorations. At the time, I thought, 'Oh my gosh, this is going to be one of those country songs where in the third verse, the card's not going to come, and that's how we're going to find out that Grandma passed away.' And I was so disappointed because I love Merle Haggard, and thought that was just formula, and so I was envisioning sort of a satire spin on that when I started thinking about writing my song. I listened to his song 'Daddy Frank' too, which is sort of a template for a rhythm structure, except not wanting to use his song, if he went to the 5 chord, I went to the 4 chord, but just started using that to get in shape, and then leading from the chorus into the verse, there's a 3-chord turnaround that he used in 'If We Make It Through December' and I threw that in there. I was trying to be conspicuous in parodying Merle Haggard, and unfortunately no one ever noticed that. It wasn't obvious enough [*laughs*]."

228   SONGS OF NASHVILLE

When he then began turning his attention to thinking about his own original Christmas song's composition conceptually, Randy, breaking the legendary song's writing down in detail for readers, exclusively offers that "the first thought was, 'We're going to do this Grandma's Dead song, and in the first line, we're going to tell that she's dead, so how would grandma die at Christmastime? In a manner uniquely seasonal,' and the very first thing was 'Well, she can get hit by Santa's sleigh!' So the best way I could think of to express that succinctly was 'Grandma got run over by a reindeer, walking home from our house Christmas eve.' From there, I started thinking 'What rhymes with eve?' and 'You may think there's no such thing as Santa, but as for me and Grandpa, we believe . . .' So then I said, 'Okay, I've got a chorus, how about a verse?' and I started dredging up memories from childhood Christmases when I was a little kid, and we would go over to Aunt Carrie's house for Christmas dinner, and as soon as dinner was finished, my grandfather and his two brothers, Uncle Lewis and Uncle Henry, who became cousin Mel in the song, would go sit in the living room, unfold the card table, turn on the black-and-white TV and watch football, and they'd play pinochle, drink beer and smoke cigars, so that all made it into the song. My grandmother wore a wig that was a color not quite found in nature, so I got the wig in the song, and I do distinctly remember one night when she was leaving our house and headed home, that she was kind of tipsy, and my dad asked, 'Are you okay to drive?' which became the line about her drinking too much eggnog. She really drank bourbon, but that was to make it Christmas-y. We were a Louisville family, so bourbon was almost a religion for those relatives that drank. So all those memories made their way in."

Spotlighting some of his personal favorite lines among the countless times audiences have sung theirs back to him during live performances throughout the years, Randy begins with "writing the lines, 'She had hoof prints on her forehead, and incriminating claw marks on her back,' I was proud of those lines. I loved the line 'Should we open up her gifts or send them back?' too, I was really happy with that. If you want to take the song seriously, that is a question you would ask, which is part of what makes it funny. The lyrics came quickly when I was writing it. I'm not really a melody writer, the words usually come first, and I'll start humming something to go with it while I'm playing chords on the guitar. So that's what came out. It's really trite to come to think about it, but I started it with the 'Jingle Bell' melody and then I ended the song with 'Jingle Bells,' and I do that when I perform it."

Rushing to his next band practice with the song in hand excited to play it for his bandmates, Randy reveals that "I didn't at first even think about performing it with my band, and then when it was finished, I thought 'That would be fun to have our own Xmas song to bring out seasonally,' so then I started thinking about performing it live and the band said 'Sure.' The first time I remember playing it live, the band was on a USO Tour in Italy, and we'd gotten taken to a Rec Hall, which was not for our usual military audience but for military families, so there were kids there [*laughs*]! We were dying in front of these kids, so we pulled 'Grandma' out for the first time."

By the time Elmo and Patsy heard it, Brooks was used to the song getting a rousing reaction from the crowds he performed it for, but had no idea it would translate so naturally live as, originally, "Elmo and Patsy were just going to play it live until three months later when I got a tape in the mail. They had gone into the studio here in Nashville with just a few musicians and had made a recording of it, and then they told me their intent was to make a .45 to sell at the front of the stage. So the next level of excitement, my name will be on the record as songwriter. Then Patsy told me, 'And my dad has a publishing company, and he can publish it for you,' and I thought 'Well, that's great, every record I've seen, you have to have a publisher,' and I couldn't get one when I was in Nashville. So all that happened, and it was still just supposed to be a record sold

230   SONGS OF NASHVILLE

from the stage, and then somebody took it into a radio station in San Francisco and it got played for the first time."

What followed was a reflection of the instantly addictive chain reaction to the song listeners had whose history-making snowball *Billboard* chronicled as "it took off—first on KSFO in San Francisco, which played it as a lark, then at more and more radio stations around the country. Trigg's parents published 'Grandma' through their Tennessee gospel-music company, Kris Publishing, which meant Brooks made money every time it sold. But [the publisher], who owned the master-recording rights, turned out to be an aggressive DIY record man, recording a full-on album containing 'Grandma' and lining up distribution through big drug-store chains. In 1983, it hit number one on *Billboard*'s Christmas Songs chart, then graduated to toys, films and TV shows. Today, it's a holiday standard."

Taking fans back inside his own response to hearing it on the radio for the first time, Randy remembers that "the first time I remember hearing it on the radio, I was driving to Dallas. I was so excited, I rolled down my windows and cranked up my volume so everybody could hear it too! I always say my reaction was twofold: the thrill of hearing it on the radio but the realization that it sounded nothing like Merle Haggard [*laughs*]!" The song's adaptability to other pop culture celebrations have included being featured on *The Tonight Show*, included in a *Family Guy* episode, and even becoming the inspiration for its own cartoon on the CW Network that airs every year there and streaming on AMC. Remembering that the call of interest in a cartoon took him aback, Randy shares that "all of a sudden, there were three different entities interested in doing a cartoon, and Elmo and I met one of the producers and he did his pitch, and said, 'If you let me do this thing, it won't be cheap, it will be quality stuff, and you won't have to worry about putting your kids through college.' We went with that producer, and it runs every year on the CW Network to this day. I put

Grandma Got Run Over by a Reindeer   231

both my kids through college with the royalties from the song and cartoon [*laughs*]!"

As he leaves for another live show where no doubt he'll be living every songwriter's dream—feeling the joy of fans singing along with his songs—Randy has advice for songwriters aspiring to be in the same position themselves one day with their own original songs and sound: "I'm not a big believer in rules, so often the people we remember are the ones who broke the rules and established their own. When you're playing a song out live, you can sort of get a sense of when you're losing people, and maybe 'This song could stand to do without this verse altogether.' So, playing a new song in front of an audience can be great feedback. But the best advice I have is never miss an opportunity to play your own songs, because if I hadn't played 'Grandma' that night with Elmo and Patsy, we wouldn't be here, that's for sure!"

CHAPTER 25

TALKIN' TO THE MOON

. . . .

Larry Gatlin

For anyone who doesn't know the familiar sound of the Gatlin Brothers, the Grand Ole Opry has introduced them as the "Grammy Award-winning trio who have dazzled audiences for more than sixty years with a lifetime of noteworthy achievements in their storybook career, including a Grammy for Best Country Song ('Broken Lady'), three ACM awards for Single of the Year ('All the Gold in California'), Album of the Year (*Straight Ahead*) and Male Vocalist of the Year for Larry Gatlin, along with five nominations for CMA Vocal Group of the Year, Single, Album, and Male Vocalist of the Year. The Brothers have accumulated seven number one singles, thirty-two Top 40 records, twenty-two studio albums and five BMI 'Million-Air' Awards. For more than sixty-two years now, the Gatlin Brothers have entertained audiences in some of the world's largest venues and from some of the most iconic stages, including the Grammy Awards, the American Music Awards, the *People's Choice* Awards, the *Tonight Show with Johnny Carson*, *Oprah*, *Hee Haw*, *Love Boat*, the *Midnight Special with Wolfman Jack*, the *Merv Griffin Show*, *Solid Gold*, the *Barbara Mandrell Show* and their own variety special on ABC with '*Larry Gatlin and the Gatlin Brothers.*'"

Behind all those harmonies was group songwriter Larry Gatlin, who took his brothers' natural sibling tonality and set it to hit after hit. He remembers back to his childhood roots: "We listened to the gospel quartets as small kids. Our grandfather was a great singer and every year the Stamps-Baxter Music Company would put out a new songbook, and my grandfather would order these books, and they'd gather them up and after church on Sunday, a lot of people in the community would have these singing conventions, where everyone would go out and eat under the trees on a blanket, and Papa would lead one of these songs. I was just a child. He would take me. I've been to several when I was a kid. Then as my brothers and I started together, we would go with our parents to talent shows. I remember we won our first one in Abilene and then a second one in Odessa, and my mother would drive us to these gigs across the state and then across the country from New York to California."

After he played wide receiver for the University of Houston, Larry headed to Vegas in 1971 and joined his first nonfamily musical group as a vocal member of the gospel group the Imperials, scoring his first cuts as a songwriter when Dottie West recorded "You're the Other Half of Me" and "Once You Were Mine," helping him land his first Nashville performing gig as a background singer for Kris Kristofferson. He signed his first record deal with Monument Records in December 1973, releasing his first solo Top 40 US Country Songs Chart hit with "Sweet Becky Walker" and "Bitter They Are, Harder They Fall," before Elvis Presley took him into the Top 10 for the first time in 1974 with "Help Me," proudly pointing to the composition as among his favorites:

> Lord, do I ever remember writing that one! I'd been in town about six months, I was twenty-three, and everybody who would hear me sing would react well, but I wasn't a star yet, and I can sing. I don't mean to brag about it, but God blessed me with an incredible instrument. I'd been doing this since I was three and could sit down with a guitar and sing my ass off. So, I wasn't a star yet and it was really discouraging and that song just poured out, "Lord, help me walk. . . ."

Rain/Rainbow would brighten Gatlin's spirits substantially in 1974 when his second solo album produced his first Top 20 hit with "Delta Dirt" while other stars helped quickly establish him around town and the country charts as a known songwriting commodity courtesy of Jim Ed Brown's "Get Up I Think I Love You," "Rain" by Kris Kristofferson & Rita Coolidge, and his first number one hit with Johnny Rodriguez's rendition of "I Just Can't Get Her Out of My Mind," winning a Grammy in 1976 for Best Country Song, "Broken Lady," which Gatlin remembered writing while on the road after "I was sitting in a cab coming from on the way to the Chicago airport. We had done a CBS promotion party up in Chicago with Herbie Hancock and some other cats, and I was in the back of the cab on the way to the O'Hare International Airport, and I started hearing this beautiful harmony, and just sang 'She's a broken lady . . .' and wrote the rest of the song from there."

Following the release of his third studio album, *High Time* in 1976, the trio of brothers made their recorded debut on *Larry Gatlin with Family & Friends,* which produced a new run of hits with "Warm and Tender," the Top 5 hit "Statues Without Hearts," and "Anything but Leavin'" off the *Love Is Just a Game* LP, which produced back-to-back number three hits with "I Don't Wanna Cry" and "Love Is Just a Game." By the time his brothers joined him in town, their winning signature vocal sound became a blend that he explains had evolved from "when we were kids. Growing up, I was singing the lead part, and our sister, LaDonna, was singing an octave higher than the tenor part and Steve was singing and we were singing four-part harmony. So, that was kind of established and then it was only natural because, when we came here, our sister decided she didn't want to do it and wanted to go back to sing gospel music. So, then we sat down and restructured who was going to sing what because LaDonna had sung the high part, Rudy had sung the low part, and Steve sang the bass part. It was natural that I sang the lead part, because I was the songwriter and I'd been here for a couple of years, and they were still in school. That's the reason they didn't come in the first place. That became the Gatlin sound that we do."

The Gatlin Brothers would prove that point when they rocketed to number one in 1978 with "I Just Wish You Were Someone I Love," where Larry credited Coach Darrell Royal and Willie Nelson's legendary golf tournament as ground zero for the song's inspiration, remembering that "we were all sitting around the pool with guitars playing, and we had a great time. Then a couple weeks later, I had these old saddlebags I brought with me on tour that I put all my junk in, and I was cleaning one of them out and saw this piece of paper. It was an envelope from the golf tournament where I'd written 'I just wish you were someone I love.' So, we were in Vegas the week the song went to number one, and Johnny Lee called me and said, 'Do you remember that I gave you that idea?' I said, 'What?' and he told me we were drunk as a bunch of goats, sitting around the pool talking about it, and I didn't even remember. First of all, you have to understand he was laughing about it. I said I don't remember it. So, I told him, 'Johnny, I'm going to look through my stuff and I'm gonna find the best idea that I have and I'm going to give it to you!' and I did."

Gatlin would continue writing hits for his own group and other artists heading into the end of the 1970s and early 1980s with "Night Time Magic," which peaked at number two, the Top 20 hit "Do It Again," the Top 10 hit "I've Done Enough Dying Today" all from the *Oh Brother* LP while the lead single off his next studio album, *Straight Ahead*, with "All the Gold in California" would earn Gatlin his next number one smash on the US Hot Country Songs Chart. Reflective of just how many country hits get written not in writing rooms but in motion on the road, Larry shares his memory within the legendary song's creation: "In 1978 I was stuck in a traffic jam at the Hollywood Bowl in LA. Right in front of me was a Mercury station wagon with Oklahoma plates, pots and pans,

236 SONGS OF NASHVILLE

kids' bags, boxes. I looked at that and my internal dialogue, which almost always goes external, I said, 'These poor Okies remind me of the Joad family in *Grapes of Wrath*. They're going to come out to California and they're going to, you know, they're going to find out all too quickly that all the gold in California is in a bank in the middle of Beverly Hills in somebody else's name. I wrote that down. I had a pencil, wrote it down on the Hertz Car Rental slip."

Gatlin's songwriting gifts would continue to decorate the charts with another era of hits throughout the 1980s as Larry Gatlin and the Gatlin Brothers over "Take Me to Your Lovin' Place," "The Midnight Choir," "Takin' Somebody with Me When I Fall," "We're Number One," "It Don't Get No Better Than This," "Wind Is Bound to Change," "What Are We Doin' Lonesome," "She Used to Sing on Sunday," "Sure Feels Like Love," "Almost Called Her Baby by Mistake," "Easy on the Eyes," "Denver," "The Lady Takes the Cowboy Every Time," and "Nothing but Your Love Matters." Others included "Runaway Go Home," "She Used to Be Somebody's Baby," "Talkin' to the Moon," "From Time to Time (It Feels Like Love Again)," "Changin' Partners," "Love of a Lifetime," "Alive and Well," "When She Holds Me," "I Might Be What You're Looking For," "Number One Heartache Place," "Boogie and Beethoven," and arguably the biggest hit of the era with "Houston (Means I'm One Day Closer to You)"—so popular it spent fifteen weeks on the country music charts. Larry counts it to date as among his favorite songwriting sojourns:

> That's a crazy ass story. You're not gonna believe what I'm about to tell you. We had done the Nebraska State Fair, and the guys got on the buses and left to go to Cheyenne, Wyoming. I had to do an interview in Omaha, then Denver. I was driving up to Cheyenne and started singing "Cheyenne means I'm one day closer to you, it's just another day on the tour." By the time I got to Cheyenne,

I'd finished the song, taught it to my brothers, and Steve said, "Man, that's terrible! We don't have time to learn the whole song, we're going to Houston tomorrow to sing at the Houston Rodeo. So, won't you put that little two-step to it. . . ." I did that, and we sang it the next night at the rodeo for the largest crowd I've ever seen at a rodeo on the face of the earth, and the crowd loved it! I've been lucky to have two in the Top 100 Country Songs and have had a very lucky life in the music business as both a songwriter and artist performing with my brothers. I couldn't ask for more.

CHAPTER 26

BRAND NEW MAN

Don Cook

When country music celebrates its heroes, that conversation never happens without not just a mention but a study of the influence superstar duo Brooks & Dunn has had over the past four decades. *Billboard,* in 2024, announced that the "Country Music Hall of Famers are set to bring their high-octane live show and stacked arsenal of hit songs to arenas in Texas, North Carolina, Illinois, and more in 2025," highlighting their iconic history that "for more than three decades, Kix Brooks and Ronnie Dunn have staged concerts that are essential viewing for country music devotees, thanks to their energetic performance style, nearly two dozen number one *Billboard* Hot Country Songs chart hits (many of which they wrote), and Dunn's always formidable lead vocals." In further measuring their legacy of singular achievements in country music, TasteofCountry.com has certified them as "the top-selling duo of all time and one of the most awarded acts in the genre."

A core member of the creative team behind the scenes, both as cowriter of many of their classic hits and the producer of the majority of them, Don Cook reveals: "When we did the first record, we had no idea if it was going to be accepted. I remember us sitting around thinking, 'Who are we going to direct this record at?' and we decided—because Ronnie's from Louisiana, Kix was born in Texas and grew up there too, and I'm from Texas—if we can just make a record that will appeal to country artists in those three states, we'll be okay."

Recognizing the superstar potential of their hit-making combination in action the first day they got together in the writing room to compose what would become the group's first number one hit, "My Next Broken Heart," Cook remembers quickly seeing the chemistry of the three men. As a trio, they lit up one another inspirationally. Sharing the same sonic and stylistic vision for the new territory they wanted to carve out in country music together, Don points to the latter hit as evidence they'd captured true musical lightning in a bottle after "we wrote that song the day Kix and Ronnie and I met. My mother was visiting, and we'd heard some tapes of Ronnie, but we wanted to get together and decided we'd try to write something and see how it felt. So, Ronnie came over to my house, and I had this downstairs where I had a music room and some recording stuff, and we wrote that song really fast, in a couple hours. Now, my mom was the absolute, most hardcore country fan and supporter of mine. She'd go up to artists in airports and say, 'You know, your career would be better if you'd cut one of my son's songs [*laughs*]!' So, we wrote that song, and Ronnie came up at one point out of the music room while my mother was sitting right by the front door and he introduced himself, and she said, 'I'll see you at the CMA Awards!'"

Arriving in Music City from the Lone Star State in the mid-1970s with the ambition at first to become a recording star in his own right, Cook remembers that "I had a band called Texas in Nashville. Harold Shedd was our first producer and ended up producing the group Alabama. But I'm not a very good singer, so I just shifted over, because I played bass and guitar and played on a lot of demo sessions until I was making enough money that I could make a living." Cook got his foot further in the door toward signing his first publishing deal "when I was twenty-two years old after a guy named Bobby Bond heard me and took me to meet Don Gant. He'd just started working at Acuff-Rose Publishing, and Don loved my songs and gave me a deal. Don was the guy that

240 SONGS OF NASHVILLE

mentored and influenced me the most, and when he left and went to ABC Records, and I did a lot of writing but didn't accomplish much, had a couple cuts and one chart record that Don produced on Kitty Wells, a song called 'Bobby.' That was my first time winning an award for a song I'd written; it won an ASCAP award back in 1974."

Finding he felt at home in the writers room as he did out on the road, Cook began developing his unique pedigree early on that would aid him consequently in his future role as Brooks & Dunn's primary cowriter and producer: "I was at Acuff-Rose for four years as a writer, but was playing at Opryland, and went on the Opryland tour to Russia as the bass player, and a high-tenor singer in a bluegrass band. I played bass for Tennessee Ford, and I was more of a musician than a writer, just because I was struggling to make a living, and didn't really have an active champion at the publishing company. So, when Don quit ABC and went to Tree Publishing in 1976, he called up and said, 'Why don't you come over here and write for me?' I couldn't believe it and was so excited! He hadn't even heard any of my latest songs, but after I went over and played him some, he said, 'I want you here.' So, I was the first or second guy to be signed to Tree when he was working there, and in a year's time, I think I got eleven or twelve songs cut, and one of them ended up being a Top 5 single on Barbara Mandrell that allowed me to quit doing anything but write songs. Curly Putman and Harlan Howard both ended up being mentors of mine, too."

Following his first Top 40 hit on the US Hot Country Songs Chart with Bobby Wright's rendition of "Lovin' Someone on My Mind" in 1973, Don's next appearance on the chart would be in the Top 5 with Barbara Mandrell's "Tonight." He continued cranking them out throughout his first era of hit-making in the 1970s and 1980s with the number three hit "Cryin' Again" by the Oak Ridge Boys, the number one smash "Lady Lay Down" and "Baby, You're Something" by John Conlee, the number one hit "Somebody's Gonna Love You" by Lee Greenwood, the number two hit "I've

Been Wrong Before" by Deborah Allen, the Top 10 hits "The Power of Love" by Charley Pride, and "Working Without a Net" by Waylon Jennings, and more chart-toppers like "Small Town Girl" by Steve Wariner, penning the Top 5 smashes "Julia" and "I Wish I Was Still in Your Dreams" by Conway Twitty, rounding out the decade with his eighth number one hit in a row in 1989 with "Who's Lonely Now" by Highway 101.

By the time Don Cook found himself sitting down with Kix Brooks and Ronnie Dunn as a trio to write what would become their first number one off of the album of the same title with "Brand New Man," Don still remembers "one of my greatest memories as a songwriter is sitting at a table at my house and the three of us singing that song in harmony and hearing the chorus sung with three parts. It was so chilling! Those two guys had started that song, and they couldn't get it off the launchpad. They'd started that song the first week they met each other, but after about a year and we'd already picked all our songs for the first album, we had one more writing session before we were set to start tracking what turned out to be the *Brand New Man* album, and they had that song they couldn't make it come alive. I came up with the line in the chorus, 'Born to love again, I'm a brand new man,' and I kind of pulled the chorus together and when we sang it. We called Tim DuBois and said, 'We have one more song we want to play you,' so he invited us up to his office, and we played it for him, and his reaction was 'Holy shit!' He got the whole Arista staff together and said, 'Okay, guys, play this for him,' and we sang that song for all of them. They went berserk, and then Tim said, 'Well, if you don't screw that up in the studio, that will be your first single.'"

Drawing off the natural creative energy of both Brooks & Dunn as they cowrote cuts like the aforementioned "Brand New Man" and "My Next Broken Heart" alongside the Top 10 career-making smashes "Lost and Found," Cook in offering his reflective insight into what both stars brought to the table, begins with "Kix, who is one of the greatest sources of human energy on the earth. When we first got to know each other, we both realized we were both really work-every-day kind of songwriters, but we worked so hard we could declare a holiday and put our guitars down and head to a golf course and finish the song on a golf cart. We had a great friendship. Ronnie's a great collaborator and writer too. The thing about Ronnie, for me, is when you sit in a room with somebody who can sing as well as he can, the problem you have is quality control because everything he sings has a certain gravitas, and you have to figure out 'Is that really good enough?' because it really sounds good! One of Ronnie's greatest gifts, along with being a great singer and great writer, is Ronnie really knows what he can sound good singing. Ronnie really knows what songs work for him."

By then, Cook had become an expert at creating radio-quality versions of his own songs while even still in the demo stage, recalling that as he began translating that skill set to the studio in what effectively became his audition for the role of producer, "when we did the record, first of all, several of the tracks were the demos that Kix and I did, so we just really did about six or seven new tracks! So, we didn't do demos on Brooks & Dunn, we didn't need to, we all understood what it was going to sound like. Part of my ability as a writer is I can write for a band; I know how to write for a particular band. So, starting with them from the beginning of the group is what was so fun about it. We cut the first album at Tree, and then finished it at a studio called The Castle. Seven million albums sold, and half the record was done at a demo studio!"

Putting Brooks & Dunn on the map as a headlining arena act overnight, they had no time to waste, writing the second album while they were still on the road promoting the first, giving Don the opportunity to see how the songs were playing with the crowd each night to keep his finger on the pulse of what fans wanted to hear, explaining that "when they played live, I'd walk around in the audience and look at people's reactions to songs. If you walk around a gig like that, you can see what songs people really love, and you can see the ones where they're not really feeling it. My whole thing—because I was on the road writing with them as they were getting more popular—was about feeding off the energy of the brand" versus partying the night away once they came offstage. Cook, Brooks, and Dunn instead channeled their creative high into the music. Cook smiles at his memory that, as they wrote for the aptly titled *Brand New Man*:

> They'd be so wired when they'd get offstage in those early days that we'd work on songs and take the energy and put it into songs. With Kix, the collaboration's just about high energy. He raises mine, and his is so high that all this stuff just comes flying out of this fountain, and you have to quickly grab pieces of it and decide what's useful and what's not, and a lot of collaborations were not like that for me. Where we'd just sit there and struggle, with Kix, you have to be receptive, and collaborating is 90 percent receptivity and knowing when you've heard something that's great.

That receptivity helped earn the band their next multiplatinum, *Hard Workin' Man*, with more than five million copies sold based on the strength of smashes like "We'll Burn That Bridge," which peaked at number two on the *Billboard* Hot Country Songs Chart and cracks Don up to this day looking back on the fact that it marked the first hit he ever wrote "on the phone! Ronnie Dunn and I wrote it while he was on the road and I was sitting at my house and we were just talking on the phone, and he told me this idea, and I got a guitar and started playing it on the phone. I was sitting in front of my computer, and was an early adopter of Bank Street Writer, so we wrote the whole song right there. Then when

244 SONGS OF NASHVILLE

he got back to town, we immediately went in and did a demo of it because the feel was so viable. The remarkable thing is, to go from just an idea at my house to me being on the bus while they were growing from a touring band into an industry, I went out with them a lot." Back on the road with the band soon thereafter, Cook points to the number one smash "That Ain't No Way to Go" as another music-in-motion moment where the song was written "in a hotel room in New Mexico. A big reason I went on the road with them a lot is because they didn't want to write at home as they were on tour so much. Ronnie had the title for that one, and if Ronnie had a little piece like that, he'd just sit and start playing it, and we'd sit down and write it."

To no one's surprise, the band kept on the rise with the release of their third studio album in as many years with the three-million-selling *Waitin' on Sundown*, which hit number one on the *Billboard* Top Country Albums Chart, driven once again by Cook's compositional contributions, in this case to the hit "You're Gonna Miss Me When I'm Gone," written once again on the road, but Don reveals not intended for the band to record: "We were in Vancouver and for some reason, we thought 'Let's write a song for Rod Stewart.' That was our motivation, and then we realized, 'Hey, this is a great Brooks & Dunn song too!' What I thought was, we were all influenced by the Eagles and classic rock music, but we were writers in a country genre. A lot of people say now, 'Jason Aldean and Luke Bryan are doing rock tracks.' Well, that's what we were doing too. They were rock-level energy tracks."

Cook took home the Country Music Association Song of the Year award in 1995 for his production work on Tracy Lawrence's number one smash "Time Marches On," which he not surprisingly cowrote, along with other hits like "Mama Don't Get Dressed Up for Nothing" off the 1996 double-platinum release *Borderline* LP, and 1998's two-million-selling *If You See Her*. Brooks & Dunn recorded their rendition of a Cook classic, "Born and Raised in Black and White," which the Highwaymen—the supergroup comprising Johnny Cash, Willie Nelson, Waylon Jennings, and Kris Kristofferson—had first recorded on their 1990 debut, and took the group to the top as a songwriter in 2000 with "Only in America" off the group's number one *Billboard* Hot Country Albums Chart topper *Steers & Stripes*, confessing at the top of his recollection of its creation that the song still brings him pride to hear, not merely because of its inherent patriotism but because "it's hard to write a patriotic song that isn't just stupid, it's really hard. What was great about that song was the inner stories, that school bus driver and the couple that moved to California to be stars and they may not be, but at least they got the shot. I wrote that with Kix Brooks and Ronnie Rogers. I was doing some writing with Ronnie, and Kix called me and said, 'We're going to do an album called *Steers & Stripes*, and we need some kind of patriotic-feeling track to go on it. We don't have one yet.' So, we just sat down and wrote that song, and we wrote it at Kix's farm, and the strange thing about that song is, those guys recorded it early in 2001, and it was their current single in the Top 10 when 9/11 happened, and people thought it had been a response to it."

Cook continued producing hits for country stars including Alabama, Shenandoah, Billy Gilman, Lonestar, Tracy Lawrence, Rick Trevino, and Conway Twitty throughout the 2000s, and with Brooks & Dunn's legacy coming full circle in appreciation in the 2020s, *USA Today* featured coverage of the "musical history" the trio made together in song and in the studio over "more than thirty million albums and winning more than eighty industry awards, including two Grammys." *Variety* in a deeper dive has affirmed the status of Nashville legends is due after "twenty-three number one records, album sales in the octuple digits and more Country Music Association and Academy of Country Music awards than any other act [Brooks & Dunn] can stake a convincing claim as country music's premier duo, past or present. In the course of their career, they have changed the conception of the country duo as well."

Reflecting on the key part he played in helping to create that country music history, Don Cook in closing points to two favorite memories made along the way as measures of how much it means to him that his songs have meant so much to so many millions of fans: "There's never an experience with the song 'Brand New Man' to equal the moment we sat in my music room and sang it in three-part harmony. Thinking about it gives me the chills, but hearing it on the radio, on the Grammys, at a restaurant, doesn't matter, there's never a greater feeling than hearing it the first time. My other is going out in an audience with twenty thousand people and hearing everybody singing your songs at the same time! Just look down a row and see a hundred people singing the words to your song is an amazing feeling!"

CHAPTER 27

PLAY IT AGAIN

Jeff Stevens and Jody Stevens

When the Country Music Hall of Fame knows your name, you've made it pretty far in a game that few players stay in for as long as legendary songwriter Luke Bryan and producer Jeff Stevens have. Stevens, a West Virginia native, recalls his childhood. He discovered a passion for performing as a boy, when he and his brother, Warren, received guitars for Christmas. Because their father was a dreamer, Stevens says, the boys entered talent shows and formed a band with their friend Terry Dotson. Jeff takes fans personally back inside his scrapbook of memories from a family musical journey and dream that began

when I was eight years old in 1968 and my dad bought my brother, Warren, and I a couple of cheap $30 acoustic guitars, and they proceeded to make country music stars out of us immediately! I grew up in Allen Creek, West Virginia, and grew up hearing what was on the radio, everyone from Porter Wagoner to Buck Owens, Dolly Parton, anybody that was out in the '60s. Dad wouldn't allow us to listen to any rock, and he didn't listen to any rock, but he was into country music and I went back as far as my dad did because he also listened to Hank Williams and Carl Smith. I'm a huge Carl Smith fan, so really I was listening to pretty much everything from the early '50s up through the late '60s when I first started. I sang in church, and me and my brother were really the only musical ones in our family, and even our extended family. My mother is very artistic with cloth and yarn, and she's eighty-one now and nonstop, but back then, she sewed us up suits, and we put glitter on our boots, and that was a way for her to be involved creatively.

The Stevens Brothers became something of a novelty act while still in their pre- and early teens as they found themselves sharing stages with the likes of "Charley Pride and Bill Anderson and Willie Nelson, just anybody who was any kind of artist out of Nashville back then, we opened shows for. We were just this cute little couple of boys who would get up there and play. My dad was our manager and was pushing us and had us on television shows and all that stuff. I finally came to Nashville for the first time in 1975 when I was sixteen years old, and by then, our band—the Stevens Brothers—was playing a mixture of country and rock and had started to write our own songs. We'd won a talent show that had been sponsored by local radio stations, Kings Island amusement park, and CBS Records here in Nashville. So, we won the local contest in Charleston, West Virginia, and then went to the next round at King's Island, where there were three full days of competition, and we won it! I couldn't believe it, because there were other bands that were better than us, but I knew how to put on a show. I imitated Ernest Tubb and Elvis, and we played an original song, and some covers, it was like a twenty-minute set, but I'd already been playing and performing at that point for eight years."

Pushing toward their dream with a mix of the kind of grit and grind that a farmer needs for a successful harvest, Jeff points to his own decision after "finishing high school and going to a couple years of college that we all committed to quit whatever else we were doing, hit the road and make it in country music. So, we played the first four or five years in the '80s all over the road in

America, anywhere that would hire us! We actually had objects thrown at us, and I've had everything from the typical beer bottles to panties, I learned early on how to read an audience. We would drive there and play, and somewhere in the midst of all that, I was writing songs. I wrote my earliest songs with a buddy I met in high school, Terry Dotson. He was in my band, and we just kept writing together and knew we were pretty good at it. At some point, around 1983, my brother—who had taken over management duties at the time—started sending our tapes to Nashville to anybody who would accept tapes. There were a lot more accepting back then, and I'd never heard of anybody on a cold tape ever getting anything recorded, but there was a fella who'd been managing Alabama named Larry McBride. We'd originally sent him a tape of the band because we'd heard he'd parted ways with Alabama, and we thought 'Maybe he's looking for a group!' It turned out he wasn't looking for a new group to manage because he was already putting one together at the time called Atlanta, and he heard one of our songs, 'Atlanta Burned Again Last Night' and they recorded it!"

Stevens's first lesson was on the difference between getting played on radio and getting paid for it. He looks back from the publishing empire he's built today and quips: "I didn't even know how to get paid; we didn't know how to do that back then [*laughs*]! I had joined BMI [Broadcast Music, Inc.] around 1976 or '77 and didn't know how to register anything, nothing like that. So, when he recorded our song, we'd been on the road all the time, struggling hard, no money, power being turned off, three children. It was a mess! I had a Ford Pinto, and every Tuesday, one *Billboard* magazine would come into the state of West Virginia, and it came into a little newsstand in Charleston. On Tuesdays, I'd drive in, and didn't have the money to buy that copy of *Billboard* but would stand there and read it. I remember telling them the first time, "It's forty on the chart!" Seeing the song on the country's singles chart and his name underneath the song as songwriter became a

250 SONGS OF NASHVILLE

road marker for Stevens as he continued touring as the front man of Jeff Stevens and the Silver Bullets throughout the 1980s, feeling he finally hit a bit of pay dirt as a songwriter after

> driving into town every week to look at the newest *Billboard* issue, and it kept climbing the charts, and it was blowing our minds, you know! We couldn't believe it, then we started hearing it on the radio, and it ended up being a Top 10 hit. Then six months later, Atlanta ended up recording another one of my songs, and it was a much bigger hit, "Sweet Country Music," which became a three-million-selling award winner in 1984. We made some money out of those songs, which was a relief. We were focused on becoming a major-label-signed country band. It helped out a little bit though, there weren't as many country radio stations as there are today, but it was a hell of a lot better than what I was making before, basically not even breaking even. Our band had a thirty-foot semitruck full of gear, and we had a station wagon or Suburban along with that, and we traveled all over the US just playing, and hadn't made any money till then.

Signing his first major label deal as an artist in the mid-1980s with Atlantic America, Jeff Stevens and the Silver Bullets' album *Bolt Out of the Blue* released in 1986, hitting his first positions in the Hot Country Songs Chart's Top 100 with singles including "You're in Love Alone" and covers of "Darlington County" by Bruce Springsteen and "Geronimo's Cadillac," and then releasing a second studio album in 1990 with their self-titled follow-up. Stevens considers it all to be invaluable experience, helping him see the reality that even though an artist signs with a major label, it doesn't mean surefire success: "Then nothing happened with the record, it never got above 40 on the charts, and we didn't have enough money to

Play It Again   251

fund ourselves going back on the road again. [The years] 1986 to 1992 [were] the toughest part of my life and my family's life. I wasn't writing anything, my confidence was gone, and I was fighting tooth and nail with the head of the label. So, I lost everything, I mean everything. Whatever we had was gone, and I even tattooed my wedding ring on my finger because I lost it to the pawnshop back then. I lost every guitar I had, and from 1987 to about 1990, I didn't have any guitars. That's after you've written hits, I didn't have anything to write with! So, I didn't write anything. Then in 1990, I remember Rick Blackburn, who had just taken over Atlantic, called me up out of the blue, and I was still signed to them technically, but just thought it was over because nobody had talked to me in two years. So, he brought me into his office, and said, 'Man, I love the way you sound, and I think you're a star. I'm going to make you a star, and we're going to make another record on you.' Nelson Larkin coproduced that self-titled record as well, and Rick signed me to do one more record, which never saw the light of day, but this time Keith Stegall produced it."

A connection would wind up turning Jeff's all-too-common down-on-his-luck story on its head—"On that record, I started to learn watching Keith, saw how he did things, and he was producing Alan Jackson at that point, so I was paying attention to how he put a record together in the studio. I had made two records before, and the A&R [artists and repertoire] process—which is primarily song selection—in those records was a joke, there was none and it's absolutely the most important piece of the puzzle in making a record! I think I saw how meticulous he was with choosing the right material. I knew it was important before, but when you're young and a fragile artist, you're so confused that you don't know which way's up or down. Personally, me having been through that thing that I see basically every artist go through, I've been through it, I know what it's like, and I use that. So, that record brought me back out off the street again, basically. In late

252 SONGS OF NASHVILLE

1992 or early 1993, I decided I'd had enough with my record deal. I was signed to Warner Chappell Publishing as a songwriter, and I'd been there about nine months total, and about six months since John Anderson cut one of my songs. At that point, my artist career was a fucking mess, and everything that could be done wrong was done wrong, on my part and everybody else's around me. It's how I've learned to help quite a few artists, because I know all of the pitfalls, I think I've fallen in all of them. So, with that John Anderson cut, I got to thinking, 'I have cash coming in the door, and here I am writing a couple songs for Warner Chappell, and one gets cut by one of the hottest guys out at the time.' John Anderson had just had a hit with 'Seminole Wind,' and so one day I made a decision, walked into my record label, got down on my knees and said, 'I want out.'"

Effectively trading one dream for another, Jeff knew he was on the right path as a songwriter after John Anderson's cut of "I Fell in the Water" peaked in the Top 20, followed by Blackhawk scoring a Top 10 hit with "Down in Flames" and Alabama finally taking him to his first number one hit with "Reckless," a moment of truth he still holds among his fondest musical memories from a seven-decade career when

> one day about six o'clock in the evening. It was spring-time, 1994. I still had no money, and was renting this funky old house I had my family living in. I went out in the front yard, sat down on a lawn chair, and turned the radio on. In the background, I suddenly heard a song I'd written called "Reckless" by Alabama come on the radio for the first time. When I'd first written that song, I had six months left on my publishing contract, and I knew Warner Chappell wasn't going to keep me around just for the fun of it. I felt this wave coming in and all the shit going out, and one day decided to walk into a fella's

office I'd been afraid to walk into named Michael Clark. He'd written "Slow Hand" for the Pointer Sisters and "Come On In" for The Oak Ridge Boys. He looked like the big hot top dog there, I didn't really know a lot about him or any of the other writers there, but he had his own room there and his own gear, and was the first person in Nashville certainly to record with a computer.

This was in 1994, and when I walked in, quaking in my boots, I said, "Man, I've got a song idea for us. Would you write it with me?" and he goes "Sure, yeah!" He looked like Burt Reynolds with white hair smoking a pipe, and I thought he'd laugh at me because my confidence was bolstered a little by the John Anderson thing, but nothing was working up till then. But I felt this urgency, and knew I knew what I was doing, but wasn't relying on myself. So, I spit out the title, it was called "Down in Flames." We wrote it first that day and I sang the demo while he produced the track. I remember we brought in Doyle Grisham to do pedal steel on it, and three or four days later Blackhawk recorded it! They'd heard it and went crazy over it, and it was a Top 10 hit on their debut album. On the strength of that, Michael Clark and I went straight back in the room together just a month or so later and wrote "Reckless," and I can't stress how much Alabama meant to me. I had done shows with them in the early '80s, knew what they were and loved what they did, they were the new energy. I remember I wrote part of that song in my car driving home one day, handed those little bits of lyrics over to Clark and we started working on it. We had an incredible demo, my voice over top of that track that he did, I used to jokingly call him the first "Track Guy," but that song went on to hit number one!

When I heard it on the radio for the first time, I remember I was looking out over the horizon, and there were some homes on it and the sky was turning some colors, and then all of a sudden, everything started turning colors. I never did LSD, I did just about everything else you can do to yourself, but had never tried acid, but everything started turning colors! It was like I had gained my purpose! So, right then I remember thinking to myself, "This is my opportunity to be who I am, do what I do, and write hits, and if I don't, I'm out of here."

Firing on all creative cylinders, Stevens knew this was a shot he couldn't afford to miss, and so aimed again for the top, writing what would become back-to-back chart-toppers recorded by country's undisputed heavyweight champ at the time, George Strait, who made number one smashes out of "Carried Away" and "Carrying Your Love with Me," with the songwriter pointing to the latter as an especially personal favorite from his songwriting catalog because "that song was inspired by just my life. I'm from West Virginia, and when I was a boy and we would travel somewhere—and we did a fair amount of traveling to these shows—a couple times, we'd go to Myrtle Beach, and any time I was in the back seat of the car, I'd look at trucks. I loved semis and big rigs as a boy, and knew all the names of the trucks, models like International Transtar, like some kids knew race cars, it was just something I did as a kid. And when I was writing that song, it was a combination of that sort of being gone / truck-driving mentality, and with musicians, a lot of it's the same thing. I was gone for years, my son Jody—with whom I coproduce Luke Bryan's records—I wasn't home when he was born. So, I'm an original old road dog, and my wife, her dedication, I used to call her 'Little Mrs. Optimistic,' so it's basically the song of my life, although Bogart contributed heavily on that. I've seen

Play It Again   255

a couple stats where they say it's in the Top 5 of George's biggest songs as far as revenue."

Putting Jeff on the proverbial map as one of the hottest new songwriters on Music Row after true country royalty, he'd round out the 1990s with other hits, including 1996's number three hit "Big Love" for Tracy Byrd and 1998's Top 10 "I Wanna Feel That Way Again," scoring his third Top 5 hit for George Strait with 1998's "True" and stay just as present on radio and the country charts throughout the early 2000s with "The Look" by Jerry Kilgore, "If You Ever Feel Like Lovin' Me Again" by Clay Walker, "Highway Sunrise" by Rhett Akins, surging back to number one in 2004 with a smash hit for Tim McGraw in "Back When."

Stevens underscores the importance of cowriting in a successful career as a Nashville Songwriter. While Stevens had written hits by himself, he was grateful for the day that "I met Stan Lynch at one of these songwriting camps Warner Chappell had started. At first, I thought it was a joke, and Buddy Jewell was there and Stan Lynch and me and Mark Green, so it was a lot of fun. Nothing came of it as far as bona fide hits, but Stan and I just struck up a friendship, and talk about a guy with experience! God, in the studio, he'd either produced or recorded with Tom Petty and the Heartbreakers, Bob Dylan, Roy Orbison! So, I just loved being around him. He'd come up from Florida and we'd write songs together. 'Back When' we cowrote with Stephanie Smith. She saw a snake in her house and the three of us were supposed to write that day, and she couldn't get rid of the snake, so I told her, 'Maybe me and Stan can come over and see if we can flush this snake out of your house.' So, we went over there, couldn't find the snake, come back over to my office at Warner Chappell, and by this time, I didn't think we'd be able to write anything after spending two or three hours looking for that snake [laughs]! There was no vibe, and her phone rang, and it was a critter catcher she'd called, and when she hung up the phone, I told her, 'You didn't have to call a critter catcher, you could have done what my grandma did when I was a kid, chopped the snake's head off with a hoe! She used to do it all the time, back when a hoe was a hoe.' Well, when I said that last line, Stephanie's eyes got big as silver dollars and she said, 'Let's write that,' so we literally wrote that song in about an hour!"

It was the mid-2000s when Jeff Stevens would encounter his next diamond in the rough that he helped polish into one of the biggest country music stars in modern history when he took a chance and decided to cowrite with an unknown Georgia singer-songwriter named Luke Bryan, regarding it still today as "such a pivotal moment in my life, I remember it like it was yesterday. Kerri Edwards, who is now his manager, at the time was his publisher there at Murrah Music, run by Roger Murrah. Kerri had called me up and said, 'I know you don't write with a lot of new writers,' and I didn't. To be honest, I've never really subscribed to the whole Nashville thing of trying to write with them young, it's just not my speed, man. I'm not much into the political thing, but she sent me a CD with some songs on it, and one of them had already been recorded by Travis Tritt, and another song on there was titled 'Good Directions,' which Billy Currington recorded first before Luke, and it became a monster hit, ASCAP Song of the Year. By then, I had a writing room at a house over here on Music Row, so after I heard that, I called Luke's publisher back and said, 'Yeah, I'll write with him.' I remember I was sitting there, and this kid walks in with this huge grin and his feet several feet off the ground, so to speak, and he sat down and said, 'I think I got us an idea!' and he takes off on me. So, I thought 'Shit!' grabbed a guitar and here I'm supposed to be the more seasoned songwriter, and we wrote a song called 'Baby's on the Way' that day, and I looked at him and said, 'Dude, I've had some luck with George Strait, I'll demo it and we'll get it over to Tony Brown and see if we can't get a George Strait cut!' So, that's the way we left it."

By then an experienced demo producer, Stevens confesses that even once he'd begun cowriting with Luke Bryan, early on, "there was no talk of producing him yet." Still, Stevens saw something extra special in Bryan, and he took yet another gamble "when we demoed the song we'd written a few days later, and Luke came up to me during the session and asked me, 'Do you mind if I sing a version?' and I said, 'Sure.' I'd recorded my version, and then he came back to the studio just super over-the-top with excitement and energy, hops in the vocal booth, and I remember going in, looking up at him at one point through the glass and telling the engineer, 'Man, I love this guy!' It was a connection that we had immediately, I think as soon as he got in that studio, so once he was done, I told him, 'We'll mix it and have you a copy here in a few days.' So, I didn't hear anything, we didn't book anything immediately, and then my phone rang one day driving on 8th Avenue, and it was Larry Willoughby at Capitol, and back then, Luke had a relationship with Capitol because he'd done a showcase for them. They hadn't signed him yet, and had told him, 'You aren't ready yet but keep bringing us music.' Mind you, I didn't know any of that at the time I got the call. So, Larry says, 'Man, Luke Bryan just left here and left me a song called "Baby's on the Way" and if you guys keep writing more like this, we'll give you some money to cut some sides on him.' I remember telling him, 'Okay, that's great!' and hung up with a big smile on my face and called Luke: 'Man, you're not going to believe this! Larry just called me and said he was going to give us some money to cut some sides,' and Luke said, 'He did!?' The next thing I immediately did was tell him, 'You and I need to get together and talk about this now.'"

Knowing he was at the crossroads in a career where he'd traveled many already, and by then had developed an instinct on which direction to head and, equally as important, *not* to head down, Stevens chose the unknown over the safe road when he rolled the dice—not just sticking with the safer path of songwriting but stepping into the role of Bryan's record producer. A vision that he articulated to Luke he at first didn't feel was fully his yet, Stevens felt the decision ultimately lay with Bryan given his career was on the line this time:

> We got together and I said: "Just because Larry believes that I'm the right guy to produce your records does not mean that I am. There has to be a real chemistry." What was going through my head was my own experience as an artist and how I had never met the right guy. There were a couple of good producers in there, but it didn't click, and I wasn't going to do it if we didn't really resonate, because I didn't want to screw this guy's career up! I could already tell, his personality—he used to make fun of me for saying this—but it was like a male Reba McEntire, he's a fucking star! I knew this needed to be handled right, so I told him: "Look, we need to write some more together, and I need to know more about you. If we continue to write this kind of song, and this really makes sense, then, hell yeah, I'm up for it!" So, we went another five or six weeks, wrote a couple more songs, and they were really good. "My First Love Song" was one of them, and "I'll Stay Me" was another. That was a funky little song, really good, and was so him! "All My Friends Say" came a little bit later.

> I instilled in him early on when we were making the *I'll Stay Me* album that "This is *your* record." The first album was kind of funny because we were recording it and weren't being pitched any quality songs because Luke was new to town. So, all the quality songs were being sent to Tim McGraw and Kenny Chesney, and we just weren't getting

any. So, I cowrote maybe four songs on the record with Luke, and there were some on there he had written, and then some songs he'd written with other writers here in town. I wrote "Baby's on the Way," "I'll Stay Me," and "First Love Song."

Luke Bryan, Sports and Entertainment Nashville:
The first song Jeff and I officially wrote was 'Baby's on the Way,' which I cut on my first album too, but 'All My Friends Say' was our fourth or fifth one. It was a really great start and really got my career going where it needed to go.

Debuting at number two on the US Top Country Albums Chart his first time out as a producer and Bryan's first as an artist, the pair would crack number one with *Doin' My Thing* in 2009 on a roll:

Jeff and Luke are the cowriters of the album cut "Welcome to the Farm" and what would become Jeff's next number one smash as a songwriter with the platinum-selling "Someone Else Calling You Baby." On the strength of those singles, sales peaked again just shy of the top of the *Billboard* charts, a trend both Stevens and Bryan would break for good by the time *Tailgates & Tanlines* took Nashville by storm in 2011. Helping Bryan cowrite the Top 5 hit "Kiss Tomorrow Goodbye," Stevens would produce number one hits with "Drunk on You" and "I Don't Want This Night to End." The songwriter-producer in reflecting back admits that amid all their early success, "That was the most stressful time for Luke and I because both of us were on the same path, and we didn't really know where we were going. But we were going forward as fast as we could, as different as we could. It was important to him and I both to be on the front end of whatever was happening in Nashville. So, I know that we were trying to break ground."

260   SONGS OF NASHVILLE

In a display of savvy that has kept him on the forefront of country music ever since as one of the most successful producers of the millennium, Stevens proudly recruited from the next generation of Music Row hit-makers-to-come when he brought his son Jody Stevens onto the team, heading into the making of Bryan's fourth album, *Crash My Party*. Appropriately credited as pioneers of bringing hip-hop elements into country's mainstream, *MusicRow* magazine has since profiled the contrast between Jeff's DIY approach coming up, that "Jody is an SAE Institute of Technology graduate and an engineer and programmer. . . . They come from two completely different generations musically. Jeff grew up on traditional country and Jody grew up on '90s country, rap, and alternative music." Drawing his own distinctions between the two generations of Stevenses that he felt made him and his dad blend so well as collaborators, Jody begins by pointing out that "me and my dad are different musically because whenever they could afford to give me a musical instrument growing up, I would have him teach me a couple chords on it and then I would take it from there. Or if it were drums, I started playing them until I thought it sounded good. So as far as playing, we both grew up in different time periods and learned how to play with different records, so we both play by ear, and definitely have such different styles musically that somehow together it meshes. Around 2012, I started doing programming stuff on Luke's *Crash My Party* LP, before I was a credited producer on his albums yet. Around then, country music finally started changing and adding elements from the pop and hip-hop world, and that made me understand that if this was going to happen, I felt like I was in a good place to be able to be of help for that. Occasionally I would be nervous, because for the most part as far as Luke and Jeff, when they kind of let me start adding all this stuff to the records, my biggest concern was obviously that Luke might not like something that I did, and that did happen! There were definitely some occasions where I would put some crazy stuff on a song and he would say, 'I don't know about that.' But I was definitely trying to do what I could to make the records cool and edgy."

Billboard magazine would appropriately credit the Stevens father–son team for helping to open "the genre's influences and steered country music in a new, lyrical, and musical direction by including aspects of urban and pop production, as demonstrated by Florida Georgia Line and Sam Hunt's dominance of the scene several years later. . . . [The song] had a huge impact on the genre's musical direction. . . . As the genre expanded over the course of the decade—ultimately transforming to include elements of rap, pop and EDM [electronic dance music]—so did Bryan's entertainer status." This was a move that Jeff reasons was an inevitable one as "sonically, in order for an artist to continue, I cheated a little bit by bringing in a coproducer in my son Jody who has kept the sound fresh, and again, in Luke's case, if and when it does happen—it has to at some point . . . I think that in that way, what I bring to the table for Luke is different. I could be wrong about this, but I believe there are some producers who have a 'sound' and that's what they do. I don't feel like I have a sound. I make it my mission with the few artists I have produced—and some that never saw the light of day that are completely different, female artists—where I consider my duty to make their record. That's very difficult, I don't have pre-set sounds, I don't have pre-set musicians, and I can see how that can yield you some hits, but I don't know if that yields you a superstar career. When I met Luke, he spoiled me in that way and that's what I shoot for. Then with Jody, I think our personalities are completely different, I'm very high-strung and very loud and can get very morose and negative real quick, and he's not like that at all. He's a very bright force in the studio, and just brings a lot to the table. He's doing alright."

Pointing to one of their earliest collaborative successes together with the decade-defying "Play It Again," the seven-million-selling,

262 SONGS OF NASHVILLE

number one smash hit as a template, Jeff credits it as a "significant breakthrough for me on 'Play It Again' where we did a lot of work on the intro, Jody and I might have spent two weeks on that intro. We kept going, and would kind of be happy with it, and of course, what's dangerous is when you get past it, and then you really fucked up because you've done all this work on it, and you've gotten used to hearing it a certain way. Then trying to unravel all that stuff, it's not like you're in the middle of brain surgery or anything, but you lose a little sleep over it. But we ended up getting it, and ended up stripping a lot out of that too." *Rolling Stone Country* instantly recognized the "utterly addictive" track where "one listen to that 'Oh, my God, this is my song' refrain and you can expect it to haunt your waking moments, especially as country radio continues to play it again, play it again, play it again." Helping his father get to that hypnotic height with the programmed elements he composed sonically to weave into the song's musical tapestry, Jody begins foundationally:

> When I'm making a beat for a song, I reference whatever demo I have, because I want to make sure that whatever it is that the artist liked about the demo is still present on the record, but I try not to copy it. I remember from the very beginning of the demo for "Play It Again," there's a reverse sound from the very beginning where I took some of the guitars that were in the record and reversed them going into the loop that starts playing. That loop was actually already there before the band started playing to it, and I knew that song was going to be recorded but sometimes I do it anyway even if I don't know a song's going to be recorded yet or not, just in case. So, I've got it already ready and try to be prepared. This was back in 2012 when I was actually working on that beat, and most of the sounds from that came from a Native Instruments

Maschine [MK3] drum controller, and I played the parts out on the pads by hand. I used a lot of the sounds that come with it, more so than finding sounds. Now, I have a library of sounds that I will dig into, and it's different for a record versus if I'm in the demo process as a song-writer. When I'm writing songs, I just throw whatever at it and it comes out sounding fine, but for a record, I try to find sounds that are the right sound for the song. The drums have to be tuned to where I feel they sound right for a song. Sometimes the kicks are in key with the song, which was the case in "Play It Again." Sometimes kicks can be higher pitched, even though a kick doesn't really have a [note], the fundamental of the sound can be higher or lower, and sometimes you have to make them sound a little bit deeper or a little bit higher.

The production team of Jeff and Jody Stevens would quickly become a unique father–son one in country music as their hybrid innovations to Luke Bryan's sound lifted him again to number one within the creation of six-time platinum number one "That's My Kind of Night," which *Country Weekly* hailed as "undeniably catchy," and Jody helped successfully cross over to a wider audience based in part on "the beat I did for that song, which they added before any of the broader instrumentation. One of the cool parts about that song to me was I don't know if I've heard a whole lot those reverse snares and also, there's another spot at the end of the second chorus in the turnaround where all the instruments go headlong into a fade and the whole song stops. It just sounded cool, and that happened after the musicians had played on the song." Luke Bryan chimed in personally on the song's importance to his growth in popular-ity in an interview with Country Music Television: "I think when you look at trying to play stadium shows and you think about the stadium artists of our genre and our era—when you look at Kenny

Chesney . . . and even George Strait, they gotta have four or five kinds of anthemic songs. And for stadiums, 'That's My Kind of Night' just works for a good time and you gotta have those, in my opinion, in your career. And it did, it gave me another element of a big ol' fun up-tempo."

Reflecting the reverberations of its influence over a decade later when *Crash My Party* received the ACM Album of the Decade award in recognition of its success as "an album that has impacted country music over the decade," the duo would continue coproducing Luke Bryan through the rest of the 2010s to hit after hit with other chart-toppers like "Drink a Beer," "Roller Coaster," "I See You," "Kick the Dust Up," "Strip It Down," "Huntin', Fishin' and Lovin' Every Day," and "Home Alone Tonight," which Jody proudly, as a credited cowriter, points to as one song where "I spent a lot of time working on it from the demo stage, and anytime you can come up with an idea and get to see it all the way through to being a hit on the radio is a lot of fun to watch! That song started in the writing room, and we never went into the big studio for that song, it was very similar to 'Chillin' It' in that respect. It has one or two studio musicians overdubbed, but I played most of the instruments. 'Kill the Lights,' the title track off that album, started as a demo, and a lot of the elements that are in the demo were part of the demo of the song we wrote. I wrote that song with Luke and Jeff, and I had something prepared that day, so elements of that track were made before we went to write with Luke. I had sort of the intro, verse, chorus, chords pre-planned out, tempo. For me, for me, the groove is more important than whatever sound it is I use to get there, so I would say I do spend more time trying to find the actual groove in a sequence than I do the sounds. With something simple like 'Fast' or another track like 'Strip It Down,' I'll add a lot more stuff than is necessary, and at some point you have to look at it, and if you can get away for a couple days and come back to it, I'll listen to the song as a whole entity and see if the elements I've added actually benefit the song and most important, try to make sure that at least from my taste and Luke and Jeff's to make sure there's not too much going on."

Properly credited fifteen years later with helping inject hip-hop elements into country's mainstream for the first time, Jody remains proud looking back and ahead that as a father–son team, they've been continually aided by his belief that "our best attributes lie in different areas to a degree. We're both well-rounded on our own, but I have attributes that I excel at, and he does as well, and we know the dance and whose best at that. So, if he's got a strong opinion in an area, like rhythm with the track, the sounds, and so on. Most people equate record production as having mostly to do with the sonic end of things. Well, yeah, that's a big deal, but there's a lot more to record production than that, and all those other things I tend to be good at, although there's plenty of times where they completely overlap. I may say, 'Gosh, I don't know if this particular thing you have going on in the beat, something's not right about that, you know . . .' and then he'll work on it. Or he'll come to me and say, 'There's something not right about this vocal,' or he knows what's not right with it. So, we work really well together."

The hits continued to roll on as the decade did with "Move," "Fast," "Light It Up," "Most People Are Good," "Sunrise, Sunburn, Sunset," "What Makes You Country," "Knockin' Boots," "What She Wants Tonight," "One Margarita," "Down to One," and on through the 2020s with a new era of hits with "Waves," "Buy Dirt," "Country On," "But I Got a Beer in My Hand," and "Love You, Miss You, Mean It." In measuring the true expanse of Bryan's success, propelled in an important part by the Jeff–Jody Stevens team behind the scenes in concert with Nashville's fellow top songwriters, *MusicRow* magazine recently admired that "during his career, Bryan has amassed a total of 21.7 billion global streams, 11.5 million global album sales and 52 million track sales worldwide. He is the most digital single RIAA (Recording Industry Association of America) certified country artist of all time with 83 million units and 15.5 million album certified units for a total of 98.5 million." Proud of their legacy to date, Jeff marvels at the rock-solid foundation still in place today of "a trust Luke and I formed almost immediately with honesty and candidness, and I think that's our strong suit. I think that belief that I'm coming from an honest place, when I'm judging his singing, when I'm judging the songs, he knows—because he can judge by example—that I've made the choice with my heart, and that's the way he does everything. He goes by how it makes him feel and I do the same thing, and that's really our bond."

Jeff stepped outside the Luke Bryan universe to conceptualize and cowrite the Jake Owen number one hit "I Was Jack (You Were Diane)," which Jody Stevens prepared for a write he had that day with "Craig Wiseman, David Ray, and Tommy Cecil. That song actually goes back to my hip-hop roots of sampling, because we wrote the song around the sample from the verse and chorus of 'Jack & Diane.' I'd thought about sampling 'Jack & Diane' ten years ago and had tried to figure out ways to put together a track that would be a tribute for a long time. 'Jack & Diane' is such a special song to me, and everybody, that I thought if we could figure out how to write a good song around that sample, then hopefully people would like it. Luckily, John Mellencamp gave us his stamp of approval."

As addicted to the rush of songwriting and creating a new number one as they ever were, Jeff admits after four billion streams and counting that "I just know, for me, I would be lying if I said that I don't want to sell records, or streams, or downloads, and those bring certain awards, but what that means to me is that I connected, along with Luke, and that Luke is connected. It's much more important that he's connecting, but personally speaking, I finally landed on the reason back that day on that walk from Warner Chappell. I realized that what really mattered to me is the connection, that moment when I'm in Montana and I walk into a 7-Eleven and hear one of my songs playing, and hear the little girl behind the counter singing it, and realize that somewhere that's happening right now. What more could we want?" For Jody, carrying the family business forward into the 2020s and beyond, he walks into the studio every morning electrified by the pure promise of new musical possibility:

> It changes every day in the writing room! There's some days when I have a musical idea, because I write lyrics and melodies as well, so there's times I'll be playing an acoustic guitar and have an idea, or sometimes it comes from someone else in the room who has a title or a lyric, or a musical idea with a melody, and every day is a new day when you're writing songs. It's fun that we get occasionally a song that gets on the radio that people get to hear, and that hopefully goes to the top of the charts, and that's awesome. But the most fun is going in and trying to create something new every day.

CHAPTER 28

THE NEW SCHOOL

· ·

Will Weatherly, Drew Parker, Josh Thompson,
Matt Rogers, and Steve Moakler

Nashville is the mecca for any aspiring country songwriter, the way New York City is for Broadway actresses and Hollywood for actors and actresses seeking to be movie stars. The difference between Music City and everywhere else is that here, those who pull into town seeking to be stars can shine just as brightly writing songs for other country acts. Songwriters are stars in this town, featured in the end credits of CMT music videos alongside the star or band performing the song, the label that released it, and the director. Still, with the rise of streaming, Nashville Songwriters have kept one foot in the writing room and the other on the stage. YouTube and Spotify have provided platforms to raise their own profiles into the millions of streams of their own original songs and albums. A hybrid model not available in previous analog-driven generations, singer-songwriters like Drew Parker, Josh Thompson, Matt Rogers, and Steve Moakler have all made the best of both worlds while the newest generation of track masters is reflected in the success of songwriter-producers like Will Weatherly, all of whom join us to reflect on their rise to the top of the new school of Nashville songwriting superstars.

Georgia has long been a breeding ground for many of Nashville's biggest millennial stars and songwriters, from Luke Bryan and the Peach Pickers super-group of songwriters Dallas Davidson, Rhett Akins, and Ben Hayslip to Luke Combs's songwriter Drew Parker, who was born and raised in Covington, Georgia. Like so

The New School 269

many Southern-reared musicians, Parker credits the church with giving him many important introductions to music and eventually performing as he'd record a number of early gospel albums while still in high school and win Male Vocalist and Entertainer of the Year from the Gospel Music Association:

> I grew up going to a little Baptist Church in Georgia. They would have what they call Fifth Sunday Night Sings where anytime there was a fifth Sunday of the month, it would constitute a special occasion. So, they would bring in a traveling gospel group or band and that was like really my first exposure to something that traveled and played music. I was six, you know, and I would want to get up and sing with the group that was there. Then when I was tenor eleven, my dad went and bought me my first sound equipment, my first speakers, my first sound board, and then we would go to Lifeway Christian store and buy Daywind soundtracks. Daywind was like a gospel or Christian-based record label who would create basically karaoke track CDs, so you could buy this CD, and it would have it in three different keys that you could sing it in, and it would have versions where it would have like background vocals. So, I started traveling around anywhere that would let me play on Saturday night on a flatbed in an Arby's parking lot and then on Sunday at the church shows. I traveled around all over the Southeast doing these shows, and I cut my teeth so early and gospel music to me taught a whole different thing because I learned how to really convey and portray a lyric, tell a story and really move the message of what you're singing about to the listener, to where they could comprehend and understand it. I think that really benefited me, doing that at such a young age, learning how to convey a lyric and match it to the melody where it would hit you

right in the face. So, I think those years early on were so instrumental in the success that I've had now. I owe a lot to those years.

Steve Moakler grew up against the same blue-collar backdrop of steel country in Bethel Park, Pennsylvania, celebrating them within the writing and release of his *Steel Town* album, which featured his first charting single, "Suitcase," and in what he called his "North Star at the time, was telling my story and looking at my life in that context, especially with the title track 'Steel Town,' that was my first opportunity to sit down and write with Casey Beathard. I had that title. I just knew most people come to Nashville, and they write that quintessential song about your hometown—one of the few topics everybody has to write. But it took me nine years to write about mine. I'd never written a song about my hometown because in the songs in the singer-songwriter world I came up in, that isn't really something you do. It wasn't in the culture of the music I was listening to, so I think it took nine years of being away from my hometown and to have traveled to so many other places to have that unique appreciation for what it is and for what it made me. When I brought the idea to Casey, he's got a grit and obviously a big football background that is so much of Pittsburgh's culture, and so it was incredibly fun to cowrite that song. I felt like we were laser focused, and he really helped me tell that story and give a proper tribute to the folks who raised me."

After playing around throughout junior high and high school and even turning down his own indie record deal in favor of moving to Nashville to attend Belmont University, Moakler, looking back years later, still expresses relief that he was patient waiting for the right opportunity versus grabbing the first record deal that came along, confirming that "I was at one of those crossroads between signing this indie record deal or applying to college in Nashville. I knew that I wanted to keep pursuing music and in Nashville, so

The New School   271

I literally just google-searched music business colleges and found Belmont. A lot of the music I was into at the time happened to be based there, and it was just a scene I was excited about, so I rolled the dice, applied, and got in. Looking back, it was really God's protection and grace that I ended up in Nashville."

Will Weatherly's journey to Nashville was via Ocala, Florida, and like Drew Parker's roots, he traces his own in both discovering music and that he had a talent for it back to growing up "playing in my hometown church. My dad played drums in the church, then met my mom through her singing in the choir and they originally met at church. She was a piano player too, so I grew up in that, and then my uncle was kind of like the life of the party, played guitar, listened to country music, which my parents really didn't growing up. So, I kind of got the country side of my influences from him. My family was all Michael W. Smith, Steven Curtis Chapman, Amy Grant, like out of the womb, just commercial Christian, so Steven Curtis Chapman and Amy Grant were like from the very beginning. I got grounded one summer and taught myself 'Walking in Memphis' by Marc Cohn, and then was into NSYNC and the Backstreet Boys, and Britney Spears. I was probably ten years old when I figured out who Max Martin was, and started looking at the songwriters and producers more than just the artist. From there, all pop music was always very influential to me, just really symmetrical stuff, but also country because of the lyrics. I was always really touched by that."

First cutting his teeth as a songwriter while playing drums in various high school bands, Weatherly got his first on-the-job training by "being one of the main contributors in the bands. I was into the melody and lyrical side of things, and then a band from my hometown [Ocala, Florida], A Day to Remember, I began collaborating with, working with them at their studio. From that, when other bands would come through town, I'd work with them at that same studio, writing for different bands. I wasn't doing very much

272 SONGS OF NASHVILLE

producing yet back then." By the time he had made the decision to take the proverbial leap of faith and relocate to Music City in 2013, Weatherly would quickly find himself living the dream:

> Though a family friend from the church back in Sarasota kept in touch and the guy that was a deacon at the church with my dad who was a mentor to my dad, and he played in the church band, well, his daughter was married to a session drummer here in town named Ben Phillips. He invited me to come to town and help him with some of his session work. Well, the first day I went to the studio, it happened to be where Josh Osborne and Shane McAnally did all their demo sessions at and here I was, making coffee. Trevor Rosen was there, and major session players like Eliot Kashinsky, Tony Lucido, and Derek Wells. They were doing the first pre-production on the first *Old Dominion* EP and so my first demos I started working on were for "Sangria" [*laughs*]! During my first weeks playing on demo sessions at that studio, I also met Ashley Gorley right as I was starting to do fuller demo tracks for unknown artists and songwriters on the side to make money. I actually was having creative say in these demos and whatnot, and Ashley heard one of them and he called me up one day and asked, "Hey, have you ever considered writing full-time?"

Representing the kind of golden opportunity knocking that any aspiring songwriter dreams of, Weatherly's next big break came when Ashley Gorley, then among the hottest songwriters in town, was first rolling the dice by setting up his own publishing house with Tape Room Music, signing Parker among a class who would feature many of Music Row's next generation of hit-makers alongside Zach Crowell, Hunter Phelps, Brad Clawson, and more. Will was over the moon that "he took a chance on me and signed me and just helping kind of guide me. He was always super supportive." Gorley chimed in with his own beaming pride as a creative headhunter that "in whatever your profession, you try to surround yourself with people that are better, and these guys turn in stuff that challenges me daily to stay on top of my game because they're so good." After scoring his earliest charting singles "Wish You Were On It" by Florida Georgia Line and "Dig Your Roots," title track to the album alongside the patriotic track "I Love My Country," Weatherly in turn points to his back-to-back number one smashes with Kane Brown over "Lose It" and "Good as You" as another two of his favorite writing room successes to date:

> I love "Lose It," because I remember at first Kane and I were striking out that day. I still have the song we were writing, and I can really tell if Kane is digging it or not. Everyone was kind of all on the same page, like "We're getting it done, but do we love this?" And I think he had ordered food or something and went to grab it and Chase McGill and I, just in a super-quick Hail Mary, said to each other "Dude, could we start a different idea real quick, mess with it, and if not, we'll bounce back to the original idea . . ." See, artists' time is very precious, so while you have them there, you try to get the most out of it. So, Chase just started kind of ad-libbing and that title popped out, and we all just kind of got on that really quick because that song was written in a pretty short amount of time.

> With writing "Good as You," we were out on the bus and that one felt pretty special in the moment. Shy Carter and Taylor Phillips especially are very animated people, and in

274 SONGS OF NASHVILLE

the whole vibe of that, it felt just like a club. Then Brock Berryhill is such an amazing guitar player, and he and I were messing around from the vibe standpoint with that lick, and we got it looping on the bus and that one was really fun to write. Hopefully the way it made people feel when they hear it live or listening to it if they drive around or something. I work with Jelly Roll a good bit, and he was playing the Key West Songwriters Festival and, being an amazing dude, he actually pulled a few of us up onstage and we played "Good as You" to like four thousand people, and they were all singing it back to me. The thing that it did to those people singing it back to me live was the way that it felt when we were all doing it on the bus. So, that is a good example of a song feeling right.

Josh Thompson moved to Nashville and first survived amid playing music by night via pouring concrete by day, confirming that once he'd settled here, "My ambitions were to do anything in the music industry that generated income so I could do it full-time. With my kids, it's strange to me because I grew up seeing my dad leave at 5:00 in the morning in his truck, and he would come home at dark tired and covered in concrete. That's what I saw growing up, and today, my kids are seeing daddy go on the back porch with a guitar, so it's a completely different experience. When I first got to town, I started out pouring concrete myself to make a living, and I was scared as hell! I'd gotten a guitar for my twenty-first birthday, took lessons for six or seven months until I could make three chords, and then I started writing my own songs. Albeit they were horrible, but I started writing. I probably wrote eighty songs, ninety songs by myself before I moved to Nashville. I was like, 'I'm going to give it a shot.'" Josh scored first charting single with "Beer on the Table" from his solo album after impressing those hearing his songs that he was not just a writer but an excellent performer, too. He landed

The New School   275

his first major label deal as a solo artist with Columbia Records with *Way Out Here*, produced by none other than Jason Aldean and Peer Music president Michael Knox, and then he toured the record by opening for Eric Church and Brad Paisley. Peaking at number seventeen on the US Hot Country Songs Chart, Josh proudly points to "Beer on the Table" as a song that captured a picture of the life of a starving songwriter investing 100 percent of his blood, sweat, and tears into the dream with everything on the line:

> At the time I was broke, literally working pouring concrete and trying to write songs and that was a night write at Ash Street with Andy, Zach, and Ken Johnson and was basically just working to put bread on the table, except we made it more fun and more of a party. When I heard that on the radio for the first time, I was on Highway 5 coming from [the] Oregon area heading down into California and I heard it with one of my label reps at time. It was like I thought he put the CD in or something, I was like, "This is unbelievable!" Then a little later we got a call from WMIL in Milwaukee, and the Senior Vice President of Programming Kerry Wolfe asked politely if I could tell my family and friends to stop calling his radio station to play "Beer on the Table" [*laughs*]!

A routine he'd become used to after his name took flight up the charts with his next Top 20 solo single, "Way Out Here," and more Top 40 singles in "Won't Be Lonely Long" and "Comin' Around" in 2010, Thompson would share the ironic experience of competing with himself as fellow country artists began making hits out of his songs, Joe Nichols being the first with "Freaks Like Me." Jason Aldean would lift Josh as a songwriter into the coveted number one single on the US Hot Country Singles for the first time with

276   SONGS OF NASHVILLE

"Any Ol' Barstool," a career-changing moment he still holds sacred among his career highlight reel:

> "Any Ol' Barstool" was my very first number one and it was greatly celebrated [*laughs*]! It was a two-way write with me and my buddy Deric Ruttan the first time we'd ever written. I had this idea called "Ask Any Old Barstool," and it was kind of weird but kind of cool because we're talking about an inanimate object. So, we dove right in and wrote it in probably two hours and sat on it for what seemed like quite some time, then eventually went in to do a demo. I had a great band there that day and it just kind of came to life. Then Jason heard it, and the rest was history.

> We went to number one on that one with Jason and with "Drowns the Whiskey," which I actually wrote seven years before that with Brandon Kinney and my guitar player at the time, Jeff Middleton. We were on my bus touring my record and wrote it just for fun. Then the same story happened as so often can with songs where it sat around for years before Brandon demoed it. Once he demoed it, it took maybe another three years and then Jason heard it. Then they really put magic on it when he and Miranda Lambert took it to a whole other level. With some songs you write, you can kind of hear how it would go, and even though it sounded like the demo, it was just a completely different song, like in another stratosphere. Jason and Miranda's two voices together was like putting butter on a piece of toast.

By then, Thompson in his own right as a recording artist was doing well, scoring a second record deal with country superstar Toby Keith's independent record label Show Dog Nashville (which

The New School 277

merged with Universal Records in 2009) for *Turn It Up* and another solo Top 40 hit with "Cold Beer with Your Name on It" before returning there with hits for Rascal Flatts's "Back to Us" and "I'll Name the Dogs," which Blake Shelton made a Top 10 hit in 2017. Steve Moakler found himself walking the same sort of line balancing hits he was writing for other country stars versus the gems he kept for his own growing catalog via studio albums like *All the Faint Lights, Watching Time Run, Wide Open, Born Ready, Blue Jeans,* and *Make a Little Room.* Counting among his favorite moments sharing his songs with his growing fan base, versus large venues opening for everyone from Willie Nelson to Tim McGraw and Faith Hill, Steve confessed that he found equal thrill from headlining his own Hometowns and Campgrounds Tours:

> I do this tour, it's called the Hometowns and Camp-grounds Tour, where I tour with my wife and my kids cross-country pulling an Airstream trailer, where we play shows directly for our fans and I initiate with our audi-ence and just do kind of direct to fan private shows. Years ago, when we did our very first one and pulled this little Winnebago camper and we did forty shows in fifty days all over the country. My wife and kids loved it when they were young, we have all these moments of the windows down, driving through cornfields, driving through moun-tains, she and I together kind of living this gypsy dream, and "Suitcase" was a song that encapsulated that. "Sid-dle's Saloon" is another of my favorites to play live, which is a song about a bar in my grandfather's basement. It's incredibly personal about my life and where I come from. My grandfather and his brothers owned a small fleet of Mack trucks, and they haul concrete block around and then they'd come back and drink at this saloon in his basement. In the fall of 2023, we headed out on our last

278 SONGS OF NASHVILLE

Hometowns and Campgrounds Tour, which has really been a pillar in my artist career. It's been a way I've been able to carve out, you know, a good living in this business and playing the music. I want to play for the people that enjoy it and be with my family at the same time.

Mack Trucks, Inc., honored Moakler's authentic blue-collar songwriting skills when they selected him to write a song for their new truck line rollout fittingly called "The Anthem." Moakler recalls the incredible opportunity: "Mack Trucks thought it'd be cool to have a songwriter write a song from Nashville about the truck, and Creative Nation suggested me, having ties to Mack Trucks through my father and being from Pennsylvania where Mack Trucks is based. So, the folks from Mack Trucks ended up coming out to my *Steel Town* album release party and basically after the album party, they pretty much interviewed me over a couple beers. They were just like trying to get to know me and seeing if I might be a good fit to write a song for them, and I got the job! I was thrilled. Before I wrote it, I had a phone call with the Mack Trucks team, I just was collecting information, like 'Just tell me everything: Tell me your taglines, tell me your history, tell me what you want this to feel like,' and it was just really an assignment to me. I was honored to have the job and 'Born Ready' is just one of their taglines that they use."

Matt Rogers has remained loyal to his own roots throughout his songwriting catalog, pointing to "I Was Raised" as one of his longtime life favorites he loves to play these days as much as when he first got going. It reminds him of where he came from, glowing in his confirmation that "this was what I call the Genesis song. That's what really started the career. I can remember almost every detail of writing that song. I was on a back porch in Blue Ridge, Georgia, in a mountain cabin overlooking the Great Smoky Mountains and, and it was just beautiful. And I was on a trip up there with my parents. I was actually gigging, believe it or not. I was playing some shows. There was a brewery and some vineyards up there that I used to play early on, and I was with my parents and just kind of reminiscing. I had just such a unique childhood. I think I was like that last childhood that was in that age where we didn't really have internet, so we played outside. Our parents just let us go, you know, in my neighborhood growing up. To this day, some of my best friends [are these neighbors], and our parents are very close. We were super involved in the church and then our parents got together almost every weekend, and we had cookouts and stuff like that. We did birthday trips together, we did camping trips together, hunting trips, everything you can imagine. We were very, very, very close. And I just kind of was reminiscing on that upbringing and how I was raised, and how we were raised and started thinking about all of those things kind of going on in the world. It was just a centrifuge of thoughts and nostalgia and it kind of just fell out. You know, it was one of those situations where I just say 'Man, thank God I was raised the way I was,' got that hook, and it was off to the races from there with imagery of actually growing up in Gray, Georgia. 'I Was Raised' is a special one to me."

Rogers represents a rare breed of Nashville Songwriter who has remained largely independent throughout his career, releasing EPs like 2017's *Richest Place on Earth*, his *Capricorn Sessions* EPs, studio album *Coal*, and a prolific run of singles throughout the 2020s like "People Are Strange," "South Dakota Sky," "Rush," "Tea Was a Little Sweeter," "Get You Off That Fence," "Whatever Keeps You Crazy," "You're My Hallelujah," "Better at Heartbreak," "Whiskey Don't," and "Never Know World." When asked among his NSAI, CMT, American songwriter-winning catalog for other favorite cuts he feels best reflect his unique singing-and-songwriting style, he begins by traveling back to the writing of "South Dakota Sky" at a moment of truth he felt he was facing as so many singer-songwriters can at different points in a career:

Man, this one was that moment of just complete self-doubt I had. I put a song out in the spring of 2021, and I was playing some shows through the Midwest, and they were just going terrible. It was the kind of shows where you go out and you do early morning radio spots to promote whatever song you just put out. You're doing like midday news segments, and playing an acoustic show in the evening to promote when you're coming back to the area later in the year with your band. One of the radio stations wasn't even expecting me and got my photo wrong. I ended the show in a small town called Pickstown, South Dakota, on the Sunday night. I remember I finished that show, and I got back to my hotel that night in South Dakota. If you've ever been in that part of the country, it's so flat. It's just horizon sky as far as you can see and I sat out there on the back porch, looked up at the sky and could see every single star. And I was just having that real moment of contemplation, because this career is tough. It's not like it's an easy path and it can really beat you up sometimes.

I was having that moment of "Am I really doing what I should be doing with my life?" and I was trying to find that motivation to push through. So, the longer I sat out there and pondered, I kind of first got that song idea about the actual roller coaster of my emotion that I had that night. That self-doubt of, "Man, am I good enough to be doing this? Can I trust my thoughts with this kind of thing?" all the way to coming full circle to realizing, "Yeah, everything in this life has put you on this path. You're exactly where you need to be right now, and you have to keep the faith, and you have to just keep chugging along and keep swinging the axe." So, as a songwriter and artist, going from self-doubting to having that confidence back has been a real thing. Ever since I wrote that song, I kinda came right back to town and started writing a ton of them and have been back in my creative cycle and have felt confident ever since. So, it comes in waves for sure, but that was one that helped me a lot to keep moving forward in my career.

Proving the "all ships rise" theory, Luke Combs's ascension to the heights of superstardom in the 2020s has been driven by his steady run of number one smash hits. Drew Parker's career benefited from such chart successes as the *New York Times* captured the sensation of the "unflashy thirty-two-year-old star [who] makes irrepressibly catchy and relatable country anthems" while *The Tennessean* has introduced him as "a blue-collar hero for a new generation of country fans." Crunching the numbers, *Forbes* reported in the mid-2020s that "Combs has now snagged eighteen number one hits on the Country Airplay chart. That's an incredibly impressive accumulation for any act, let alone one who has been collecting leaders for less than a decade. The superstar's track record is impeccable, as he's scored a total of twenty-one Top 10 hits on the ranking of the most successful tracks at country radio. All but three of those have soared to number one." Responsible for some of the major rockets that made it to the top, Parker helped write the five-time platinum number one smash "Forever After All" on both the US Hot Country Songs and US Country Airplay charts and number two on the US *Billboard* Hot 100 Singles Chart, cowritten with Rob Williford and Combs. This song took home the BMI Country Award for Song of the Year in 2022, alongside "1, 2 Many," which featured Brooks & Dunn, "Nothing Like You," "Doin' This"—which earned Drew his first Grammy nomination for Best Country Song—and "This One's

282 SONGS OF NASHVILLE

for You." Describing his songwriting synergy with Combs as one rooted in their friendship that predates his superstardom by years, Parker—who by then had realized his own dream of signing a record deal with Warner Nashville, releasing two EPs with *While You're Gone* and *At the End of the Dirt Road* and cowriting the Top 5 hit "Homemade" for Jake Owen—recalls a relationship with Combs that travels back over a decade:

> This kind of goes back to 2014 before I moved to Nashville. I got a call from a promoter down in Georgia named Bradley Jordan on a Friday afternoon. I was still working in the hospital, and he said, "Hey, my opener for this show in Rome, Georgia, tonight has bailed. Is there any chance you could come open the show?" And at the time, I was trying and taking every opportunity I could get to perform and so I was like, "Yeah, I'll be there." It's a two-and-a-half-hour drive to Rome, and I called Bradley on my way there and asked, "Hey, who am I opening for tonight?" He told me his name was Luke Combs, and I had no idea who Luke was at the time. I got there and maybe sixty people had bought a ticket to the show that night, and we were in the green room before the show, hit it off and we've been really, really, really close friends ever since. I consider Luke one of my best friends."

> He'd just moved to Nashville, and we hit it off enough for him to say, "Hey, why don't you come to Nashville? Let's write some songs together," and honestly, he was the first person that I knew in Nashville that had ever invited me to come write songs. So, I started doing that and I thought this was my chance to go there and not be too afraid because now I know somebody who's willing to write songs with me.

That was in 2014 and then ultimately I moved in September 2015, and we kept writing together ever since. The first song that we ever wrote together was a song called "Lonely One," which was on his debut record, and I remember I didn't even have a publishing deal when that song was recorded, and obviously we've had a lot of songs written together since. I think we are both on the same page about everything, and Luke is one of the best singers I've ever heard. We worked well together because we wanted to say the same things, we wanted to write the same kind of songs, as much as I'm a fan of clever songs, he's a fan of clever songs.

When I met Luke Combs, he was driving a Dodge Neon. So, literally every aspect of "Doin' This" when we wrote it was true and so many people related to that song! I still get compliments from songwriters, which is really cool, about that song, and people were also able to put their own story into it, even the guys still living in a small town. Because if Luke or me or any of us weren't doing what he's doing, he'd still be doing it in some capacity, right? Something that you're passionate about, whether that's being a dad, being a songwriter, whatever that is, you find passion in that and you find a way to do it because that's what you love to do. That's what "Doin' This" was about. When we wrote "Nothing Like You," that's a song that took about four writes, even though that song is very simple if you listen to it. Luke was early on in his relationship with Nicole then, and traveling a lot, and we wanted to put that situation into a song, "I've been all around the world, I've seen everything, still I haven't seen anything like you . . ." But there are parts of that song that just melodically and lyrically we could not get to just marry each other, and so that's what

284 SONGS OF NASHVILLE

I think took a little longer. With that song, I was trying to make the lyric match the melody, which is super important and so fortunately, about the third or fourth time we tried on it, we finally, finally nailed it to the wall.

By the time Combs was a superstar, Josh Thompson had similarly shared in being part of riding that same wave as a key member of country music's other new bonafide superstar. Morgan Wallen also rose up those same charts to stadium status, scoring two singles with Luke Combs with "Angels Workin' Overtime" and "New Every Day" before scoring a place on the team responsible for cowriting a generation of Morgan Wallen hits. Songs likely to comprise much of his first Greatest Hits album include Top 40 singles "Quittin' Time," "Rednecks, Red Letters, Red Dirt," "Whiskey'd My Way," "Your Bartender," "Whiskey Friends," "Dying Man," "Neon Star (Country Boy Lullaby)," and the monster number one "Wasted on You," which hit number one on both the US Hot Country Songs and US Country Airplay Charts, moving eight million copies. Taking fans back inside his memories of writing this titanic hit, Josh recounts "writing 'Wasted on You' back right when the pandemic hit. People were locked down, but we still went to town and wrote that with Ernest, and we had a track from Charlie Handsome. He wasn't there, but he sent a track and we're like, this is awesome. So, we just sat down, and I forget whose idea 'Wasted on You' was, but it fell out somehow. And the way that that chorus goes, you know, it just kind of amps up and amps up and amps up. Morgan can get up on the microphone and pretty much spit a song out, and you really just dial in the little intricacies of it. I mean, he's really fast. He's a phenomenal songwriter. I knew at that point, like, that was going to be something special somewhere down the line."

Turning to the writing of other hits from his massive 2020s run of chart successes, Thompson has been responsible for highlights like Jon Pardi's "Ain't Always the Cowboy," which peaked at number

The New School   285

six, the Top 10 hit "Whiskey and Rain" by Michael Ray, "Brown Eyes Baby" by Keith Urban, "Stars Like Confetti" by Dustin Lynch and "Young Love & Saturday Nights" by Chris Young, and Luke Bryan's "One Margarita," which rocketed all the way to number two. Ordering "One Margarita" up off his menu of songs he had the most fun writing by the very nature of the subject matter, Josh shares that "we were just setting out to write something fun, like a party, summertime, something that you didn't have to think a whole lot about, and it started somewhere else. First I think we were writing about a beer song, and somebody said the line, 'One Margarita' and then we just went 'One Margarita, two margarita, three margarita, shot,' and it was, 'Man, that's it!' Then we just played some feel-good music to it and painted the picture of being at the beach and drinking margaritas. Writing about back roads and beaches and then mountains, those are those locations that work for country music." Thompson's run of smash hits with Thomas Rhett has been equally impressive, including "Growing Up," "Angels Don't Always Have Wings," and the Top 10 hits "Half of Me" and "Be a Light," with Josh pointing to the latter pair as two of his personal highlights:

With "Half of Me," that was what we call a "bus write." Thomas is probably one of the most prolific songwriters I've ever been around. My first weekend and time writing with him, we wrote ten songs in three days. It was like a songwriting boot camp, and he can pick up a guitar and come up with ten different songs, ideas, and arrangements in like five minutes. I mean, he's just wired for a song. I mean, it's amazing to watch and how productive— it is refreshing. He was actually going to go work out, but he came back ten minutes later and said, "I don't feel like working out today. Half of me wants a cold beer," and I said, "The other half does too . . ." and then we just wrote it: There was the hook, and we had somewhere to go.

We wrote "Be a Light" on his bus two years ago in Canada. He came back from doing a meet and greet and was like, "I had this idea" and then he pretty much sang the chorus just off of like this idea that was going on in his head. So after the show, we sat down and wrote it [in] probably twenty minutes, did a few fixes on it as the weeks went by, just via text. Then talk about a happy accident: He put Keith Urban and Reba McEntire and just put it out, not as single and radio but I guess based off the message and the fact that the legends' voices were on there, and they just picked it up and ran with it and it became a hit.

In honing that instinct, these five members of Music City's New School of hit-makers offer the following guidance in closing to any songwriting students new to the game and just learning how to write songs they hope get play, in the writing rooms on Music Row, on record, and eventually hopefully on radio to equal heights as number one Nashville Songwriters:

Drew Parker: If you're in the position of writing a song for another artist, you have to understand their fan base as much as you understand them. I think that's very important. If I'm listening to a demo, I want to hear somebody really good singing it to me. That's what sells the song. It's also important to remember that the hard work comes easy if you want it bad enough. In your lifetime, there's going to be opportunities presented to you, there's going to be doors that get open for you, and you have to be willing and ready to walk through them and find out what's on the other side of it.

The New School 287

Will Weatherly: I think that you should just write the song, and as long as you leave the room that day wanting to listen to it over and over, then you accomplished something that day. So, find the smaller victories because the things that you think are big victories and what success means generally are very fleeting emotions. They're cool for about one second and then the reality hits you that once you have a hit song, now you need to figure out how to do it all over again. Definitely don't chase what other people do. Do your own thing.

Steve Moakler: My first memories of interacting with music was really in my dad's office in our basement. He worked at home pretty much my whole life, and his music collection was and still is some of my absolute favorite music. I know it's a blessing to be an artist and a songwriter, and finding a great publisher is really key to any of our success, that's why I'm so lucky to work with Luke and Beth Laird at Creative Nation. The music business can be a very harsh reality, and when you first move to Nashville, you are going to be overwhelmed and intimidated by the talent that you encounter. I've seen it happen where so many times, people come here and get discouraged, but if you can resist the temptation to be jealous and intimidated, just let it inspire you. Let that greatness inspire you!

Josh Thompson: If you're a songwriter who's also a performer, being authentic is just so important, so cling to your roots, what you grew up loving, what made you want to be a songwriter in the first place and just take that and melt it into your style with your voice. So, just be honest when you're writing, whether it's about going to a bar or matters of the heart, because that's timeless.

Matt Rogers: People can sense when you're genuine. People can sense when you're singing a song that means something to you. The fake stuff sometimes will get through, but I feel like it's on a pretty shaky foundation. So, unless you deliver something that really lets people have an insight into who you are and what you're about, it's not going to have any staying power. Clint Black's a great example, he's like "I'm going to do what I do," and I've always come back to that because that's such a big part of this industry: If you go chasing trends, you're in trouble. By the time you catch up, it will have turned already.

ACKNOWLEDGMENTS

Thank you first and foremost to the amazingly talented song-writers who have devoted their cosmic talents day in and day out on Music Row to giving generations of country music fans the soundtrack of their lives, including Ashley Gorley, Cole Swindell, Sonny Curtis, Dallas Davidson, Shane McAnally, Craig Wiseman, Dean Dillon, Matraca Berg, Freddy and Catherine Powers, Merle Haggard, Jelly Roll (congrats on blowing up!), Hillary Lindsey, Liz Rose, Lori McKenna, Natalie Hemby, Vince Gill, Buddy Cannon, Bobby Braddock, Sonny Throckmorton, Colt Ford, Dallas Frazier, Clint Black, Kinky Friedman, Earl Bud Lee, Jack Tempchin, Wayne "The Train" Hancock, Willy "Tea" Taylor, Jim Weatherly, Tim DuBois, Rock Killough, Mark Irwin, Larry Cordle, Jim Lauderdale, Wanda Mallette, Jim McBride, Carl Jackson, Randy Brooks, Larry Gatlin, Don Cook, Jeff Stevens and Jody Stevens, Will Weatherly, Drew Parker, Josh Thompson, Matt Rogers, and Steve Moakler, and for opening up to me about your personal stories and those behind many of the amazing hits you've given us throughout the decades. Thanks to Jon Conner and David Ray for your help with facilitating the Jelly Roll interview; thanks to Beth Laird and the entire team at Creative Nation; Tape Room Publishing and your amazing team; Big Loud Shirt's team; and everyone else within the publishing and management arenas who helped facilitate the interviews with your respective songwriters here throughout the book.

Thank you to Frank Weimann at Folio Management for the past five amazing years of representation. I couldn't ask for a better representative to be handling my third decade in the book business;

thank you to Keith Wallman at Diversion Books and his amazing team including Amy Martin, Nina Smetana, Beth Metrick, and Jeff Farr for taking a chance on this book, and to Simon & Schuster for doing such an amazing job pushing it out to retail; and everyone else involved in making this book a success.

Personally, thank you to my wife, Carrie Brock-Brown, for your tireless love and support of my very unusual (lol) career, and our wonderful Westie Molly for sitting beside me late into many nights grinding away to finish this manuscript; to my parents, James and Tina Brown, for continuing to be two of my biggest cheerleaders over the past twenty-five years pursuing my creative endeavors; my brother, Ret. Sgt. Joshua Brown, and sister-in-law, Jenna, and nephew, Greyson Liam Brown; my in-laws, Bill and Susan Brock, my brother-in-law, Christopher, and their furry buddy Gizmo; the extended Thieme (Auntie Heather, Deb, Vick, Jeff, Steve, all my cousins and their amazing families), Brown and Schweiss (my beloved Aunt Sharon RIP, Bernie, Bob, Colleen, Anne, Sharon, their amazing families, and the third generations of cousins); my *About the Authors TV* team (Ray Riddle, Alan McCall, Peter Bacigalupo, Ed Seaman, Tiffany Bailes, and others at MVD Entertainment Group, Tubi TV for believing in the show from day one, Ben, owner at City Square, Hendersonville, TN, and everyone else involved in making this the success it's become); my indispensable assistant, Ellie Schroeder, I couldn't do what I do without you; my extended lifelong circle of friends who continue to have my back, Alex Schuchard, Andrew McDermott, Cris Ellauri, Sean Fillinich (and Megan "Megatron" Fillinich), Bob O'Brien, Richard Kendrick, Joe Viers, my longtime musical collaborator Aaron "Whippit" Harmon, old-school St. Louis peeps I grew up with (John McElwain, Britton Clapp, Tim Woolsey, et al.), Paul and Helen "Bizzle" Watts, and the most amazing publicist I have ever worked with, Samantha Downey, for reinventing my career for a third decade with your brilliant 2020 COVID

Acknowledgments   291

50th Book Campaign; Teddy Riley for the opportunity to cowrite your forthcoming memoir, a career highlight for me as a lifelong fan, and Charles Suitt at 13A / Gallery Books / Simon & Schuster for believing in our project; Ed McDonald for the opportunity to collaborate on your upcoming memoir; Tony and Yvonne Rose at Amber Books for giving me my start in 2001; and anyone else who has read the sixty books I've been fortunate enough to write over the past twenty-five years.

ABOUT THE AUTHOR

Award-winning biographer and *About the Authors TV* host and creator Jake Brown has published sixty books since 2001, in eleven countries around the world. They include bestsellers and collaborations with rock's biggest legends, including 2013 Rock & Roll Hall of Fame inductees Heart (with Ann and Nancy Wilson), living guitar legend Joe Satriani, country music legends Merle Haggard and Freddy Powers, late hip-hop legend Tupac Shakur (via the estate), late metal pioneers Motörhead (with Lemmy Kilmister), and Smashing Pumpkins front man / founder Billy Corgan, and the critically acclaimed *Nashville Songwriter* and *In the Studio* (Dr. Dre, Rick Rubin, Tori Amos, Iron Maiden, and more) series. His extensive TV work includes series like *Music's Greatest Mysteries* on AXS TV, *Breaking the Band* on REELZ Network, on-air narrator for much of BET's smash hit *The Death Row Chronicles*, Bloomberg Network's *Game Changers*, and FUSE TV's *Live Through This* series, among others. Brown is creator/host/producer of the first-of-its-kind streaming television show *About the Authors TV*, airing on Tubi TV with three million viewers and counting. His work has been covered by *CBS News*, the *Hollywood Reporter*, *Rolling Stone* magazine, *USA Today*, MTV.com, *Billboard*, *Parade* magazine, Country Music Television (now known as CMT), *Variety*, and many other prominent national news outlets. In 2012, Brown won the Association for Recorded Sound Collections Awards in the category of Excellence in Historical Recorded Sound Research.